Neighborhood Caretakers

Stories, Strategies and Tools
for Healing Urban
Community

Neighborhood Caretakers

Stories, Strategies and Tools
for Healing Urban
Community

by Burton C. Dyson, M.D.
and Elizabeth U. Dyson, M.B.A.

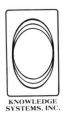

KNOWLEDGE
SYSTEMS, INC.

Published by Knowledge Systems, Inc.
7777 West Morris Street, Indianapolis, Indiana 46231

First Edition

10 9 8 7 6 5 4 3 2 1

ISBN 0-941705-08-0

About the Book

Much of the 20th century has been devoted to doing things bigger and faster. From breakthroughs in technology, we've built global megasystems for transportation, communication, doing business, controlling disease, and the 24-hour financial market. But when one person's electricity became another's acid rain, we realized that systems that seemed to work well for economic or political reasons at global or national levels were not as beneficial to lifestyles at the individual and community levels. As the GNP rises, the quality-of-life index falls.

Thus technology's victories, and shortcomings, created another major trend of the century. There is an emerging consensus—now being tested—that all the earth belongs to all the people: all the resources, all the decision-making processes and all cultural inventions such as art, language, skills, data and knowledge.

Social pioneers have been busy inventing and applying increasingly sophisticated *social technologies* based on this *new consciousness of what it means to be human*. The evolving recognition of our interrelatedness is impacting the search for remedies for plagues of the mind and spirit that show up in our social structures: Daddy can't read; the Jones baby has a bruise on her head again; Mrs. Quinn is crazy and won't come out of her room; the ground water supply is polluted. Examples abound of how individuals have changed the career rat race into high vocational adventure, or how families have become powerful missional units, or how neglected inner-city neighborhoods have begun thinking of themselves as prototypes for the future.

This is a how-to book of stories, strategies and methods which are creating new social vehicles and structures in a wide variety of social laboratories. When, why and how does a "new social vehicle" come into use? How are people trained and sustained in new styles and methods of leadership? What are the belief systems, or new spirit modes, that undergird social creativity? And what does all this theory look like when translated into practical programs in housing, community business, land use, media, education, and health care for fragile urban and rural populations? In short, how do we create authentic social change?

Acknowledgements

We wish to thank all of the readers and writers among Those Who Can Make Good Things Happen who contributed stories to the *Neighborhood Caretaker Journal*, and without whom this book would not have been possible.

We appreciate especially the vision and experience of Knowledge Systems staff who in bold faith saw the potential of hundreds of NCJ stories over a period of six years and pushed us forward to write this book. Our thanks also for their editorial skills used in ordering the chaos of the whole struggle to write well!

Particularly we want to thank our Indianapolis Family, John and Anita Gibson, and Jesse and Mollie Clements, for their loving support in the highs and lows of daily living; and the many colleagues whose paths we crossed at Earthcare Indianapolis with whom we experienced life as celebration.

Table of Contents

**Introduction: Coming of Consciousness
          in Community Medicine   13**

Healing 20th century social diseases—plagues of the mind, spirit and social structures—calls for new approaches by those who care. Healing emerges when a group uses appropriate social, spirit and leadership methods and understands itself to be acting on behalf of the whole community.

Chapter 1.   The Path of Renewal   23

How does social change happen in our complex society? Introducing Those Who Can Make Good Things Happen and how they empower their vocational communities and the essential structures of society. From numerous success stories, methods and replicable models emerge.

Chapter 2.   Weaving the Fabric of Society   35

Social pioneers have created a "new localism"—a powerful vision of a neighborhood caring for its own needs in health, education, economic growth, affordable housing, and in cooperation with other neighborhoods. We catch a glimpse of the awesome interconnectedness of life.

Chapter 3.   Leadership for Social Cohesion   62

The style of the servant leader and new empowering social technologies release orderly, real change. We examine characteristics and costs of authentic leadership and four powerful revolutionary tools that empower persons and groups in all social classes.

**Chapter 4.   The Social Laboratory:
          Social Medicine for the 1990s   86**

The bridge between social theory and real world acceptance of new approaches is the urban social laboratory. Borrowing tools from epidemiology—the study of who gets ill and why—a new, empowering neighborhood science is applying remedies that work in complex situations.

Foreword

As we enter the nineties, a fundamental shift is taking place in discussions about the future of the planet. More and more people know that we face the certainty of revolutionary shifts not only in our technology but also in our social systems. As people confront the massive changes which are inevitable, they are looking for guidelines for thought and action and ideas about how to change systems so that they can support a more compassionate society.

Neighborhood Caretakers provides a framework for looking at the new society. It is a timely book because not only are national leaders concentrating their attention on what can be done locally, but also because economic and social trends are causing people to spend more time in their neighborhoods. After a long period in which we believed that national decision making could solve all problems, we are coming to understand that much of the action has to take place at the neighborhood and the community level.

The nineties should be a period of ferment with many different ideas being tried out within a cooperative framework. The Dysons have provided a great many examples of action possibilities which can be adapted to the needs of varying communities. They are well aware that one does not simply transfer a model from one community to another: They see their writing—both in this book and the journal—as a method of pollinating ideas from community to community. They are also aware of the importance of providing mentors for change.

It is all too easy to look at the many difficulties we face and feel they are overwhelming. The Dysons show that bite-sized pieces can be created and effective action mounted. They support the key insight of Willis Harman and others—that change of the magnitude we require today does not come about as a result of orders from one great leader but because a great many people do a lot of things in slightly different ways.*

I have long encouraged the creation of communities which concentrate on the quality of life rather than the standard of living. In recent months and years, I have seen movement in this direction. One particularly exciting effort is in Spokane where a large number of people have been working together in "Linking Economic Development and Community Values."

Quality of life neighborhoods and communities bring people together to grasp possibilities while they exist and to prevent problems from becoming acute. Working in this way means the development of a profoundly different pattern of decision making than currently exists. It will require the implementation of all-win strategies which care for *all* those involved. It will recognize that the welfare and safety of any one of us depends on the welfare and safety of all of us.

This pattern of behavior is not possible within industrial-era norms and values. We are being forced to create a totally new set of conditions and systems. The compassionate era into which we are moving will be very different from anything that has gone before. I am using the word "compassion" in its original sense of "with passion." This is not a weak word. It does not mean treating everybody with gooey sympathy. It means being a hopeful realist. It means uniting a tough head and a caring heart.

The compassionate era will be very different from anything that has gone before. The agricultural era was self-contained and its dynamics were heavily dominated by peer pressure. It was largely conformist, but often had a surprising tolerance for eccentricity. The industrial era was based on maximum economic growth. In recent years, as the industrial era has begun to break down, the economy has moved toward maximum labor force participation and drawn more and more people into jobs. This has increased the stress in the culture and reduced the energy available for neighborhood and community support.

In the compassionate era we will rethink fundamentally the way we spend our resources and our time. We shall come to recognize

---

* Willis Harman, *Global Mind Change: The Promise of the Last Years of the Twentieth Century*, published by Knowledge Systems, Indianapolis, 1988.

that we need to rebuild a "community" of honest communication and caring in the sense that this word is used by Scott Peck in his book *The Different Drum*. We need to share our joys and our sorrows, our glorious moments and our tragedies with each other. Today, all too often, people want to hold a job because there is no real human contact in the neighborhoods.

If we are to create this new form of neighborhood and community we shall have to use different forms of leadership. The compassionate era will be based on very different success criteria than the industrial: Helping people see this reality will be difficult and require highly creative teaching.

In addition, the compassionate era requires that we learn to live with uncertainty: to realize that we must "live in the question" rather than seek slick answers. In addition to the specific ideas for action, the reader will find much wisdom in this book particularly with Old Doc's discussions and dialogues.

This book is a feast. Most of you will not read it in one sitting. But you will return to it again and again for reference and ideas. Enjoy!

Robert Theobald
Wickenburg, Arizona
July, 1989

Intro

Coming of Consciousness
in Community Medicine

octor, I've been reading your journal called the *Neighborhood Caretaker*, with the intriguing subtitle *Converging Science, Art, and Vocation*. How did you and your wife get started in journal writing?

OLD DOC: In 1974 when I was 52 years old and in good health, I retired from 25 years work in medical pathology to seriously take up medical care in the urban neighborhood. Those years in clinical pathology had passed in an intellectual landscape marked by miracles of 20th-century science. Mass sanitation, better nutrition, immunization, antibiotics, mind-helping drugs, and the wealth-creating information age were transforming the whole world. The clinical laboratory was the heart of hospital-based medicine, which was the reason 80 percent of us had escaped the plagues of earlier centuries only to face a new universe of social plagues.

MEDICAL STUDENT: Didn't you miss the daily excitement of the pathology lab?

OLD DOC: Not really. My wife Betty was involved in comprehensive health planning and issues of poverty, and it was becoming clear to us that social diseases, rather than biological illness, were responsible for most person-days lost from work, from family life, and from chosen interests. The same social diseases disable First World people everywhere: accidents, abandoned elders, addictions, adolescent pregnancy, assault, deteriorating housing and neighborhoods, family collapse, joblessness at all ages and in all classes, senility, youth alienation and suicide. Laboratory medicine was not addressing these.

12

MEDICAL STUDENT: If these are the manifestations of illness, what did you discover were the underlying causes?

OLD DOC: Underlying these signs of sick systems of human settlement are the contradictions of fragmented "specialty" services; abandonment of the poor; nonfunctioning public education; impotent local and national government; work without meaningful engagement; and meaningless old symbols and public stories in church, state, and family that are powerless to direct the common life or give dignity to life's struggles and transitions.

MEDICAL STUDENT: A blanket indictment. Medical science surely has no mandate to deal with the entire culture.

OLD DOC: On the contrary. Medicine, in the sense of rational inquiry, experiment, and appropriate technologies to heal or help the major causes of human pain and disability, has precisely this challenge. Community medicine then became our new arena of work. My new laboratory was a storefront primary-care center in the black ghetto of Chicago's West Side, described at that time as the most dangerous square mile in the world.

MEDICAL STUDENT: What did your family think of your move to the ghetto?

OLD DOC: Our youngest had left the nest by then, and all the children were supportive. Betty and I saw ourselves as a missional family, working together in this new field. While I was grounding my social theory in the real life of the city, she was getting her master's degree in business administration, having discovered that 30 years' community volunteer work is not enough background to address the major challenges in creating healthy neighborhoods. We both decided that the focus of the human services in the late 20th century needs to be the primal community.*

MEDICAL STUDENT: What is a primal community?

OLD DOC: It is the intentional net of human relationships that does the civilizing and conserving work of the old natural village and kinship ties. Integration of fragmented lives and human services in most cases will be based in geographic neighborhoods. We are

Every man bears the whole stamp of the human condition.

—MONTAIGUE

---

* *primal community:* an underlying sense of wholeness in human settlement. It is a basic understanding of life shared by residents of a particular piece of geography. This common understanding is the foundation that gives rise to the cultural, economic, and political structure peculiar to that community. It is held in being by common (not individual) symbols that point to the nature of life in a given locale.

betting on healthful neighborhoods as the social design that will care for all the needs of all the people living in them. We don't expect to be proven wrong.

MEDICAL STUDENT: How long did you work in your ghetto primary-care center?

OLD DOC: Only 18 months. We said this was our first generation social laboratory. I came to see that the levers for moving our health system towards remedying the modern epidemic of social diseases do not exist in the ghetto, or in the county health-care establishment. So I looked for a better base of investigation, a second generation social laboratory.

MEDICAL STUDENT: And you chose?

OLD DOC: A state public health department. In 1977 I began a four-year job with the Illinois Department of Public Health in Springfield as chief of a statewide chronic disease control program, while Betty launched a year-long pilot program to establish alternatives to institutional care of disabled elderly persons (in home support services funded by the state Department on Aging).

MEDICAL STUDENT: That makes sense, since public health has always focused on environment, and since high blood pressure, diabetes, and lung diseases have important social and environmental components. What did you discover?

OLD DOC: My question was: can government, responsible for the wellbeing of all the citizens, serve the new health needs effectively? I soon discovered that bureaucratic paralysis at all levels, public and private, effectively blocked cooperative action necessary for data gathering, tracking, remedial action or evaluation, regardless of how much money we had.

MEDICAL STUDENT: Looking back, do you regret the time you spent working for a state agency?

OLD DOC: No. It was an opportunity to see a side of medicine I had not appreciated before. In medical school I was led to believe that medical science belongs to the whole society, and that the priorities of applied health sciences are set by the pressing causes of disability in a given time and place. In 1977 I realized that priorities were set by the funding sources.

MEDICAL STUDENT: What was Betty doing at this time?

OLD DOC: In a local community forum meeting we heard residents and agency representatives identify gaps in human services. Building on her learnings in the one-year Comprehensive Alternative Care program which she directed during our first year in Springfield, Betty and I set up a small home help business, called Elder Power: Professional Home Helps. Elder Power provided essential assistance in bathing, cooking, cleaning, laundry and shopping.

MEDICAL STUDENT: Where did you get your funding?

OLD DOC: Mostly from our own pockets initially, with fees for service—including state contracts and donations, as the business grew. We discovered that an average of ten hours per month of support services were enough to keep many disabled elders out of nursing homes. It was at this time we started *Neighborhood Caretaker* as a one-page newsletter of Elder Power, to focus attention on the societal challenges facing our aging population.

MEDICAL STUDENT: What kind of challenges?

OLD DOC: Three major ones in 1977 were loss of sense of community, loss of significant engagement, and the institutional bias of third-party payers. Generally, there still is no adequate public funding for home support services, which are more needed than home nursing.

MEDICAL STUDENT: But after four years you moved on. Why?

OLD DOC: Whatever the objectives of our statewide government programs, the implementation had to be at the local level, by cooperating groups of the public and private sector. Elder Power was a going business by then, and a demonstration of just such cooperation. It had a dedicated board of directors; financial angels; caring workers; collaboration with voluntary, public, and private organizations; and grateful clients: a wonderful sign of hope. But one of anything can be an accident. Was it replicable?

MEDICAL STUDENT: You mean you just dropped it, after you got it going?

OLD DOC: Yes. We wanted to move on to our third-generation social laboratory. Betty resigned as executive director. When we left, Elder Power employed 32 full- and part-time workers. A year later this had grown to 100 workers in two urban centers. We wrote, phoned, visited dozens of groups in cities across the U.S., telling the Elder Power story, inviting them to check out the operating principles we had used to fill a gap in needed neighborhood structures of human care. Most gatekeepers of existing agencies listened politely without follow-up action. However, in Dallas, Texas, and in Coraopolis, Pennsylvania, new Elder Power-type businesses came to life and prospered.

MEDICAL STUDENT: What made it replicable?

OLD DOC: Each is sponsored by a local council of churches, funded by private individuals and groups and by fees for service, with little or no help from existing social agencies.

MEDICAL STUDENT: Why did you choose to move to Indianapolis?

OLD DOC: Here we joined a group of other missional families—called a cluster—churchmen and women with experience in community development methods which we see as necessary for developing healthy neighborhoods.

MEDICAL STUDENT: And what is the mission of your missional family cluster?

OLD DOC: We collaborate with local groups to deal effectively with the issues identified as priorities by local citizens in their home neighborhood settings. *The Neighborhood Caretaker* changed its focus from the elderly to the emerging interface between local residents developing their neighborhoods and the new discipline of community medicine. One of our operating principles is that engagement in the social process is what most of us would call good health.

MEDICAL STUDENT: That accounts for the variety of topics you cover.

OLD DOC: We try to uncover gaps both in family and community medicine and in the holistic health-care movement by reporting what is happening in many kinds of social laboratories, in the context of our definition of health. We run stories about:

- architecture and community space design that support lively safe social interchange (including affordable, low-income home ownership);
- community medicine and nursing using new texts and agendas;
- conflict resolution;
- crime control and better correction programs;
- ethics that make sense and command responsibility;
- journalism and social art that hold up stories and symbols of integrity* and wholeness;
- learning for all ages, especially literacy for adults;
- macro- and microeconomics that lead to thousands of new kinds of jobs;
- psychology that understands community dimensions of individual thinking, feeling and deciding;

---

* *integrity:* wholeness, coherence, inner shalom; a person who "has his act together."

- social work that helps the poor and guides them into the mainstream; and
- university departments which are developing new working models and field tests.

MEDICAL STUDENT: What is the unifying factor in all this? Is it networking? Are you just sharing approaches that work?

OLD DOC: It is more than networking. We know that information alone never changes behavior. The underlying questions are: What starts and sustains the core groups behind each new venture that is working to shape the new world? In the midst of information overload and innumerable choices, how do these groups come to know and trust each other when their collaboration would be mutually helpful? And where in all our glorious diversity do we trace the one unifying reality that sets the limits in our varied and free living?

MEDICAL STUDENT: I take it that by core groups you mean missional family clusters, and you want *Neighborhood Caretaker* to link them together. The questions around sustaining core groups sound to me like another experiment for your social laboratories. Who is going to pull together the varied resources to deal with all the disorders in one community?

OLD DOC: You are right about the role we wish our journal to have. Readers are beginning to contact each other about questions raised in the stories, half of which come from our readers. The Indianapolis core group of half a dozen families is our primary social laboratory now. Together we are committed to giving social form to needed cross-disciplinary collaboration in neighborhood sciences. We think of this as urban homesteading.

MEDICAL STUDENT: Do you all live under one roof or operate under one financial budget?

OLD DOC: Each of the families has done this in the past, and may again in the future, as a matter of economy and convenience. More important is our shared office space which fosters close coordination of our several concerns with the neighborhood—affordable housing for low and moderate income families, adult literacy, entry-level job- and life-skills training for jobless women, rebuilding urban church congregations and citizen groups as neighborhood caretakers, and publishing *Neighborhood Caretaker Journal.* Even with our busy schedules, we manage to eat together several times a week.

MEDICAL STUDENT: What are the advantages to each of the families in your close association in this missional cluster?

OLD DOC: Urban homesteading is hard work. Few individual

17

families should attempt it alone. The work is sometimes discouraging and costly. Each of the families needs a secure financial income apart from the innovative projects we are pushing and the groups we are helping. We understand each other's joys and sorrows, and often can help each other with our particular skills or other gifts. Our "Venture Loan Fund" has sustained several projects through otherwise very lean start-up times.

MEDICAL STUDENT: What are you learning about covenants that hold a core group like your Indianapolis missional family cluster steady on its course?

OLD DOC: Together we are working on that important question, and will offer some tentative thoughts in Chapter 8 on Core Family Clusters. I think we all have experienced surprise and pleasure at the fun of working together in this project.

MEDICAL STUDENT: Thank you, doctor.[1]

■ Our vocational journey

In our own vocational journey* in medicine over 40 years we have encountered, as a residual of the old world passing, the collapse of structural care; the contradictions of fragmented "specialty" services; abandonment of the poor; nonfunctioning public education; impotent local and national government; work without meaningful engagement; and meaningless old symbols and public stories in church, state, and family that are powerless to direct the common life or give dignity to life's struggles and transitions.

We have come very strongly to believe that medical science, in order to deal effectively with the actual, underlying causes of the more visible symptoms of human pain and disability in our society, must work with our entire, diseased culture. Thus, for the past 14 years, the social laboratory of community medicine has been our arena of work, less through the medical establishment than through the *dynamic* of the church that throughout history has cared for society.

---

* *vocation:* one's calling, coming as a recognition of a human need to which one has the ability to respond.

Pioneer role of the church dynamic in society

Theologian H. Richard Niebuhr saw the church as that part in any society which, in the midst of general chaos, is the first to despair, first to repent,* first to see and hold up a new vision of resurrection† (see Appendix A). Unhappily, those in the churches who now are ready for social repentance△ have few modern, working models of how to rebuild lives and neighborhoods. Surely they cannot do the whole task alone. But just as surely, we argue, no one else is as well placed to invite the many gifted, middle-class persons (in or out of the churches, we do not care) to come together in task forces and work groups to accelerate all the scattered efforts at human and neighborhood development. Churches, synagogues, mosques, and temples are present in every part of American life. Where government, educators, professionals, agencies, and business organizations generally get low marks, their churches still are trusted by many people.

This book, then, is for the new church: that pioneering part of every society that lives in continuity with the past through relevant rites, rituals, and symbols,** and in its own life embodies with profound awe the way life really is. This book is for those people who want to get beyond their single-issue passions to comprehensive enhancement of our common life. It is for those who are ready to work together for the convergence of science, art, and vocation in local settings, knowing that economic development always needs social and spirit†† development and vice versa.

■ A global spirit movement

In our search for colleagues, we were drawn to the Order: Ecumenical (O:E) in the Ecumenical Institute which was embody-

---

* *repent:* to change direction, turn back. An action, not a feeling.

† *resurrection:* to have unlimited possibilities for a new life style where no such possibilities existed before. A concrete situation, not a feeling.

△ *social repentance:* an organized change in group behavior. An action, not a feeling.

** *rites, rituals and symbols:* see a good dictionary.

†† *spirit:* the earthy reality of human experience which in its totality goes beyond material, thinking and feeling contact with the world of the senses. Today, we find that concerns of the spirit appear less in ecclesiastical settings and more in secular vocations such as commerce, medicine, homemaking and education

ing the pioneer role of the church in the urban chaos of Chicago's west side as part of a global spirit movement. (We were stipended members of the order in 1974-75.)

A broad-based social and spirit movement, as manifested in the European Ecumenical Lay Academies, and communities like Iona and Lindesfarne in Great Britain after World War II, spread to North America. Like the dove flying out of Noah's ark looking for a landing place, this movement developed several political, social and religious forms. In Chicago in the late 1960s, the Order: Ecumenical, a family order along with full-time staff of the Ecumenical Institute, became one of the powerful expressions of this movement. (Later, when O:E began working in non-church and non-western communities, the name Institute of Cultural Affairs [ICA] was adopted.) The 2,000 or more generally young, educated people in this order directed their passion for justice and renewal of the common life into disciplined research, teaching and demonstration that invited established churches to work together for total parish renewal. Living out of a common purse, on stipends at or below the poverty level wherever in 50 nations they went, the rapidly-growing, multinational order created a social parallel for the intellectual and theological revolutions of the early 20th century.

Not surprisingly, organized religious bodies in general did not embrace the poverty and simple life style of the Order: Ecumenical. Its members found themselves isolated from most congregations in the churches. The stipended, full-time troops (they used military analogies a lot in those first heady days) then reached beyond established ecclesiastical bodies to create "urban houses" in about 35 cities in five continents. Living and working with the poor in Hindu, Muslim, Buddhist, Christian and secular societies, the O:E troops believed they were making an "end run on the church," pioneering in methods of local community economic and social development which the congregations of all the world's great religions one day could embrace.

The O:E continues with its original vigor in India, Japan, Latin America and Africa. In North America much of its drive has been transformed into a decentralized, almost invisible collage of now-matured pastors, educators, healers, and community pillars quietly pursuing the dreams of the Ecumenical Lay Academies: the transformation of the common life of all humankind. Many persons without formal religious affiliation share vigorously in this 20th century enterprise.

Our intent in writing this book is to help the O:E and similar groups complete their "end run on the church," the holy dream of their youth. Our perception is that most of the major church denominations of Christendom have completed their update of 20th century theology and have an increasingly well-read and interested laity. Many who in the past two generations have fled the inner city for the good life in the American suburbs are pretty certain now that they are called to some kind of social repentance serving the whole city, including especially its illiterate and unemployable youth in non-nurturing families, its abandoned elders, and its disorganized and dilapidated neighborhoods which are such easy prey for psychotic and vicious criminals.

Independence and decentralization have tended to be a strong bias for many pioneer groups. However, our isolation can rob us of the opportunity to learn from and gain strength from the similar efforts of others and can prevent them from benefitting from our experience and wisdom. We hope that local groups—in their communities, congregations, task forces, committees and councils—can discover how they can work with other like or unlike groups to get on with the whole civilizing enterprise. This is a question of polity (appropriate decision-making structures). Just as a working global polity will be created by those who understand the interdependence of the whole planet, so, at the local level, those who can learn and use the methods of convergence and cooperation will create the local framework for the global spirit movement in the 21st century.

Earthcare Indianapolis

For six years, through 1988, we were part of Earthcare Indianapolis, an inner-city intentional community which also served as the regional office of the Institute of Cultural Affairs. The core group of about a dozen families (three living under one roof; others visiting frequently around their interactive concerns) regularly planned together and shared the weekly celebrations. From this base we published the *Neighborhood Caretaker Journal* with its success stories of social transformation efforts occurring around the globe. From such stories, visits with colleagues across the country, and the Earthcare community experience, we learned much that we felt should be shared on a wider basis.

It is our hope that through this book, new dialogues will be catalyzed between groups of socially concerned individuals engaged in social care across the whole planet, and particularly in North

America. That they will have the opportunity together to ask each other: What can dialogues with other caring individuals involved in similar efforts tell us about our own careers, our vocations? What have we learned in our efforts? Which of our local experiences and learning supports or throws into question what others are saying? What learnings are so often mentioned as to suggest newly-emerging or newly-recognized natural laws? With that in mind, we invite you to read on, to revel in the following stories of successful ventures in the arena of social transformation, and to look for colleagues with whom you might like to share or from whom you might like to learn.

The questions in Appendix B will facilitate your reflection, learning and decision for action if you utilize them either alone or with others at the completion of reading each chapter.

Chapter 1

The Path of Renewal

As the song says, we are in a new world now. We never can go back. The light of the new still blinds our eyes. As they say after a good funeral, life goes on.

The era of the printed page, steam power, cathedrals throwing stone and glass to the heavens to reflect the order and beauty of the firmament, nation-states growing out of the barrels of cannons, communities of faith divided by great systems of religious belief, commerce organized globally around great banks: What shall we say? Let us say, "It was good. And now it is over."

In the pages following we will encounter dozens of players creating the new world ahead. Artists, bankers, children, crazy folk, elders, heroes, homemakers, organizers, poor folk, preachers, prisoners, scientists, teachers, and zany comics in a hundred ways are making the new world happen.

Our stories are about Those Who Make Good Things Happen. More generally, let us call them Those Who Can, TWCs (pronounced Twicks). Where we can, we will give their addresses and phone numbers. Where they are really making things happen, a good rule is that TWCs want to talk to other TWCs. They make time to help each other.

Hundreds of thousands of TWCs of all ages, vocations, and backgrounds are giving substantial money, time, and thought to one or more parts of a diversely organized movement toward:

- A *new social value system* supporting decentralized power and leadership aimed at creating a whole new social vehicle of civilization;

We are in a new world now, we never can go back.
Our eyes have seen a thousand years,
Our minds have bridged the gap
And here we stand, we hear the cry, creation surging on.
Our hearts beat wildly, and they sigh, no thing to lean upon.
We are in a new world now, the light still blinds our eyes...
Like clowns who merge with time and space,
Who run and jump and fall,
We beckon to the endless race, we play the fool for all.

—FROM EARTHCARE SINGS, A SONGBOOK OF THE INSTITUTE OF CULTURAL AFFAIRS

23

- *Profound* spirit refreshment,* in a mode that honors the deep values of many traditions, looks to the future, and enables an authentic life journey for every person and group; and
- Stable, sustaining *core groups†* of individuals and families, who act as the essential engines and laboratories of social change△ toward nonviolence, ecological harmony, economic sufficiency and total neighborhood care in the wider society.

■ Old Doc: Where have we come from? Where are we going?

DR. PRIMUS: From all sides I hear that "we are in a great age of transition," that a breakout in mass human consciousness is underway; that we must go beyond our origins in sect, class, nation and race in order to realize an ancient drive to peace and harmony in the midst of this turmoil, to find our way to our lost Eden. I don't think we will ever find it. In fact, the universe has always been in an age of transition.

DR. TERTIA: We and the dinosaurs, in the same situation: an unreliable climate, overconsumption, too much competition, and exploitation of the environment. I can just hear little groups of Stegosaurus here and there muttering, "There's gotta be a better way to make a living. Let's get out." It was a radical shift in consciousness that required them to go beyond their origin, stretch

---

* *profound:* speaking to us below the merely intellectual or emotional levels; carrying a message related to our self-images of maleness/femaleness, work, play; our chosen values. Profound messages, when heeded, change our lives by changing the way we see the world.

† *core group:* stable sustaining groups, usually of a dozen persons or less, who over years lead and hold-in-being a neighborhood, business or other enterprise. Varying degrees of intimacy characterize core groups. In some their association is all business related; in others, the whole group functions like an extended family, perhaps living out of a common purse.

△ *social laboratory:* social inventions (e.g., community land trusts) should be tested in a controlled setting before being recommended to the general public. Social engineering has a bad reputation for lack of prudent, small-scale social laboratory testing of new social designs. Should we spend our limited resources in money gifts to poor families, or in sex education of grade school children, or x, y, z efforts, or any combination of these approaches, to reduce the personal and community tragedy of unwanted adolescent pregnancy? Controlled social laboratory studies of relative cost effectiveness of many possible action plans can lower the volume of outraged moralistic rhetoric.

their limbs and fly, or perish. So they transisted into pterodactyls and flew into the unknown to get a totally new perception of themselves and their role in the universe. Ah, the mystery of the genetic code!

OLD DOC: The human journey is analogous. In the age of telecommunication, of mass literacy, of political struggles for peace and justice, there is a global consensus being tested: that we are one planetary people in an era of one God,* and that the earth belongs to all beings. From the dawn of the preliterate era our consciousness has been formed by visions of wholeness. And through every transition our consciousness as a race has grasped a foundational Word: The struggle we experience is good.

We can see now, looking back, that we have emerged from a millennium of rule by world empire hegemonies, empowered[†] by the likes of Galileo, Napoleon, Edison and Eisenhower. At times Eden seemed beyond grasp; at times the whole enterprise seemed to self-destruct. But as a race we knew that life for Everyman can begin all over, at any moment. The quest for Eden allowed the experience of a life of meaningful expenditure—in the laboratory, battlefield, nursery, orphanage, academy, or wherever.

DR. PRIMUS: Why are we talking about Eden?

DR. TERTIA: I think because the Eden myth[Δ] is talking about our human separation from the wholeness of creation and from our own mystery, depth and greatness.

> The cosmos is the primary revelatory experience of the divine.
>
> —*THOMAS BERRY*

---

* *God:* no system of belief or worldview is implied. For some persons in our pluralistic, secular society God is the ultimate ground of our being (Tillich); the inscrutable Other; the One (Islam and Judaism); the Father of all humans (Christian and many folk religions); the final Mystery. In an age pulling back from sectarian divisiveness, "God" may not be used to legitimate any belief or commitment. "So help me God" is generally perceived as a quaint archaism.

† *empower(ed):* as an end in itself, asserts a reverence for human freedom which threatens powerful systems of state, church and commerce which glorify manipulation of people. Although freedom is a central affirmation of every world religion, reverence for human freedom is quickly lost, gained again only at cost in life and treasure. This will be true in the New World as in the old world that has passed away forever.

Δ *myth:* multidimensional truth or experience of life conveyed in story form. The story need not be considered literally or historically true to be profoundly empowering. An American example: Patrick Henry said, "Give me liberty or give me death."

DR. SECUNDUS: This is an astonishingly simple truth about human consciousness. Prince or slave, one option is ours that no other human can give or take away. Expressed in a thousand varied vocations, the option is faith. Like a successful virus which can enter the plant or animal body to join and transform the very genetic code itself, faith transforms human consciousness instantly and permanently. Faith is common in children, the lasting jewel of the old, an option for Everyman.

DR. TERTIA: Are you saying that faith is the key to transformed consciousness and the door to Eden; that is, to transcending our separation? But you also said faith is like a virus that transforms the genetic code, which means it is ethically neutral because the genetic code is neutral; or doesn't faith have ethical values?

OLD DOC: Well, a man from Nazareth once said, "Why do you call me good? Your faith has made you whole."

DR. PRIMUS: Words like faith, hope and love lack meaning for most of us.

DR. SECUNDUS: Pity. They reflect a basic attitude toward life. Faith can be defined as venturing with confidence into the unknown. Hope is trusting in the goodness of Being in a climate of unbelief. Love is the stance of forgiveness.

DR. TERTIA: So now the lord of history, like a child gleefully smashing her castle of blocks, is ending the thousand-year hegemonies of our world empires, institutions and social pillars. Turn ye away from illusions of safety, from covenants that bind us to the city of destruction. Repent! Join in enterprises of faith for the future!

DR. PRIMUS: And what are these enterprises? What will replace the social order of the People of the Book? or St. Benedict's model for the interior decorum and polity of a thousand-year civilization?

DR. SECUNDUS: Among the social structures that may house a new global age of faith is the urban neighborhood, ecumenical, with gifts from a thousand cultures past and present. Faith, beginning in the caretakers of that neighborhood, transforms its common life as quickly as affordable housing for all or local sanctions for liberty and justice for all. Without faith, the interior life of the neighborhood is chained to the terminal illness of the millennium that is dying. Within each ecumenical faith neighborhood will be numerous interdependent core groups, mutually assisting each other.

DR. PRIMUS: No matter how many excellent core groups there are, they cannot impact the larger community by themselves. They must act in coalitions.

OLD DOC: True. Winning at research into schizophrenia will not happen in the individual neighborhood. One of the quality-of-life issues in urban living will be how many broad action coalitions will find support in any given neighborhood. In some neighborhoods, some mutual-help groups and some coalitions will take on the hard task of global myth-making that will point our children and grandchildren to the truth about life, about faith, hope and love. The convergence of these three in ecumenical-faith neighborhoods has the potential for another Great Awakening.

DR. TERTIA: Myths are made from the stuff of human experience. How will the theologians and ordinary household saints integrate all the treasures of the world's wisdom? What is the story that will make a village or neighborhood co-terminous with the universe?

OLD DOC: We stand on the shoulders of giants. We can imagine the nameless creators of the ancient Vedas of India smiling encouragement at our struggles to give appropriate form to the Song of God for our time. We can be sure that the Hebrew psalmists would admire our praises of God's goodness if they lift the hearts of our people. Mohammad's pillars of social order and holiness were not fulfilled sufficiently in the old world of Islam: They command further observances in our time.

DR. SECUNDUS: In every age we are called to take down the idols that limit our consciousness and freedom, and replace them with a vision of wholeness, infinitely varied and intricately interdependent, for a global-mass age of faith. Who of us can imagine the world our grandchildren will build? Will it last a thousand years?

■ The path of leadership

The normal and major flow

The path of leadership into social change in the new world is in two directions. Moving with the normal flow of the world are the frequent creative bursts of inventiveness by Those Who Can Make Good Things Happen. In the diagram on the next page, this is the major, clockwise flow.

A. Normally TWCs first work through small groups, then later larger ones, to build social consensus and cohesion around the new. The new social inventions are gradually adopted by whole groups.

B. Next, the old and new are integrated within intimate groups or families. The internal work of the family, along with birthing, nurturing, mutual help and defense is a multilevel pulling together

He has half the deed done who has made a beginning.

—*HORACE*

27

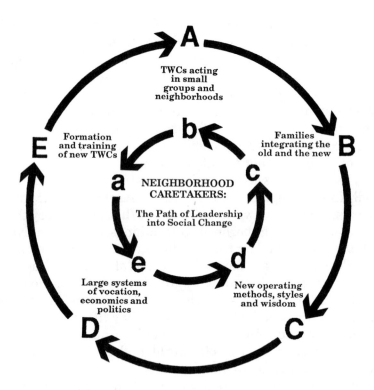

FIGURE 1-1: THE PATH
OF LEADERSHIP

of old and new values: order/freedom, assigned roles/selected roles, conserving/destroying. It is often in the family that information is developed into knowledge—where "I think," "I believe," and "I wonder" are as meaningful as any statement of fact. It is in family where knowledge is developed into wisdom, where "my neighbor can't read" develops into "all learning belongs to all people."

C. Out of the developing wisdom of families and groups there appear conventions, traditions, and ways of talking about the world we experience. The notion of Gaia, of the earth as a living being, is capsulized in a televised vision of earthrise seen from the moon. Vastly expanded knowledge of psychology and sociology provides new spirit contexts as ancient religions incorporate the new data.

D. Armed with new future-looking myths and contexts, TWCs, frequently in intentional core groups, increasingly address the challenges of the world of work and politics.

E. As they win in these struggles, they train new leadership, new TWCs appear, and the process spirals ahead.

The minor reverse of normal flow is important also

With each of these normal transitions there is, as in the back and forth flows of ions in classical inorganic chemical solutions, a lesser reverse flow.

e. A few individualistic TWCs choose not to work through the normal flow (A-E) of group processes, but move immediately in reverse of the normal flow to take on the challenges of their vocation alone. Individual doctors try to correct the wrongs of the health system; students rebel in inappropriate schools; the oppressed poor run amok.

d. Divisions appear within the worlds of work and politics as TWCs insert new organizing images and call forth new energies for restructuring the institutions of those arenas. Families whose lives revolve around particular arenas of work are caught up in the struggle for appropriate change.

c. Sacred and secular congregations empower families with new contexts and myths.

b. Neighborhood caretaker families—families that have made the health of the community and of the planet their lives' work—create the ordered communities in which they choose to live.

a. Local groups produce new TWC leaders.

In this book we look at both the normal and the reverse-normal social flows among these five dynamics of the new world community and at explorers and leaders of both directions of social change.

We discern key characteristics of leadership and some social methods that release orderly and real change. From real life examples and reflections, we trace the foundational affirmations that all life is good, the past (all of it) is received, our present reality (all of it) is approved by that which is greater than we are, and we each and all are free to live the only life given to us.

We meet several kinds of family, and look at the integration of information, knowledge, and wisdom in core groups and families.

We see emerging outlines of new myths for the planet's one human community, myths that energize leaders to move with power around contradictions* which blight our experience of wholeness.

---

* *contradiction:* also called challenge, is a powerful but often quite hidden active force which prevents desired results or changes. On the border is the root challenge poverty? which is due to what? or racism? which is due to what? corruption of bureaucrats? due to what? What is the probable hidden cause of misery and oppression, which, if removed, would release the creative and reconciling energies of the local people to realize a good life?

We look at examples of TWCs transforming the complex systems of our intellectual and political life.

To summarize:

TWCs, operating through cohesive social groups, empowered by family understanding and new wisdom, guided by new myths and refreshed religion, will address the real challenges of an intransigent world: Daddy can't read; the Jones baby has a bruise on her head again; Mrs. Quinn is crazy and won't come out of her room; the ground water supply is polluted. The new social ethics* and actions around these challenges call forth a new generation of TWCs. We conclude by asking—will we do it?

■ Preparing for the journey

There are two requisites for a community of people about to set out on the journey into the compassionate era,[†] with its unknown terrors and undemonstrated benefits:

First, the journeying community needs many, many messages that the old ways are not working, that new ways are possible, and that they—not the mayor, nor the minister, nor the school superintendent—are the ones who are going to make the journey happen.

For example, the following story on homicide against children shows that the old civilizational values really need fixing but also suggests the power of the science of epidemiology in naming problems, discovering the critical variables, setting priorities among remedies, evaluating allocation and use of resources, and developing the criteria for public accountability.

The second requisite for starting the journey is that the community needs leaders who are recognized by the group as good, experienced, wise, and powerful in ways that really matter.

What really matters? The second story, "Serviglesia," from the U.S.-Mexican border, provides examples of leaders who can develop social cohesion from use of sound social and spirit methods, inte-

---

* *social ethics:* As Bonhoeffer reminds us in "Ethics and Freedom" on page 33-34, and as the foundational images of every world religion teach, each person and each group are responsible for choosing obligations and inventing appropriate action responses to the always ambiguous real and particular world of available real choices.

† *compassionate era:* no one name has yet emerged to describe this new world we are entering. The term "compassionate era" comes from Robert Theobald's work *The Rapids of Change.*

grate family and core group values, create new myths and spirit refreshment, and make powerful moves against powerful contradictions.

Leaders who are willing themselves first to traverse the way of uncertainty, to live with doubts, in constant struggle and inner growth, also have a strong ethical base acceptable to the times and the community. The third piece on ethics and freedom provides a model for a workable ethical base.

> Do not take council
> of your fears.
>
> —UNKNOWN

Childhood homicide: A leading cause of death [2]

Homicide accounts for one death in 20 in the under-age-18 group in the United States. Infanticide, fatal child abuse and neglect, and homicide in the community have increased dramatically since 1925. In all groups more males are victims. At all ages half the victims are black. Deaths due to arson are highest in the 5-9 age group. The proportion of deaths due to firearms increases with age. Prevention will include measures to strengthen families and their community support systems.

Serviglesia on the border [3]

Driving south along the Rio Grande, our first impression of the El Paso-Juarez complex was, on the Mexican side, increasingly crowded shacks in the vast desert surrounding Juarez; and, on the U.S. side, the Tibetan architecture of the university campus and downtown high-rises. Over coffee with our hosts, Carol and Bill Schlesinger, we learned the following:

U.S. companies here operate twin plants in Juarez, employing thousands of young women, while husbands, fathers and brothers remain jobless. Undocumented adults cross the border by the thousands each day for work, a source of cheap labor, subsidizing U.S. industry. In spite of the veneer of prosperity in El Paso, both sides of the border share all the problems of a third-world city: poverty, illiteracy, lack of water, bad sanitation, spotty health care. These conditions and traditional Anglo-Hispanic hostility have severely strained the structures of family and community.

While both U.S. and Mexican governments have looked away at pressing problems elsewhere, churches on both sides of the border have stepped into the chaos, calling people to love God and neighbor. Begun in the early seventies, Project Verdad is sponsored by the National Presbyterian Church of Mexico, the Presbyterian Church (USA) and the Cumberland Presbyterian Church. It has developed

31

nine "serviglesias" (serving churches) in the poorest neighborhoods ("colonia") on the outskirts of Juarez and El Paso. Of its four co-directors, two are Mexican and two are American. Cross-cultural relationships are developed through sister churches and participation of volunteers and work teams from across Mexico and the U.S.

The congregation of each serviglesia learns how to make decisions as a group, how to plan for their own needs and growth, and how to understand their lives in the light of their faith. Each serviglesia provides direct services to the community and participates with other groups in local community development. The pastors are supported half by the congregations and half by Project Verdad.

The serviglesias provide a variety of services including clinics, preventive health education, breakfast feeding programs, kindergartens, building materials and other assistance to improve housing, and emergency food supplies.

Our first stop on the tour was a meeting with the two co-directors, a doctor and public health nurse. The doctor has created a network of volunteer physicians and a laboratory to serve patients referred by the serviglesias. Next we visited a class of Health Promoters, ten attentive women meeting in one of the church buildings. In the course of their training two of them had found head lice on children in one of the serviglesia kindergartens. Their instructions were successful not only in getting rid of the head lice, but also in adding two new mothers to the Health Promoters class.

Each serviglesia works with other community groups to improve the neighborhood. Our tour took us through the poor neighborhood of Felipe Angeles (population 40,000) which had never been connected to the city water system until the serviglesia pastor organized a community water committee. With the help of UNICEF, USAID, and organizations interested in border health, the committee persuaded the Juarez Water Board that connecting the neighborhood to the water supply was possible. Temporary pipes now provide water a few hours each day, until city water is connected.

In Felipe Angeles we bought hot bread for lunch from the cooperative bakery, one of several production cooperatives and self-help activities sponsored by the Project. In other poor neighborhoods, new businesses include cement block making, woodworking, sewing, and a laundromat. Adult literacy, scholarships for secondary education, and training in family financial management are also offered in each of the communities served.

Ethics and Freedom[4]

Theologian Dietrich Bonhoeffer provides a context for TWCs as they struggle with societal transformation in the real world:

> Responsibility and freedom are corresponding concepts. Factually, though not chronologically, responsibility presupposes freedom, and freedom can exist only with responsibility. Responsibility is the freedom of men which is given only in obligation to God and to our neighbor.
>
> The responsible man acts in the freedom of his own self, without the support of men, circumstances, or principles, but with a due consideration for the given human and general conditions, and for the relevant questions of principle. The proof of his freedom is the fact that nothing can answer for him, nothing can exonerate him, except his own deed and his own self. It is he himself who must observe, judge, weigh up, decide, and act. It is man himself who must examine the motives, the prospects, the value and the purpose of his action. But neither the purity of the motivation, nor the opportune circumstances, nor the value, nor the significant purpose of the intended undertaking can become the governing law of his action, a law to which he can withdraw, to which he can appeal as an authority, and by which he can be exculpated and acquitted. For in that case he would indeed no longer be a truly free man. The action of the responsible man is performed in the obligation which alone gives freedom, and which gives entire freedom, the obligation to God and to our neighbor as they confront us in Jesus Christ. At the same time it is performed wholly in the domain of relativity, wholly in the twilight which the historical situation spreads over good and evil; it is performed in the midst of the innumerable perspectives in which every given phenomenon appears. It is not to decide simply between right and wrong and between good and evil, but between right and right and between wrong and wrong. As Aschylus said, "right strives with right." Precisely in this respect responsible action is a free venture; it is not justified by any law; it is performed without any claim to self-justification, and therefore without any claim to an ultimate valid knowledge of good and evil. Good, as what is responsible, is performed in ignorance of good and in the surrender to God of the deed which has become necessary and which is nevertheless, or for that very reason, free; for it is God who sees the heart, who weighs up the deed, and who directs the course of history.

NEIGHBORHOOD CARETAKERS

Those Who Can, the TWCs, are present in every group that is growing and serving the social order. Caretakers and pillars of neighborhood or company cohesion, they may be present as individual persons. More often they are a rather small core group living and working within their larger social community. They create community order, reach out to regional and global colleagues, maintain the fragile spider webs of planetary interchange in a hundred arenas of life and consciousness. In the next chapter we'll look at some of their successes.

Chapter 2

Weaving the Fabric of Society

Old Doc: The Woof and the Warp

DR. TERTIA: Doctor, I'm amazed at the number of different ways people try to express the transformation that is going on everywhere. Who really has the keys to the kingdom in this day and age?

OLD DOC: Your question is, I think, who is reweaving the fabric of society? In this intransigent world, many TOACs (Those Of Arrested Consciousness) seem to be in positions of power, often in the majority. These principalities and powers of this world, if left to themselves, are moving us all to the brink of destruction. They are the "warp" of society. They will always be with us.

DR. TERTIA: Some of us call them the reactionary establishment. And all too often their rebel opponents offer little real improvement. Neither confrontation nor compromise moves us toward safer, more satisfying ways of living together.

OLD DOC: Try to avoid despair. Moving in a different direction are the creative, aware, intentional TWCs, throwing over old ideas, reempowering dinosaur institutions, inventing new structures, shuttling back and forth among the TOACs, creating the designs of the future. In short, being the "woof" of society's fabric.

DR. TERTIA: We used to call them reformers or even revolutionaries.

OLD DOC: There are TWCs in the establishment too. I think the question we are asking is: What are the decision-making structures for woofing through the planetary warp? What do the shuttles look like? Are they an intentional community,* a movement like the Greens, a mainline church congregation, a global servant order?

DR. TERTIA: I expect we need all of these and more, since each group has strengths and weaknesses. But leaving the weaving metaphor aside, what do you mean by your terms the old and new church? Are you saying that with our new consciousness of our perishable planet we are creating a new church? With an earth goddess, perhaps?

OLD DOC: God forbid! I firmly believe that Cosmic Consciousness is totally uninterested in our belief systems. Old Ezekiel (Ezekiel 37) saw the new church as new flesh and spirit on old bones. Whenever the TWCs cause a part of society that is despairing over its old images and forms to repent, to see a new vision of the resurrection and to start implementing it in their own communities, that is the new church. I see this happening again with our modern TWCs woofing across the whole world.

DR. TERTIA: But, Doctor, today there are so many different kinds of movements, institutions and helping systems, all trying to make the good better. How can anyone measure their effectiveness? An intentional community, a local church congregation, a Green movement, and a global order are all very different. How can they ever really learn to work together?

OLD DOC: Each of those movements needs what we as individuals need. Each needs core groups that nurture their members. Each core group needs spirit refreshment and a ritual life † that empowers it to serve others. Each needs social ethics, effective methods, and actions for justice. Most groups will be stronger in one or two of these arenas, making their greatest contributions to society from their positions of strength

DR. TERTIA: To the extent that they recognize their lacks and link up with others who can compensate for their lacks, they are being

---

* *intentional community:* a group associating by choice, not by natural kinship or geographical settlement. Some vision of the good life not presently realized in the general society is shared by its members, who choose each other's company and mutual help.

† *ritual life:* any practice, form or procedure with which a group acknowledges its common history, its present reason for being together and the vision of its mission for the future. Examples: a birthday party or an annual stockholders' meeting.

In care there is no excess.

—*Bacon*

the new church dynamic, the woof of the new society. We do not expect any one group to meet all the needs of all kinds of people.

OLD DOC: Doctor, why not examine these woof groups as if they were our patients? First affirming their strengths, let us also probe for their weaknesses. In which arenas do they have relatively little to offer? Where are they interested in getting stronger? What could strengthen them?

DR. TERTIA: We can begin with the Greens. I would say their strength is in social ethics. They have a passion for justice and ecological responsibility. They are less strong in core groups, but their loose structure allows networking with many single issue groups, to their mutual benefit. Their weakness could be in spirit refreshment. They could learn much from the world's great religions.

OLD DOC: The gap could be filled by collaboration with those intentional communities with empowering ritual, and down-to-earth reverence for the mystery, depth, and greatness of human life.

DR. TERTIA: Some religious groups that are strong in spirit refreshment have their greatest weakness in social ethics, effective methods and actions for justice. They could learn about social and ecological justice from the Green movement, and from intentional communities which are nurturing their members and putting into practice new ethical values. They could find power and relevance in working coalitions with neighborhood caretaker groups.

OLD DOC: The question is, how can intentional communities be effective in the modern city? Some are a bit inept in the technologies of social change, but are good company. Less good company are the highly efficient and disciplined groups which are somewhat fanatic. What is your prescription, doctor, for those core groups that are disciplined, well-organized, experienced in social change, with a strong sense of mission? What is it that makes the tapestry beautiful and not just strong?

DR. TERTIA: I think you are talking about a few revolutionary cadres and about most successful business groups.

OLD DOC: Strange bedfellows, but yes.

DR. TERTIA: Most sooner or later take up the sword of ruthlessness. Then they turn on each other and will perish by that sword. Their remedy? Old fashioned courtesy as a standard operating procedure. Honoring one another in every way. Openness and honesty. Decision making by consensus. Celebrating life together. The skills of primary community.

The universe is wider than our views of it.

—*THOREAU*

■ Six components of the new localism [5]

At first, nothing need change visibly in a neighborhood under-going transformation. The images in residents' thinking about their neighborhood can be shifted after they receive enough images of change and local control. When the neighborhood, for all its short-comings, is seen as "our home, to be improved," residents can work together to rebuild their lost selfhood and power. Gardens appear again. Housing stock is upgraded. Streets become safe. Learning is valued. Life overcomes death and decay. And they learn to tell others of their experiments. Linkages are formed that are mutually reinforcing and synergistic.

The new localism, or neighborhood power base, involves at least six arenas:

1) developing neighborhood vision and communication;
2) developing health, education, and other services;
3) creating a local vision through neighborhood organizing;
4) promoting growth in the local economy;
5) upgrading housing; and
6) inter-neighborhood cooperation.

Let's take a look at some examples in each of these areas.

■ Developing neighborhood vision and communication

More is required of newspaper leadership than front page and editorial cheerleading. In any corporation, effective leadership alters agendas so that new priorities receive necessary attention. The structure of the media limits the kind of information disseminated. The gatekeeping activity of newspapers tells readers what is important. To be socially responsible, a newspaper must be an intentional instrument of social cohesion and a facilitator of the sense of community.

Sprouts! [6]

A free monthly newsletter published for several years by the Community Self Reliance Center is a delightfully cheery combination of local ads and a community bulletin board with notices of the community festival, arts council, war tax resistance group, the city-owned community garden, an upstate New York regional co-op conference, the alternative Federal Credit Union, attractive full page inserts by community groups, and answers to a set of questions by candidates in a local election. The staff also published updates on appropriate technology (energy, health care, small food gardens). The credentials of the Center's new director (in 1986) were: Cornell engineering degree with attention to appropriate technology, work in Minnesota's Common Sense Energy System, volunteer and paid work in peace groups. The Self Reliance Center also sponsors a Local Employment and Trading System (LETS)* to generate and manage a local currency independent of and parallel to the federal monetary system.

COM 351 - Mass communications ethics [7]

Secret taping, embarrassing photos, checkbook journalism—these are a few of the ethical issues in mass communications that Purdue University students are addressing in Journalism Professor John Webster's unique course COM 351.

Objectives are to help students recognize ethical issues through lectures and case studies, sharpen their analytical skills, and heighten their sense of obligation and personal responsibility in decision-making. In team workshops students articulate their hopes and dreams for the future of ethical mass communications, analyze the obstacles to achieving their vision, and create strategies to remove or get around the obstacles.

Each student also writes an essay on "My Search for Mass Communications Ethics." The essay must first address the present reality, and the forces that downgrade or upgrade ethics in mass communications. Only then can the student comment on the trends in the field, decide what the fundamental moral issue in mass communications is, and comment on the changes he might make in his own consciousness to be effective in the future of his chosen field.

■ Developing health, education, and other services

The limitations of an institutionalized welfare system are painfully and economically obvious; the following two stories demonstrate communities beginning to take back the task of caring for their own people.

A bridge away from welfare [8]

In 1974 the Fremont Public Association (FPA) of Seattle was created to supplement city services to the poor. A coalition of public,

---

* See page 48, for an explanation of LETS.

private, voluntary and neighborhood groups provides a growing array of direct and advocacy services primarily on Seattle's north side through a central office where the staff coordinate the many programs. In 1985, 72 percent of FPA's $2.6 million budget was funded by public monies; 28 percent by 20 corporations and foundations, 33 businesses, 27 community organizations, 258 individual donors, and 239 volunteers.

FPA has participated in city and statewide coalitions to help victims of plant closings, to prevent cuts in programs for the poor, to prevent demolition of downtown housing, and to secure health care for the homeless. A key question now is how to continue but also go beyond crisis intervention and direct services to the empowerment of people.

"Now I'm a taxpayer, just like you!"[9]

My name is Germaine Allen. I'm the mother of two beautiful kids; I have a job with a future; I have friends who care about me; and most of all, I care about myself because I know I can be anything I want to be!

That may not sound so unusual to you, but believe me, it wasn't that long ago that I was stuck in a rut where every day was just like the day before it and I had absolutely nothing to look forward to. I was a single parent living from welfare check to welfare check and surrounded by people with no ambition. One day I made up my mind that I'd had enough!

I started out by applying to enroll in clerical training at Indiana Vocational Technical School. The course was okay, but all I could think of were the two years it would take to graduate.

It seemed like such a long time and what I really wanted was a job. My kids were growing up without the things I wanted for them. I couldn't afford to take them to the state fair. When my son needed new shoes he had to "wait 'til the check came in." I just decided I had to make things happen faster. I called an organization known as Training, Inc.*

---

* *Training, Inc.:* an entry-level clerical job skills training program which uses all the social and spirit methods described in this book, and more. The curriculum was first developed by the Institute of Cultural Affairs in 1975. Over its seven years in Indianapolis, Training, Inc. has graduated and placed over 85 percent of its 500 entering trainees, with a 90-day retention rate also remarkably above the rates achieved by almost all other programs in this difficult field of job training.

They said the next class would start in October. The 14 weeks that followed were the beginning of the rest of my life.

I was like a sponge, soaking up everything my instructors taught me. Accounting, data entry, personal presentation, effective communication, all the things the want ads ask for when they are trying to fill a clerical position. The staff also worked on my head. I know I looked motivated to an outside observer, but secretly I didn't know if I could do it. My confidence in myself was fragile, and to make it worse, my "friends" tore me down every chance they got. I had almost no encouragement from family or friends. I became an outsider to people I had known all my life. I found I had to withdraw to survive. The staff and trainees at Training, Inc. became my new support system. I kept going and in December I graduated.

I put in job applications all over the city and then in January I got a call from American Fletcher National Bank for a part-time temporary position starting at $3.65 an hour. I took it to get experience but still I had not reached my real objective which was to get off the welfare system that I had been on since I was seventeen. *That* didn't happen until six months later when I was hired full-time at Indiana National Bank in the installment loan department for $4.00 an hour. On June 4th, I celebrated my one-year anniversary with INB. I'm now making $4.25/hour and am due for a raise soon.

Another important day for me was when I received my first income tax refund. I am now a taxpayer just like you! To me that means I want to do what I can to get others off welfare. I tell them, "Look: welfare should be temporary! Don't let it be a way of life for you! You'll never get ahead with it! It will make you lazy! It will screw up your mind if you let it!" I tell anyone who will listen that training is the way out! I've physically taken people downtown to sign up for training. An acquaintance (I now call her a friend) just got off welfare too. She's working at National Underwriters. That's one less person *we* (that's you and me) support with our taxes.

Well, that's my story. It took me 24 years to get my life together, but it's going pretty good. My friend John (also a single parent) is an electrician and he's been showing me how to do electrical wiring in case I should decide a nontraditional career would be good for me. He alone has been beside me all the way, and who knows—maybe we have a permanent future. For now, I like my children to see me hustle, so they'll have someone they can look up to as they are growing up. I want them to say, "My mother did it and so can I!"

Old Doc:
Psychosocial depression—burden of young and old

MEDICAL STUDENT: Doctor, I wonder if the common experience of depression, occurring in all age groups and social sets is a factor in the desperation of jobless, poor youth and in the hopeless withdrawal of senility in the old.

OLD DOC: Germaine Allen's testimony tells of a turning inward when the demands of her life in socially structured poverty appeared overwhelming. Likewise, when old and retired persons abstain from meaningful engagement in new work and love, depression is a common condition.

MEDICAL STUDENT: How can I help depressed patients to see that the cure, or return from embracing death in depression, is to re-embrace life, beginning with trusting a caring human being? How can I help them get over the self-blame, ultimately reaching suicide, which damages the emotional motor, the physical organs, the social self, and the spirit quest? After a time, reparative energies may not be enough to sustain the struggle of life to hold off death.

OLD DOC: Meaningful hard work, appropriate for the person's age and station, reintegrates the isolated victim into caring primal community—into networks of responsibility, accountability, absolution,* acceptance. Those with needed gifts and skills may be called to expend the rest of their regained lives in building caring community for all of us.

Neighborhood care of schizophrenics [10]

What is "schizophrenia"? About one percent of the human race suffers from this lifelong disorder of perception which baffles scientists, fills mental hospitals, provides the underworld with entry-level workers, and tragically robs the world of great creative gifts of many of its victims.

Commonly appearing in early adult life, the disorder is marked by better and worse periods over many years. Most schizophrenics

---

* *absolution:* the ending by whatever means of shame and guilt over one's offenses, for which one freely takes complete responsibility. Examples: heroic acts make up for cowardly acts; acknowledged responsibility plus restitution make up for theft. For many acts which have harmed others, no sufficient restitution is possible. In such cases, absolution depends on the mercy of the One who is greater than ourselves. To refuse such mercy is the arrogant sin of hubris, presumption of equality with God.

lead orderly, reasonably happy and productive lives. Marriage and good family life are particularly helpful to the schizophrenic person, who more than most of us is harmed by excessively solitary living.

What does schizophrenia contribute to the "multiproblem family" so troublesome in neighborhoods? To learning disabilities, unemployment, loneliness? To underworld exploitation of illegal drugs, prostitution, alcoholism, domestic violence? How do those so afflicted, who are disturbing to the community in these and other ways, differ from the majority who lead peaceable, reasonably happy and helpful lives?

Can community care offer more than family, domiciliary, or agency care for persons handicapped by schizophrenia? One hopeful report is from San Francisco. Half a dozen patients in a home-like residence share decision making and daily tasks with two resident staff. Medications are little used. Two matched groups of unmarried schizophrenics ages 16-30, have been followed for two years. Costs equal those of the control group given traditional hospital care, but outcomes look better. Is this a new cottage industry for capable neighborhoods?

Community for the chronically mentally ill [11]

Author Lynn Jones sets out a forward-looking approach to treating the chronically mentally ill, from 14 years experience first as a nurse, then as a team manager in community interdisciplinary long-term care of several hundred persons disabled by schizophrenia and bipolar illness. The book, *A Matter of Community*, is written in three parts: for persons experiencing these disorders, for those spending time with them, and for researchers.

History of a treatment community

We have developed the Community Support Systems Program (CSSP) as a network of people within places to live, work and gather. After the public funding cuts in human services in the late 1970s, we decided that the same staff would do day programs, case management, medication management and residential outreach. Crucial to survival of a program like ours are persons with business management skills and political finesse.

We developed a concept of functioning levels and used it to design programs, to set criteria for admission and evaluation. We focused on three kinds of structures for the integrated empowerment of clients: residence, work and center. Our 370 clients have varied talents and want to do meaningful things. Attendance and participation are voluntary and the community offers a natural flow of reinforcement for this.

Philosophy of treating long-term mental illness

Following their discharge from public hospitals two decades ago, our clients have had the precious freedom to come and go. Most of these persons can live successfully in a community setting, given appropriate structure and support. Those disabled by schizophrenia and bipolar illness need: protective care including emergency, short-term, inpatient, hospital alternatives, and long-term inpatient services; highly structured community care in residential settings, time structuring, medical care and rehabilitation services; outpatient community care including appropriate assistance with housing, medication, work activities and outreach.

We see three goals of community treatment: ... give clients tools to be as effective and comfortable as possible in dealing with self and environment;... evaluate realistically areas in which each client is unable to be effective and comfortable;... fill in gaps with appropriate support and care so that the client can still maintain safe and humane functioning in a community environment.

I have some expectations of my clients. They will be honest with me, have respect for other human beings, and expend some energy and caring in the treatment process. Awareness of self and acceptance of illness are also necessary.

We call too many things "mental illness": marital and family problems, school problems, adjustment to loss and physical illness, social maladjustment. It is fine to help persons with these conflicts, but not from funds intended for mental illness.

How to develop a treatment community

1. Describe the situation. What are the target clients like? How many? Ages? Diagnoses? Length of illnesses? Do not include developmental disability, primary drug and alcohol abuse, organic brain syndrome, or habitual antisocial behavior.

2. Using an evaluation matrix form, record functioning scores to determine kinds of services needed.

3. Existing community resources need to be drawn into the treatment community, including privately-owned boarding homes and nursing homes. Continually develop new funding.

4. Decide on structure, including: relationships; places, buildings, things; time; rituals, activities; information, instructions,

rules, limits; food, clothing, self care; values, thinking structures, beliefs; rewards, opportunities, support; physical restraints.

The Center is the hub of the community, with clients from all residential levels feeding into it, and owning it. Without it clients become isolated at their residences. Here values are developed and maintained; special events are held. Clients share activities and information. Work opportunities are structured for a variety of functioning levels. Client productivity becomes defined as community productivity. Everyone can feel good about it.

Documentation reflects the pattern of each person's illness over the years. Research is looking at psychotics' awareness of physical disease, their trust in health-care givers, and their disorganization as it affects health-seeking behavior.

Asbury Park's new economic base[12]

Can a small town absorb a large influx of mentally-ill persons newly released from the state hospital? The newcomers create a large demand for additional municipal services. In 1979 Asbury Park, New Jersey, a faded residential community of 15,000 persons, agreed to work with the Urban Health Institute, a not-for-profit consulting firm, to develop local planning. The community required new resources to care for 1,200 recently settled, deinstitutionalized mental patients (a number greater than the patient population of any psychiatric hospital in the state).

In a series of interviews and public meetings the Institute was able to find out how many discharged patients lived in the community, and where they had come from. The Institute also identified individual and institutional perceptions that were blocking solutions. Absence of a common language had contributed to furious public disagreement. A public meeting allowed all parties to believe they had been heard. Regular follow-up meetings were set for informed debate. In this way, local leaders entered dialogue with state and professional authorities who had assumed wrongly that local leaders understood and welcomed the responsibilities of caring for the mentally ill, including developing new service network.

Local planning dispelled pervasive hopelessness and led to appointment of a new city manager. The new municipal care duties were transferred from the fire department to a strengthened health department. Grant funds were secured for expanding services.

That which is not good for the swarm, neither is it good for the bee.

—*MARCUS AURELIUS*

45

■ Creating a local vision through organizing

Experiments in social change are rarely overfunded, but as the following stories show, there are always enough resources when everyone participates in leadership.

Research the neighborhood: then act boldly[13]

In the 1940s Cedar Park neighborhood in West Philadelphia was all white. During World War II the young adults left. Aging residents sold to absentee landlords who divided their aging homes into apartments. In ten years all renters moving in were black. Crumbling housing, low residential income, fleeing business, and neglected public services created a disaster area. The bishop saw a quarter million people without a Methodist church, and allowed a young pastor to move in, but only after spending $8,000 to replace windows and other vandalized parts of the Calvary Church manse.

In the first year a handful of local residents joined in porch-sitting visits and research, and pulled together in weekly team reviews what residents saw as their visions, realities and priorities. Scores of block meetings looked at other new business ventures that could bring jobs, job training and stability to the area. Neighbors trusted the outsider pastor as their one focus for self-help. The first big argument came over setting boundaries for their ten-year total development covenant. Six arenas emerged with local support for action: human rights, economic development, education, cultural effectiveness, health, and urban maintenance. Carefully, they selected housing rehabilitation (rehab) on one street as an initial effort to restore hope. The University of Pennsylvania and Calvary Church became principal depositors in a credit union to start construction. Other businesses came in and began to prosper.*

A model for the homeless from a shantytown[14]

Villa El Salvador district is a shantytown of 300,000 people on the edge of Lima (population seven million), the capital of Peru. This "Town of the Savior" recently won the Prince of Asturias Peace Prize (Spanish) for its system of solidarity and self-management. Its strategy of collective survival is a model for the homeless and deprived of the Third World. In 16 years this stretch of sand has become the country's sixth largest urban area, with asphalt roads

* The Cedar Park story is continued in "Need housing?..." on page 52.

and thousands of trees, a colossal undertaking carried out ant-fashion.

In 1971, 4,000 refugee families from an Andean village destroyed by an earthquake were dumped by the army in the desert outside Lima, without roads or water. They set up their straw shacks and began to manage their existence collectively, together building a track to permit access by water trucks and other vehicles. Next they built a parish church, primary and secondary schools, and a clinic. Amateur masons are slowly replacing straw shacks with bricks, corrugated iron and concrete.

The town has mushroomed but in a planned, orderly manner. Villa El Salvador now has electricity, a sewage system, 34 schools, 150 daycare centers, nine clinics, three higher education centers, 22 markets, dozens of dispensaries and sports grounds, a town hall, 40 kilometers of paved road and 500,000 trees.

"Everyone's a leader here," explains the mayor, a former Marist brother who was one of the original refugees. The self-managed Urban Community (CUAVES) practices a unique form of democracy. Every family has been allocated a plot of land; 24 families form a "manzana" or block. Sixteen blocks make up a residential group. Today there are 105 such groups, divided into four sectors. Each block appoints five people to be in charge of health, education, production, marketing and security. Each residential group holds general meetings at which eight board members are elected. All of these meet in congress to choose the 11 executive members of CUAVES and its countless secretaries. A multitude of associations, parallel to CUAVES, cover the social interests of the community, including 500 sports clubs and 54 cultural groups for youth.

This collective organization, a synthesis of ancestral traditions, the trade union, and the cooperative experience of Lima's marginal inhabitants, is an effective response to centuries of oppression and neglect. The people continue to struggle against an implacable economic system that causes 70 percent of the active population to be underemployed, with the consequent malnutrition and disease. To improve the diet, 500 committees hand out 50,000 rations of milk and cereal to children leaving for school each day. The residents have also organized over 200 community kitchens, using food purchased from food cooperatives.

To solve the problem of transportation to work in the city, CUAVES has arranged for eight bus lines now serving the district. The community's next priorities are to operate its own industrial

If a tree dies, plant another in its place.

—*LINNAEUS*

47

park and to expand its agricultural zone which is irrigated with oxy-genated, used water.

■ Promoting growth in the local economy

Redirecting community economic resources is where some of the most creative and compassionately hard-headed work is taking place. People creating their own local money, a financing system for businesses that won't allow a business to go bankrupt, imaginative local coalitions, and new technologies coming into use—all now available at a neighborhood level—are creating the belief that economics can be controlled by a community instead of being something that happens to it from outside.

Local Employment and Trading System (LETS) [15]

The LETS system recycles green dollars in our community. If you want to be sure the money you spend stays nearby, spend the money in green dollars. Federal dollars are not simply transaction markers. They carry the story of sagging international trade, of the immense federal budget deficit, of expenditures for war supplies. Green dollars are impervious to unemployment, to inflation and the trade deficit. Green dollars rely on your being able to provide a service that is of use to someone. Green dollars don't have finance charges, nor do they engender cash flow problems. Two potential problems, however, are taxes (individuals must report to the IRS income made in LETS trades) and defaults. In order to avoid defaults by LETS members, we have set a maximum-owed balance that is allowed in any LETS account. This insures that we will operate at a level that is safe for us.

The entrepreneurial poor [16]

In 1976 a group headed by an economics professor at the University of Chittagong in Bangladesh reasoned that the landless poor (50 percent of the Bangladesh population) might become highly productive if they found the resources to get something started. The Grameen Bank Project provides loans to five-person borrowing groups in villages, totalling 30,000 landless persons, 40 percent of them women. They help set up nonagricultural businesses that are an essential part of rural life: weaving, mat-making, peddling, tai-loring and scores more.

Each member of the five-person group must be from a different family and own not more than 4/10 acre of land. Initially only one or two of the members may borrow $30-$50 each. All must agree to a strict repayment discipline—and learn to sign their names. They meet weekly with a bank representative to make payments of two percent of the loan plus enough to cover 13 percent annual interest. And they must put a penny a week into savings for the group. After establishing their credit worthiness, the five-person group may join with five other groups to form 30-person borrowing centers. One center qualified for $1,000 to purchase a pump-operated tube-well for irrigation, making possible an extra crop of rice during the dry season. The loan is being repaid by $1 weekly installments from each center member.

Young bank workers travel far to do the lending and collection of repayments. While helping villagers remove the blocks to regular repayment of loans, they encourage such social changes as better sanitation and health practices, smaller families, improved nutrition, the revival of traditional family crafts, elimination of excessive dowries, and an end to wife beating.

Third world bank in the U.S.A.[17]

Women's World Banking (WWB), a pioneering financial service for women, has offices in Kenya, Ghana, Sierra Leone, Uganda, Jamaica, Thailand and 16 other countries, as well as in Charleston, West Virginia. WWB began seven years ago to offer women entrepreneurs in Third World countries access to credit to start small businesses or expand existing ones. WWB places deposits in a local commercial bank and then helps women-owned and -managed businesses obtain money through a guaranteed loan. The West Virginia affiliate was founded in 1984 by several women active in job training and small business development for women. It is a membership organization, currently run by volunteers. Contributions are used solely for the loan fund. Some 25 percent of each loan is raised locally by the WWB affiliate. The WWB International in the Netherlands contributes 50 percent. The local bank assumes the other 25 percent. Applicant businesses must be at least 50 percent women owned and managed. The owner must have at least 10 percent equity in the business, be willing to accept technical assistance or training, and share management information as determined by the loan review committee. WWB-WV has given two loans, both repaid, and has thirty "active" files of women applicants.

Mondragon's bank doesn't allow a business to fail [18]

Mondragon is a Basque village in Spain, the center of a highly successful association of cooperatives whose main purpose is the creation of jobs. The cooperative Bank, with 500,000 local depositors, was started in 1958 by Father Jose Arizmendi in a church basement. It has created over 21,000 jobs, guaranteed for life, in over 200 cooperative enterprises owned by the Mondragon community: 101 industrial, six agricultural, 14 housing and 43 school cooperatives. Providing additional services are four secondary cooperatives: the Bank's Entrepreneurial Services Division, Technological Research Institute, Business and Professional College, Social Security and Medical Services. In spite of low salary scales—no one may receive a salary plus overtime in excess of five times the lowest wage—the management is among the most aggressive and innovative anywhere, and the other worker-owners are found to be highly motivated and fulfilled by their jobs. Low wages may be offset by worker-owners' share of profits, distributed according to salary scale.

The Bank has a near-100-percent success rate at forming business cooperatives and avoiding loan defaults. It assumes every new business will succeed and makes a commitment to the business until it does. Someone in the Entrepreneurial Services Division of the bank first interviews the partners (never individuals), who want to go into business, and enters into a partnership with them. All parties are committed not to abandon the others until the business is running smoothly. Each member of the project must loan the business a substantial amount, so all partners are at risk. If the initial product ceases to be viable, a new one is chosen, even if it requires more capital, which the bank will loan at *decreasing rates* of interest. Once the business succeeds, it pays back the loan. Seventy percent of the profits are distributed to managers and workers (owners all), as allocations to their internal capital accounts and are regarded as a loan to the company at 6 percent interest which each worker-owner receives in cash. Ten percent of profits are donated to charity; 20 percent are reinvested to create more jobs for worker owners.

The structural basis of Mondragon as established by Fr. Arizmendi is relationships of love and cooperation rather than competition and enmity. The community sees itself as in business together; *it has reversed the capitalist and socialist order of priori-*

ties among the factors of production—from capital, product, manager, worker to worker, manager, product, capital.

Similar groups of enterprises have arisen in Poland, Asia, Africa and South America. In the U.S. several companies have copied the Mondragon system. They are leading us beyond capitalism and socialism into a "Third Way," in which Gandhi's vision of humanistic economics may become institutionalized in a new social order of worker-owner cooperative communities.

A successful hospital-community development effort [19]

Bronx Community Enterprises (BCE) is an example of professional groups working in collaboration with neighborhood residents as a desirable improvement upon many hospital public relation programs, which in fact do little to empower their immediate humble neighbors. BCE was formed in 1983 to stimulate Bronx business development with the purchasing power of Montefiore Medical Center, the largest employer in the borough, and with technical aid and loans to assist these businesses. The Montefiore Child Care Program enabled 40 Bronx residents to set up their own businesses. Mosholu Preservation Corporation gives technical help to housing owners, buys and renovates apartment buildings, and rebuilds investor confidence. Over 315 apartments have been rehabilitated.

Greening the city: An energy recovery model [20]

Earthseason Urban Farming Institute, of Santa Cruz, California, is looking for an ecologically-minded city neighborhood group that wants to field test in partnership a working model for sustainable urban farming, The Earthseason Flow System. Based on five years' technical research, this system reuses three energy streams available in inhabited buildings: food scraps, greywater from washing, and blackwater from toilets.

An additional and essential component in the model is the community radio station. The Solar Family Radio News Service invites listener participation and generates support for the project. Programs include an educational series on the main components of the Earthseason system: employment, composting, greenhouses and food production. The Urban Farming Institute provides practical instruction in such components of the system as building earthworm beds, composting beds, alcohol still, and small scale generator. The Institute will help organize a bicycle-cart route to collect table scraps.

51

The Institute provides expertise for utilizing the secondary streams of wastewater and (perhaps more importantly) the cost/benefit analyses necessary to get the cooperation of city officials. The values of this integrated resource recovery system are several: 1) enrichment of the soil in the neighborhood; 2) an aesthetically more interesting neighborhood, with gardens and trees in vacant lots and retrofitted buildings; and 3) increased property values and improved economic base. To be economically self-sustaining, the community must develop sufficient sources of food waste to make the soil factory, alcohol still and food production commercially feasible.

■ Upgrading housing

Building affordable housing is a complicated process. It requires large amounts of capital, mastery of local politics, and the frequent necessity of moving against powerful trends such as gentrification and "urban renewal" (bulldozing housing stock to build highway systems). For these reasons perhaps nothing demonstrates a community's desire to renew itself better than a successful record with housing.

Need housing? Start a credit union![21]

In 1972 the new pastor assigned to Calvary United Methodist Church and a few members put the glass back into the windows of the solid grey stone building on the corner of 48th and Baltimore Avenue in West Philadelphia, and began strategic planning to restore the economic foundation to the neighborhood (population 15,000), which was considered a disaster area. The church staff spent the first few years establishing community linkages and holding hundreds of town meetings—in every church, civic organization and 51 block clubs—to discover what the community wanted. They purchased—for $1.00— a local bank that had closed, to create the West Philadelphia Community Federal Credit Union. With management assistance from the University of Pennsylvania Wharton School, assets rose from an initial $165,000 to over $2 million. Today, the Cedar Park neighborhood has a community development corporation (West Philadelphia Fund for Human Development), created by the church and neighborhood organizations, which owns the credit union, along with a radio station, a comprehensive care program for elders, a state-of-the-art printing business, and a neighborhood school of economics.

To increase the local supply of affordable housing, the credit union loaned the West Philadelphia Fund for Human Development $15,000 for construction of the first group-shared house in the city— where people of different ages live together as a community. Seven tenants rent rooms for $135-$245 per month and participate in family-style group activities. For this the Fund spent over $100,000 of grants and loans from churches, other financial institutions, and the city of Philadelphia.

Four-sector partnership forms housing task force [22]

In 1985 two clergymen (Episcopal and Methodist) approached the leadership of seven communities of faith (Episcopal, Roman Catholic, Lutheran, Methodist, Baptist, Presbyterian and Jewish) to consider the need for 10,000 additional housing units in the greater Wilmington area. These seven faith communities sponsored a luncheon to which they invited corporation executives, foundations, city and state authorities, and the Enterprise Foundation. They presented the need for housing as a public challenge to each sector. The religious groups pledged $15,000 seed money and created the Interfaith Housing Task Force to create a plan.

In January 1986 their leaders charged the denominations to raise $1 million and to be the key elements to bring the rest of the power structure on board, including a fragmented Black community.

Early funding came from DuPont ($25,000), Enterprise ($100,000), and the churches. The Task Force hired a researcher for the planning process. The initial plan, released in July 1986, called for 1,000 new units of housing in five years.

In the first two years, 30 houses have been rehabilitated as a result of bank challenges under the Community Re-investment Act, $5.3 million has been commited for low- and moderate-income housing. The Delaware Community Investment corporation will make loans at 9.5 percent fixed interest over 15 years to developers of affordable housing. E.I. duPont de Nemours & Co. is investing $400,000 as a limited partner and the state of Delaware has created a Housing Development Fund. In each of the neighborhoods, where the task force works, local residents are recruited to the housing team, along with representatives from churches and community organizations.

The community land trust [23]

In 1982 real estate in Burlington, Vermont, was appreciating faster than the median income levels of its residents. The last affordable housing stock and public access to the waterfront in the Old North End was threatened by gentrification. In 1984 the city provided $200,000 seed money to a private group incorporated as the not-for-profit Burlington Community Land Trust (BCLT), which acquires properties and resells the structures while keeping the land through a long-term CLT lease. Local banks and a community loan fund offer low-interest financing to CLT leaseholders. Community Loan Funds pool philanthropic and socially responsible investment dollars of foundations and corporations for high social impact and diversification of the risk inherent in community development.

Several eastern cities now support CLTs for their ability to preserve community resources and to build community coalitions. The CLT gets public subsidies to develop affordable housing, develops without displacing, provides rent control and housing cost stabilization without a city ordinance, uses private planning and resources to protect and upgrade valuable space, returns property to the tax rolls, and puts land to good public purpose.

Great cities of the world have been destroyed and rebuilt many times over the centuries. Archeological digs uncover treasures of succeeding groups of people who chose this same place for their homes. Permanent values reside in the site: good water, climate, security, access to trade or resources. Urban land, even more than the most productive agricultural land, is a renewable resource which can be preserved for the use of present and future owner-residents, protecting their rights to its value and desirability. Land has been created without human action, in contrast to property values that humans create by their own work (crops, goods, homes, enterprises). Good laws carefully distinguish group and individual rights over land and over property.

Modern cities everywhere are endangered by social disorder: street crime, abandoned elders, disengaged youth, dysfunctional education, neglected job skills, erosion of trust in public offices, and disillusionment with inherited customs. Absentee land ownership leads to property deterioration as social controls erode. Except for the land speculators, everyone loses, resident owners most of all. Flight to prosperous suburbs accelerates urban decay and the estrangement from neighborhood.

An urban land trust is a democratically-structured nonprofit corporation with a membership and a board of trustees. The trust acquires land by purchase or donation with the intent of holding title in perpetuity. Interests of resident property owners are protected in articles of incorporation and bylaws. Benefits include assured buyout by the trust should the owners wish to move, at a price recognizing improvements and inflation. Zoning remains in local hands. As the trust prospers, it can underwrite development of desirable local businesses. Its major "disadvantage" is that sellers reap no windfall profits as the neighborhood property values rise. Increases in land values benefit *all* the owners of the trust who remain and reside in that neighborhood.

Housing and the homeless minority [24]

The fastest growing minority in many of the world's most prosperous cities is the homeless: Amsterdam, Los Angeles, New York, Tokyo. Their exact numbers are not known. The estimated U.S. totals range from 2.5 million down to a tenth of that number. Around the world, wars, fires, depression, and even well-intentioned programs like urban renewal have forced people into the streets. The evidence is in every U.S. city: the elderly pushing shopping carts loaded with their possessions, down-and-outers aimlessly wandering the streets.

Up to 50 percent of U.S. homeless are believed to be mentally disturbed. Effectively addressing homelessness could contribute much to stimulate a return to good health among the neglected unsheltered. Investments in shelter create jobs, raise incomes, and improve living standards. A strong construction sector benefits the whole economy, says UN's HABITAT.

Responses in developed countries follow conventional lines: public housing built by construction companies at high cost. Building standards, often overspecified and out of date, like Banquo's ghost, continually haunt efforts of industrialized nations to drive down construction costs.

Less developed countries have utilized low-cost self-help efforts of future occupants. World Bank experience is that a dwelling upgraded by self-help costs one fifth that of the lowest cost public housing built by construction companies. For each public housing unit built, five families are excluded from upgraded shelter. In addition to the cost advantage, self-help offers participants the opportunity to play major roles in designing their neighborhoods

Lead, follow, or get out of the way.

—*OLNEY, TEXAS COMMUNITY SLOGAN*

55

and dwellings. Claims made on the public sector are usually minimal. Governments must register titles and protect property rights, and usually build infrastructure roads and utility connections. The time has come for industrial nations to import methods which third world nations have found workable in solving their homelessness problem.

■ Interneighborhood cooperation

No matter how great a community's desire to solve a problem, some solutions are more easily worked out when neighboring communities are brought in.

Vermont towns pool resources for elders [25]

A group of residents in the five Vermont towns of Granville, Hancock, Rochester, Stockbridge and Pittsfield, with a total population of 3,000, in 1985 organized to provide for the changing needs of their elderly population. Their project is currently called Rochester Community Care Home. Instead of a large, single community-care unit that would meet "all" needs in one place, this is a continuing care community: a coordinated network of services and housing options in the five towns. They refer elderly residents to existing services. Also they develop gap-filling programs such as visitation, meals, transportation, house and yard maintenance, exercise programs and dental care. In addition to volunteer, shared housing, eight new units of congregate housing will be built. They will formalize opportunities for elders to be active in the community through the senior service network, churches, libraries and schools.

Four Worlds Development Project [26]

Native elders, spiritual leaders and professionals from native communities met in Lethbridge, Alberta, Canada, in 1982 and dedicated themselves to the elimination of alcohol and drug abuse in Canadian native societies by the year 2000. They saw that the solution had to come from within the native communities themselves, each community taking control of its own development. They said that a learning enterprise would "systematically educate human beings from the time they are in their mother's womb until they pass out of this world."

The elders designed the Four Worlds Development Project. Their professional colleagues developed a curriculum package and a system for supporting communities seeking to transform themselves.

The Alexander Reserve in Alberta was one of the first pilot communities to use the Four Worlds approach. Only one student had graduated from the high school in the preceding 15 years; the system was irrelevant to native people. At the new Kipohtakaw Education Centre, the attendance now has gone from 50 percent to 95 percent in two years. A Cree cultural center with a Resident Elder program is one of the many evidences of an integrated school and community life. The staff is 80 percent native.

In spring 1985, about 150 people gathered at the Alkali Lake Reserve, British Columbia, to begin planning "Sharing Innovations that Work": a two-year plan for sharing resources and methods among native communities and for developing their own consultants.

The Alkali Lake Reserve is now virtually an alcohol-free community with an 80 percent employment rate after a decade-long fight against alcoholism, based on the rediscovery of life-enhancing values of traditional culture.

■ Old Doc: The church and urban health

DR. TERTIA: Doctor, did I hear you say that it is the four pillars of church, state, commerce and the family that make society work? In a new age of physics, pillars are much too static to describe social structures. Can we talk in terms of dynamics?

OLD DOC: Let us say instead that church, government, business and family must be in creative tension for a community to be healthy. Industrial-age communities are no more. The world from now on will be cosmopolitan, urban and diverse, and new social forms will have to emerge to make our neighborhoods human.

DR. TERTIA: Let's begin with the church. How will the old institutional forms, the denominational structures, translate into the new age consciousness? Won't they be destroyed?

OLD DOC: Some will change and take up new servant roles; some will very slowly disappear. Change happens much more decisively in commerce and in government. Even family forms change more rapidly than a church that resists new calls to service. Remember, however, that the normative life of the church is resurrection and providing pioneer leadership as new human needs require.

DR. TERTIA: I can see that in the world coming to be there may be

no Presbyterian urban parishes,* no Roman Catholic counties, whatever our American denominational history. What basic social dynamics are you pointing to in "church?"

OLD DOC: Three dynamics are important for neighborhood health. The church as I see it is a covenanted congregation[†] of people within a defined geography, the parish. And within any alive congregation, as well as in the parish, there are the sensitive, responsive core groups that call and empower the congregation and parish to serve the whole community and the world. It is the congregation/parish/core tripolar church (Fig. 2-1, below) that we need as an organizing force in the neighborhood to address the social diseases which account for 85 percent of all our disability days.

DR. TERTIA: You mean that the core groups within the congregations or a parish get together and link up established congregations

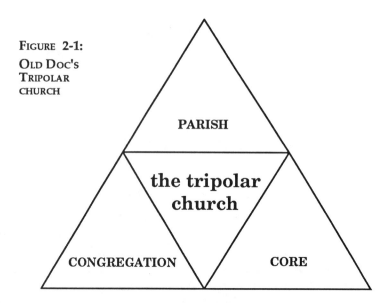

FIGURE 2-1:
OLD DOC'S
TRIPOLAR
CHURCH

PARISH

the tripolar church

CONGREGATION

CORE

---

* *parish* here is synonymous with neighborhood, a place with defined borders, where residents and others recognize a common history; often will have an informal name, e.g., "Pigtown" in downtown Seattle, "Frogtown" in St. Paul, "Fountain Square" in Indianapolis.

† *congregation:* a people who gather. Sacred congregations gather for regular public worship. Secular congregations more often call themselves an "association," "fraternity," or "club," or may come together for a single event, such as an annual business meeting.

with local businesses, government and families to deal with all the issues of the people living and working in the neighborhood?

OLD DOC: Only then can we begin to get breakthroughs to healthy neighborhoods instead of bandaids.

DR. TERTIA: What would I see happening in such linking?

OLD DOC: In my vision, the resurrected urban neighborhood is where people of many races, traditions, beliefs, temperaments and religions live together peaceably. Missional family clusters living together in the neighborhood will be the core church of the future parish.

DR. TERTIA: In family structures we already have nuclear, extended and intentional family groupings. Is missional family* cluster a sort of urban holon?[†]

OLD DOC: Yes. A miniaturized fragment of a whole planetary society, these intentional family groupings of several natural families will lead the whole church into new forms of urban service.

DR. TERTIA: To whom will they answer?

OLD DOC: To the local community, to some regional judicatory of the historic church, and to some global network. The holon covenant[Δ] will look more like a business contract than a statement of belief or doctrine.

DR. TERTIA: A business contract?

OLD DOC: Say four congenial families invest their savings in a multifamily residential condominium plus common and business space, perhaps with the blessing and backing of a respected neighborhood entity, such as a local council of churches. Call this a holon house. They then recruit a parish board of directors who also invest (not give) $1,000 each. Also buying investment shares in the holon would be a global network, like a regional denominational church body. Local health then would be tied to global development. The parish would become a social laboratory.

---

* *missional family:* a family by common consent dedicated to an external task or mission.

† *holon:* a term from laser light physics, where from any part of a three-dimensional holographic image the whole image can be reconstituted. The part contains the whole. A Holon House, further discussed in Chapter 8, contains the whole planetary excellence in its living rooms and work areas.

Δ *covenant:* an agreement worked out wholly by the participants, a device for protecting the group's freedom from any outside coercion by church, state, or colleagues.

DR. TERTIA: Would you find support for this among health professionals?

OLD DOC: We have a track record of responsible leadership in the quest for wholeness for all persons. With most of the middle class we share in the guilt of flight from the neighbor in need in urban neighborhoods. I think some of us are ready for socioeconomic restitution in an urban life of service.

DR. TERTIA: So you say pick up the investment risks, join a holon house, rebuild the neighborhood and the world, and live the fulfilled life?

OLD DOC: It will be the holon, with its local and global linkages, that will integrate the resources of the other three essential pillars of state, commerce and family to deal comprehensively with neighborhood health.

MEDICAL STUDENT: Doctor, we could have urban health if we had a common urban value system, which a cosmopolitan neighborhood now does not have. How can the church change that?

OLD DOC: I think the need is for new covenants.

MEDICAL STUDENT: Few neighborhoods now have covenants except as a way of excluding undesirables. What should the new neighborhood covenant look like?

OLD DOC: The covenants we need will look more like business deals than statements of belief, more like city charters than charismatic cliques, more like conservative self-help than liberal philanthropy.

MEDICAL STUDENT: We could look to the Old and New Covenants in the Bible for models.

OLD DOC: Absolutely. Learnings from the past are not forgotten, but the limits of the past are transcended. The covenants of the new age will be multidimensional commitments of mutual interests, the intentional mergings of economic, decision-making, and cultural relationships.

MEDICAL STUDENT: That sounds very complex. Can you give me a simple example?

OLD DOC: Here in Indianapolis an ecumenical group of six congregations in our racially and economically mixed neighborhood formed a council to sponsor a city-funded youth employment program, to pool resources for an affordable housing corporation, and to sponsor programs for youth and elders. The success of each program rests on the commitment* of the parish core groups working on that project.

MEDICAL STUDENT: I think many congregations do not see the parish as part of the church. They feel threatened by getting too close to the problems around them.

OLD DOC: Perhaps. It is the core groups that can take the risk of controversy and move the church into new covenants to upgrade the social and economic health of the neighborhood.

---

* commitment: a deliberate and announced decision made by a person binding himself to a stated course. A unilateral covenant, a freely undertaken obligation. Until I have personally made them my own by my free commitment, I am not bound by claims made upon me by others on the basis of my age, sex, race, class or community. Example: "I will be a gentle man."

Chapter 3

Leadership for Social Cohesion

The Gothic arch of the church or the dome of the courthouse once showed where the society's pioneer work of caring for all kinds of people was going on. More suitably for our secular, cosmopolitan world-come-of-age, a new style of leadership and revolutionary new social and spirit tools are available to the emerging caring community. The new style, called servant leadership, and the new tools are leading to the empowerment of persons and groups in all social classes. We'll examine the characteristics and costs of authentic community leadership and then look at groups and leaders using these powerful tools.

■ Called to lead

Most of our society's energies and resources are spent in maintaining our popular culture of hi-tech, economic growth, resource consumption, welfare bureaucracies, and nuclear war strategies. Nevertheless, a significant number of individuals and groups have heard a new Word, have broken away from the majority, and have begun building structures of a new, more humane and sustainable society. How does this breakaway happen? These persons experience something, gradually or suddenly, that shifts their view of reality. It can be a mystical experience, a world-shattering defeat (from alcohol, drugs, divorce, or loss of status), or a process of education. Whatever the cause, the result is a destruction of old illusions and a rebirth into a new view of reality, with the freedom to choose a new relationship with themselves and the world.

Of course, they could have denied this freedom to change, blamed their external situation, and retreated into an isolated lifestyle to lick their wounds. Instead, by mysterious grace, they woke up, embraced a new reality and chose a life of care, creativity and commitment. They have read and written new books; established new communities; learned respect for the cosmos, for the earth and global cultures; and formed action groups, networks, and alternative structures. They have awakened to an expanded realization of Being.

■ Ethical context

Twentieth century ethics asks: What does (not *ought to*, but *does)* it mean to be human? One answer is that to be human means to be in a consciously chosen relationship to the Final Mystery through myths, rites and symbols, and to affirm that life is good. It means to be conscious of my own relationships, for *I am* the attitudes I take to my relationships. It means to care for the whole world (humans *do* care, not *ought to* care). To be ethical, or moral, is to be decisional. I am free to decide that every situation and every relationship I am in is significant. The authentic (servant) leader models the fully human person. (See page 33, "Ethics and Freedom," on freedom, obligation and responsibility.)

■ Authentic leadership style

There is a difference between legitimate and authentic leadership.* The legitimate authority of a leader is conferred by the people led. It appeals to customs, values and symbols generally honored by that group. The scoutmaster, in citing the Boy Scout pledge ("A scout is trustworthy, loyal, courteous,...brave, clean and reverent.") is calling for application of the generally honored values and sanctions of that particular group. He acts as the legitimate leader of the boys' group.

Authenticity, beyond legitimacy, comes from self-consciously assuming responsibility for one's own deeds.

The authority of the authentic leader comes from a power outside the group, to which the group is drawn for the benefits of the relationship. The scoutmaster who lives his manly values by show-

---

* *legitimate authority:* explained and illustrated in the text. *Authentic authority:* authority related to something outside the group, as compared with legitimate authority which belongs wholly to the group alone.

ing respect for symbols and being successful in his own family and vocational commitments, serves as a role model for boys who want to become men. Authentic leadership calls the group to something outside itself.

> Leo was one of our servants (who were naturally volunteers, as we were).... This unaffected man had something so pleasing, so unobtrusively winning about him that everyone loved him.... He did his work gaily, usually sang or whistled, was never seen except when needed—in fact, an ideal servant.[27]

Leo, in fact, was truly serving as an authentic leader of the group. Such leaders define their role as doing and being whatever is necessary, in order for the group to get the job done, to reach its goal. The leader creates the climate of the group and helps others to develop interior resources to become leaders.

The authentic leader enables the whole group to observe, reflect, interpret, decide and act in any situation—through group processes that will shift their self-images to ones of confidence, intentionality, caring and ability to reach consensus—in order to perform as a team. Such leadership is often shared. A leadership panel (several experienced leaders acting together) can act as a corporate motivator, guide, orchestrator and sustainer. The panel can lead the whole group to be a powerful team.

■ Leadership style: Using life methods

The discoveries of science and events of history in the 20th century have radically shifted our worldview and the operating images out of which we live. We no longer see the world as hierarchical, but as interrelated centers of influence. We no longer see reality as objective, but as multiple perspectives, each of which names the reality it points to. To be an educated person today means to be skilled in *life methods*—methods for thinking, for creating one's own destiny (selfhood), and for participating in the global-social process wherever one is. To educate is to enable others to manipulate these skills so that their whole lives are a process of learning and growth. The imaginal educator* (motivator, guide)

---

* *imaginal educator:* one who is able to use, create and change mental images, or, pictures in the mind of "the world out there." The picture, or image, determines our thinking, feeling, deciding; we can perceive the

understands that one's images determine one's behavior and therefore intentionally and self-consciously uses a wide variety of tools and methods to beam messages that challenge a person's or a group's old, limiting images of self and the world in order to open the way for new, enabling images and new, more successful patterns of operating.

Direct messages

Using all the recent discoveries of how people learn and new techniques to accelerate the learning process, the motivator or guide repeatedly sends new information that intrudes directly on old images and invites the learner to change and grow.

Rational and intuitive exercises, the use of all the senses, meditation and visualization, mind mapping, and discontinuous periods that encourage creativity, as well as the intellectual methods of analysis and synthesis—all are tools that the motivator finds useful as she or he seeks to strengthen the ability of others to relate to life's situations with confidence and effectiveness.

The environment

We are, however, constantly receiving indirect messages from our environment and our relationships that either motivate or depress us. Messages that motivate us are those that extend our interior sense of time, enhance our sense of space, and expand our relationships. Responsible leaders understand the importance of indirect messages as well and utilize them to reinforce new ideas, new images, being conveyed or built upon. For instance, the leader seeks to expand the interior sense of space and time of the group by careful attention to the meeting space. The seating arrangement of a meeting room is a clue to the self-image of the leadership (hierarchical or egalitarian, flexible or rigid). What mood is conveyed by the color of the walls and the lighting? Is there a chalk board and wall space for display? What decor is on the walls? Decor should be inten-

---

external world only filtered through and interpreted by this picture in our mind. For example, in Cervantes' Don Quixote, the girl Aldonza throught of herself as "just a whore." When Don Quixote insisted he saw her as "My Lady," Aldonza reacted with anger, until her own self-image was modified by Quixote's persistent messages that she was a person of dignity and beauty. Only then did her feelings and behavior change from that of an abused whore to a lady.

tionally related to the subject of the meeting, reinforcing its objective. The meeting room's decor might include: a year's time line that the group has created and a picture of Earthrise on the wall, an enlarged street map of the neighborhood, a globe and a blowup of a microorganism, and art objects from other countries. The image of standing on a bridge, related to all past and all future, puts the group's involvement in the world in an historical frame that gives meaning to its work.

The leader also utilizes group experiences that enhance the sense of time and space. Two exercises that give a new awareness of time are *The Timeline of My Life* and *How I Spend My Week*.

The Timeline of My Life (chart on page 67) begins with the year of my birth and ends with the year of my death, which I decide. The line is divided into decades with the present year marked. For each decade I put important world trends, important people and events in my personal life, and rites of passage and turning points. I then choose a title for each decade, naming the importance of that part of my life to me—affirming what is past and choosing what will be.

In *How I Spend My Week* (chart on page 68), each participant colors in a chart* of the 168 hours of their week with five colors representing sleep, personal time, family time, job/work, social/recreation, and community/world engagement—first, as it now is; and a second chart, as they would like it to be. All the varicolored charts are displayed on the wall and reflected upon by the group.

The group discussion following these exercises gives participants a new appreciation of their relationship to all of time and the possibility of setting new directions for the future.

The leader also pays careful attention to the time design of meetings and the longer, over-all rhythm of the life of a group, understanding its importance in motivating and sustaining the group. Key factors in creating a schedule which is motivating are establishment of a rhythm that alternates more intense and less intense and discontinuous activities; celebrations of accomplishments; and, perhaps most importantly, making time for reflection on and coalescing of group learnings or experiences—bringing them clearly into the self-consciousness of the group—at the end of an activity.

---

* Suggested colors are yellow for sleep; green for work; red—family; orange—personal time; purple—social/recreational; and blue for community and world engagement.

The Timeline of My Life

Title _____

Years	Birth				Death
Titles					
PERSONAL					
FAMILY					
COMMUNITY					
WORLD					

How I Spend My Week—Time Log

Date _____

	Mon	Tue	Wed	Thur	Fri	Sat	Sun
12:00 mid							
1:00 am							
2:00 am							
3:00 am							
4:00 am							
5:00 am							
6:00 am							
7:00 am							
8:00 am							
9:00 am							
10:00 am							
11:00 am							
12:00 noon							
1:00 pm							
2:00 pm							
3:00 pm							
4:00 pm							
5:00 pm							
6:00 pm							
7:00 pm							
8:00 pm							
9:00 pm							
10:00 pm							
11:00 pm							

In addition to the intentionality of the space design and the eventfulness of a time design, team-building within the group is critical to a motivated student body or community group. To be effective in the 21st century, corporateness is necessary, with a 21st century twist. The corporate leadership style is shifting from boss to facilitator of the team.

The team

The team must operate out of a common model. The leadership orchestrates the process of defining the vision, finding the contradictions, proposing strategic directions and creating the necessary implementing steps. Consensus is created when the team members look at the issues, decide the common values to hold, and consider alternative models of action until they can agree on one or more.

Critical to sustaining the life of the team is the overarching story that relates their tasks to the needs of the world. The sustaining role of the leadership is to help the team create an operating context and operating images through team symbols, songs and story. To be a guide to the team involves looking at the journey of each member, his/her gifts and vulnerabilities, and structuring opportunities for members to support and motivate each other. The effectiveness of the group then becomes greater than the sum of the parts.

Neighborhood residents, awakened to practical visions of dramatic upgrading of the quality of their living through cooperative ventures, have the motivation for serious, long-term learning and effective team actions. The theory of the four leadership methods described in this chapter is only a beginning. Real excitement happens when the methods are used in leading a group, as one sees concrete, doable plans emerge and concrete progress takes place.

■ Old Doc: Leadership needs bold spirit

DR. TERTIA: Doctor, everybody talks about leadership these days, but why is it so hard to find leaders for our neighborhoods?

OLD DOC: People are reluctant to take on the awesome role. No one will follow a superficial leader today. We wait for leaders who, though they may not know all the facts, have wrestled with the profound social, intellectual, and spiritual issues of our time.

DR. TERTIA: How about charisma?

OLD DOC: If you mean do our leaders need integrity, compassion and boldness: Of course they do.

DR. TERTIA: You say there are four roles people expect of trusted leaders. Should one person try to fill all four roles, or plan to work in a leadership team?

OLD DOC: Team is always better, but you may need to begin alone.

DR. TERTIA: (reading) "There are four leadership roles to be considered in your relationship with the group: the Guide, the Motivator, the Orchestrator and the Sustainer.

"As guide, your most powerful tool is the Basic Discussion Method. This is a disciplined, step-by-step way of talking together about a mundane situation or statement. It is not often used in our schools or public discussions. Your job as leader is to practice the method yourself, insist that your group follow the four steps exactly, and look for the surprising depth insights in ordinary simple disciplined talking together. Lead your group in listening for the profound in the mundane."

OLD DOC: Listening carefully and speaking clearly are powerful tools for any group. The leader who teaches this kind of group conversation deserves to be followed.

■ Using life methods

This chapter sets forth four intellectual and social methods* leaders can use to guide, motivate, orchestrate and sustain groups:

- *The basic discussion method*—used to enable a group to understand a movie, book or other shared experience in depth;
- *The image shifting workshop*—used to form group consensus;
- *Strategic planning*—used for taking a set of unstructured realities, making sense of them, and forming a plan which all the group can buy into and agree upon to bring their combined leverage to bear on the situation; and
- *Celebration*—used to help regain a healthy perspective on life or on a particular task; helps people to see the magnificence of the forest after spending the last week taking inventory of the trees.

The reader is advised: These methods are best learned in front of real work groups, with the help of an experienced mentor. They are more than a series of "how to" procedures. They are a distinctive, interior, spiritual stance on the part of the leader. From this stance comes the leader's power.

---

* These methods were developed by the Institute of Cultural Affairs and used in 35 countries for the past 20 years. They work!

Regional Mentor Panelists (see Epilogue) who are using one or more of these four methods in their own work offer you their assistance in getting inside these methods and testing them in your own setting. Much of the "magic" of effective group leadership is the result of using a few key methods like these four, experiencing their internal dynamics, and thoroughly internalizing them so that they become "second nature." Later we will describe these four methods as the distinctive hallmarks of the new church dynamic. In their function of affirming the goodness of life as it is given to each of us, their empowerment of each participant and of groups learning their use, these four methods are becoming as characteristic of the new spirit movement as were the Gothic arch and other architectural features of the medieval social institutions.

Leadership is more than methods. The leader's self-understanding and image of his/her role in group decision-making is critical. This can be called leadership style and is critical to the development of group competence and confidence. More and more good leaders are using these basic life methods—tools for group thinking and analysis, participation in decision-making, and deciding and creating one's future.

■ I. The basic discussion method[28]

Søren Kierkegaard's insights on the process of becoming a self provide the basis for the structured experiences that create new images and change lives. He understood that a person becomes free when he faces his life situation, takes a relationship to it, and self-consciously appropriates that relationship. In so doing he avoids becoming a victim of his situation or of his relationship to it. The same process applies to groups.

Moving from the objective level (the situation), to the reflective (taking a relationship), to the interpretive (appropriating the new relationship) releases a new level of understanding and action (decisional level). This process is transferrable. It works in the classroom, in leading a meeting to get consensus, in discussing a work of art or a story, in a problem-solving workshop, in strategic planning, and in conflict resolution.

Old Doc: Making conversation that counts

DR. TERTIA: My friend and I nearly had a fight with my department chief over the movie "Salvador," a semi-documentary on U.S.

When you cannot see what is happening in a group, do not stare harder. Relax and look gently with your inner eye. When you do not understand what a person is saying, do not grasp for every word. Give up your efforts. Become silent inside and listen with your deepest self. When you are puzzled by what you see or hear, do not strive to figure things out. Stand back for a moment and become calm. When a person is calm, complex events appear simple.

—JOHN HEIDER; THE TAO OF LEADERSHIP

involvement in El Salvador in the '80s. He asked what the movie was about, and while we were trying to tell him about it, he dismissed it as propaganda. An outrageous way of dealing with an unpopular truth!

DR. PRIMUS: He allowed his ideology to govern his thinking, which we of course never do, do we? How did you handle it?

DR. TERTIA: We stopped talking. Why is it that he is so overbearing and dogmatic in ordinary conversation and so open and fair when he is teaching medicine?

DR. PRIMUS: You can hardly treat a movie like a clinical case. How should he have talked with you about something he'd never seen?

DR. TERTIA: Well, he could have asked us what we remembered about the story. Who were the main characters? What were some of the incidents? Who said what? Just beginning with objective observations focuses and sharpens our memory. Isn't that how we start taking a patient history and doing a physical exam in a new case?

DR. PRIMUS: Okay, say that we've heard some objective data: scenes, characters, plot. What is next?

DR. TERTIA: Next are feelings and reflections. Hearing events recalled by others, we start making connections. That movie had lots of emotional content. He could have asked us where we laughed or felt depressed or angry. He could have asked what similarities and differences there were to other movies we'd seen. Just as in medical diagnosis, exploring the similarities and differences among particular sets of signs and symptoms, in a variety of conditions, is how we discover what is going on.

DR. PRIMUS: I've noticed a strange phenomenon. The more highly educated a person is, the easier it is to jump over the objective recall and reflective analysis, and to expound on one's own interpretation of whatever the subject is. We doctors ought to know better, since we usually insist on an extensive discussion of all the possibilities before making a diagnosis.

DR. TERTIA: We have no right to interpret a situation until we have looked at all the objective data and reflected on it. After giving due consideration to the textbooks and experience of others, we are led to a probable diagnosis. After that we can decide on a treatment plan. My first question to the patient is not "What's the diagnosis?" I ask where it hurts.

DR. PRIMUS: Aha! And you don't start with, "What's the movie about?" If you really want to learn, you start with, "What do you remember?"

DR. TERTIA: Right. I can't tell you what it is about until I've had a chance to discuss with someone else what happened and how we felt about it, and how it fits into the social consciousness. Then I can decide what relationship I am going to take to the movie. I've decided it is more than propaganda.

DR. PRIMUS: It takes effort to use a rational method, going from the objective to reflective to interpretive to decisional levels of discussion. We don't use it perhaps because we don't want more than a superficial conversation. Like "Hi, son, how was your day today?" Answer: "Oh, okay." Communication stops.

DR. TERTIA: You might surprise your son one day by starting with "What did your teacher wear today?" or "Name one thing that happened on the playground." It might lead to a conversation that goes to deeper levels.

DR. PRIMUS: Come to think of it, I could avoid a lot of arguments by beginning with objective questions.

How and why the basic discussion method works

The Basic Discussion Method (also referred to as Focused Conversation or the Art Form Conversation) structures interpersonal communication in a natural, productive way. It is "natural" because it follows the path the mind takes when it acknowledges and responds to stimuli. It is "productive" because it leads to decision and action.

This way of "talking" may seem awkward at first, partly because it requires us to be conscious and purposeful about an activity (communication) which we would prefer to do spontaneously. Another reason the model may seem awkward is that the Western social and educational systems have stressed abstract concepts and theory. In school and at work, we are seldom asked to describe something and/or relate it to previous experience. We have often been encouraged to "jump the gun" in our communications with others by assuming a mutual knowledge of facts, common images or similar experiences. We are often asked to evaluate quickly or judge things—a poem, a political system, a person's promotional potential, the source of a problem. This frequently leads to misunderstandings and poor judgments based on faulty or incomplete information.

The Basic Discussion Method was originally developed for use in guiding group discussions. It can equally well provide the structure for one-on-one discussions and for developing effective statements of praise or correction. It can also be used to organize reports to management on the need for decisions or on the results of decisions.

The method consists of a sequence of questions (or statements) directed at four "levels of consciousness (or discussion)." The four levels are:

Level 1—objective: "What words or phrases do you recall? Scenes? Persons or events?" Some well educated people have difficulty beginning with objective answers, which they consider "too simple." Actually, jumping to answers at the interpretative or decisional levels may be a way of avoiding real dialogue.

Level 2—reflective: "What feelings did you experience? What other events, stories, or memories came to your mind?"

Level 3—interpretive: "What is this story about? What is its meaning for our time?"

Level 4—decisional: "How does this affect me? Do I change my thinking or actions based on what I now know?"

Group conversation begins with first level, objective questions and answers. After everyone has spoken at this level, the conversation proceeds to the second level or reflective questions and answers. Several responses are needed, but it is not necessary to wait until

The Basic Discussion Method				
Levels	1–Objective	2–Reflective	3–Interpretive	4—Decisional
Questions	What objects, colors, action, words, phrases, scenes, persons, events, music, smells, etc., do you recall?	What were your feelings? What other events, stories come to mind? What colors or music would you add?	What is this story about? What is the meaning for our times? Where do you see this going on in your life?	What response are you going to make to this experience? What would you say back to this situation?
Context	The external situation	Internal response	Enlarging the context	Image of what is necessary
Function	Get clairty on the data	Relate self to situation	Relate self to larger context	Respond to a larger context
Dynamic	Common group experience	Composing a larger picture	Expanding the encounter with event into life	Active participation

each person has spoken before going on to level three (interpretive) and then to level four (decisional). Sometimes a level four answer is offered by someone in the group as a natural consequence of the conversation without the direct questioning of the leader. In any event, the conversation should always end at level four.

Protecting the freedom and integrity of the individual

Good leaders regularly use the Basic Discussion Method, although not always under that name, to guide groups through deepening levels of discussion to achieve greater levels of awareness that lead to new images of themselves and their world. These levels of discussion allow and empower each participant to shift images in accordance with his/her own developing value screen. The consistent use of the Basic Discussion Method lessens interpersonal conflict, helps the group get beyond immediacies, and sends the message that each member is responsible for thinking through his/her own decision to participate.

Success with this technique requires more than careful thought for the questions to be asked. In leading such a discussion, leaders needs to be conscious of the images they are projecting—in their style of conversation, dress, and mannerisms—and what kind of messages the group is getting. Does the leader's bearing affirm that life is good? That we can live our lives in spite of limits? Does the leader, by constant affirmation and encouragement of individuals, enhance their participation in the group?

The responsible leader cares for the journey in consciousness of each member of the group. Solitary meditations, journal writing, singing and numerous other rituals that expand awareness can be used in meetings to raise the energy level of the group and to help, as well, to improve the quality of the work produced.

■ II. The image shifting workshop

It is my image of the world that largely governs my behavior. Every time a message reaches a person, his image is likely to be changed, and as his image is changed his behavior patterns will be changed likewise. *The meaning of a message is the change it produces in the image.* This means that for any organization there are no such things as facts, only messages filtered through a changeable value system.[29]

> All the great civilizations had one thing in common, a positive image of the future, infusing the present with purpose and expectation.
>
> —ROBERT BUNDY

Messages designed to shift interior images and behavior have been used by advertisers for many years. Information, concepts and ideas may stimulate thinking. But unless thinking is translated through a value screen into messages that shift the receiver's image of the subject, thinking has no effect on behavior.

The group leadership or the teaching team decides, out of their own context, what new images are needed to replace old ones (from "We are victims" to "We can do something"). Given the trends in our world, and the future needs of our community, what new images does this group need to be effective? What will make the group receptive to these new images?

Scenario:
Changing attitudes at a neighborhood meeting

On the opposite page is a chart of how leaders might begin to analyze their group situation in order to improve it. It could be a classroom, an office, a home or organization. The workshop is based on the supposition that images determine behavior; messages can change images; and new images change behavior.

In this scenario, a few members of a neighborhood association are meeting in a home in a depressed inner-city neighborhood where residents feel neglected and disconnected from the larger city and world. The members wonder how they can turn the situation around. They know that for anything to happen in the neighborhood, people's attitudes will have to change. They have a good leader who asks carefully chosen questions, requires short answers, encourages each person to participate. They set up a chalkboard, and one member keeps careful notes which will be copied for all to have before the next meeting.

First, they decide what to focus on. Should it be the neighborhood association or the neighborhood as a whole? They agree on the latter. Then other basic questions: What is the self-image of the neighborhood? What messages are residents getting that reinforce that self-image? What changes in their self-image are needed for change to happen? What is blocking that? What new messages are needed to shift from old attitudes to new attitudes, and thence to new behavior?

This meeting will be followed by individually assigned homework and a further meeting in two weeks, to decide how to beam the messages needed in the neighborhood. Engagement reinforces new self-images. Real social change becomes possible.

Image Shifting Workshop

Opening Conversation	Full Group Brainstorm	Two Team Workshops	Full Group Reporting	Reflection and Next Steps
Facilitator begins the meeting with questions: 1. Objective: Name one problem you see in the area. (E.g., fallen street signs, trash....) 2. Reflective: What operating images do these reflect? ("It's the city's fault.") 3. Interpretive: Why do we have these images? ("I've called and they won't do anthing here.") 4. Decisional: What can be done about it? What could we do about it? —Go into brain-storm—	1. Individual brain-storm, silent, listing several attitudes of residents and leaders towards the commu-nity. 2. Scribe writes all of these on board as they are volunteered. 3. After all are up, the facilitator helps the group cluster simi-lar items, and name the clusters. 4. Choose 2-4 atti-tudes or operating im-ages that need to be changed first ("We can't control vandal-ism.") 5. Choose those negative images, that if they could be turned around, would lead to real breakthroughs.	1. Break into two subgroups, each group to deal with one or two attitudes that need changing. 2. Each subgroup uses 2 worksheets: Worksheet I asks what *messages* are we get-ting that *reinforce* the old image? From the city? From the envi-ronment? From our-selves? Worksheet II asks what *new attitude is needed* to replace the old one? And, what *messages* are required to make the shift? (What change in the environment? What new self-story?) Write the attitudes and images on index cards to put up in front of whole group.	Reassemble the two teams into the large group. Put up the new atti-tudes required. Each team reports. List on board all the messages needed to achieve the new im-ages or attitudes. Group discussion: What strikes you? Where are there over-laps? What are the hard-est? ...the most do-able? What have we learned from this exer-cise? What are the impli-cations for the commu-nity? ...for us?	1. Facilitator brings meeting to a close with a ques-tion: "What did we accomplish in the last two hours?" (Important to get feedback.) 2. What are our next steps? 3. When is the next meeting? Who will be host and who will be facilitator?
15 minutes	30 minutes	30 minutes	30 minutes	15 minutes

■ III. Strategic planning—A motivating event[30]

With decreasing participation, declining membership or falling sales, what organization has not faced the challenge: *Change or die!* Leadership may have lost its vision and the organization its mission to address a need in society. The challenge is to address the collapse of old values and symbols that once provided a framework for the mission and operations of the organization. How can one create effective strategies for change in the midst of past failures and future ambiguities?

Answer: begin with the present, the indicative situation; get all the necessary players around the planning table.

Strategic Planning is a participative process of strategic and tactical thinking elicited in a group by a facilitation team trained in the Basic Discussion Method, the Brainstorm, Gestalt, and Contradictional Analysis (see Figure 3-1, page 80). The indicative planning process is applicable in corporate board rooms and village squares. At the end, whether the process takes three hours or three days, the participants take home a plan they themselves have just created and are now motivated to implement.

Keys to motivation are affirmation of the group by the facilitation team, discontinuous celebrative events in the planning process, and the reflective conversation using the Basic Discussion Method after each workshop.

The planning process

Simply put, the process asks and answers five questions:
1. What is the focus question or what is the arena of planning?
2. What is your vision? What does the group want to have happen?
3. What are the challenges you face? What is blocking your vision? Why hasn't your vision happened?
4. How are you going to remove the blocks? What are the strategic directions?
5. What are the implementing steps, by whom and when?

Step 1: The practical vision

Through a directed conversation, visualization or brainstorm, the group articulates its own self-understanding in relation to present and future trends. The Vision Statement clarifies the direction the group wants to move in terms of specific activities or structures.

Step 2: The challenges (contradictional analysis)

Group members brainstorm all the irritations, negative attitudes and actions which they perceive as frustrating or blocking the realization of their practical vision. The aim of the challenge workshop is to identify the negative forces and to name them as a web of challenges. Defining the challenges is the most difficult part of the planning process, but this part must *never* be omitted. The real blocks to change are never superficial. They are usually related to negative attitudes, symbols or self-story. The facilitator must push the group to articulate the *why* behind the obvious irritations and external obstacles. (*Why* is it that we lack money, members or time?) It is most important to identify the underlying issues or contradictions. To do this the facilitator helps the group organize the brainstorm into groups or clusters of similar items.

The group is then asked to name the contradiction underlying each cluster, which is worded as a challenge (e.g., unexplored financial resources). Discussion continues until the group agrees on the contradiction, which may be a struggle. Once the the challenge is identified, there is a feeling of release, like understanding the root cause of one's symptoms. After consensus is reached, the group is ready to break for some discontinuous activity: refreshments, singing, or muscular exercises.

Step 3: The strategic directions

The group divides into subgroups of five to seven persons. The task of each subgroup is to think of several concrete actions that, if implemented, will remove the blocks and open the way to realizing the vision. Each subgroup brings its proposed actions, written on index cards, to the total group in a plenary session. The whole group clusters the proposals into different strategies, according to their intent. Again, they must come to consensus on the title or name of each cluster. Under questioning by the facilitator, the group decides which strategic directions are most critical to changing the situation, and which are needed to support the former. A diagram can show the relationship of all the strategic directions agreed upon.

Step 4: The implementing workshop

The amount of time for such a planning group to get through the Strategic Directions phase is from three to six hours. An additional two- to three-hour workshop is usually needed to develop and schedule the practical programs to implement the strategies; to answer the questions who, what, where, when and how.

WORKSHOP METHOD

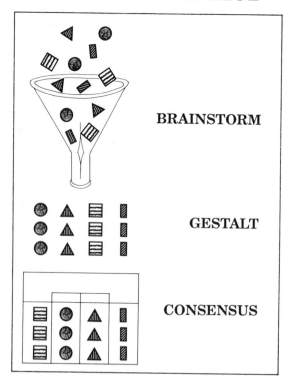

BRAINSTORM

GESTALT

CONSENSUS

FIGURE 3-1:

THE WORKSHOP METHOD

This leadership tool is central to both the Image-Shifting Workshop and Strategic Planning.

1. A brainstorm of ideas from all members of a group encourages a good selection of raw material. By writing down all contributions, the leader signals that everyone's participation is important.

2. The gestalt distributes brainstorm data into similar groupings. Ideas which may have seemed unrelated, or even stupid, often get transformed into jewels when combined with supporting data in a logical matrix.

3. Consensus is reached by talking through the gestalt matrix: Which groupings are more central to doing what the group wants done? ...How do the groups relate to each other?

This indicative planning process, when all the relevant players in an organization or community group participate, is a powerful tool in reducing the resistance to change. The experience gives the whole group a new vision of possibility and ways to achieve the objectives which they themselves have decided upon. In the Implementing Workshop, for each strategic direction the group creates several tactics which are scheduled over a given time period (e.g., a quarter or year). With little wasted time or energy they have created a plan and are motivated to act on it.

Step 5: The document

Rather than have outside consultants take away the brainstorm of goals, objectives, good ideas, and problems of a group, later to return with recommendations, this strategic planning process ends on the last planning day with distribution of the participants' own words in a completed document. Those in the meeting who have created their own vision, challenge statements, strategic directions and implementing steps have this material before them in print. Included in the document are the products of the workshops, list of participants, acknowledgement of those who helped put the event together, and a cover symbolizing the identity of the group. This becomes a reference point for those who will implement the plan.

Strategic planning is a cyclical process. Once the plan is put into action, the situation changes. New visions are possible, and new blocks arise that require new strategies to overcome. The process is repeated as needed. A design conference with key leaders before-hand can select the kind of facilitation team and length of planning needed for the purposes of the group.

■ IV. Celebration

OLD DOC: I saw a greeting card in the store that said "Let's celebrate!" on the front, and inside against a background of explod-ing colors, was "Anything!" It was saying something about our impulse to celebrate. I bought it.

DR. TERTIA: Fiesta! Let's do something different! Perhaps it's an invitation to escape from the day to day.

OLD DOC: I don't think so. Celebration is the opposite of escaping life. It is embracing and affirming it, in a special way. A thoughtful person would have written "Everything!" instead of "Anything!" It is different from a party, though some parties are great celebrations, just as recreation is different from entertainment. It has to do with consciousness.

DR. TERTIA: Celebration is a churchy word. Celebrate mass, cele-brate communion, as a way of getting reconnected with the source of life. And the Jews have a blessing for everything, which I suppose is a way of celebrating life, *"L'chaim,* to life, *l'chaim!"* Singing, dancing and telling funny stories, and making toasts!

OLD DOC: Singing, dancing (kneeling, processions), telling stories (homilies), and making toasts or offering prayers—in one form or another celebration is in every culture. It is part of being human. It's a way of connecting with the past and anticipating the future. And above all, it is a community activity. I don't know if I can celebrate by myself.

DR. TERTIA: I think I can. If I feel especially good, I can celebrate anything, or everything. In spite of the tremendous diversity of celebrations in different cultures, the occasions to celebrate seem similar. There are the rites of passage: birth, puberty, marriage, graduations and death; national holidays, religious holidays, and

81

seasonal holidays. I've noticed, however, that people don't necessarily look happy at celebrations.

OLD DOC: People's feelings may not be the most important element. It is their decision to participate that counts. The closer the festivities approach the sacred celebration of life, the more authentic they are.

DR. TERTIA: What are the elements then? Are they basically all religious? If I celebrate my anniversary by going out to dinner and a nightclub, is that a party or a celebration? Church, it isn't.

OLD DOC: Sacred* liturgy rehearses the dynamics of living in relationship to the divine, and to all of creation: praise, confession,[†] absolution and dedication.[Δ] These same elements are part of secular** celebrations too.

DR. TERTIA: And how do you see that going on in a nightclub?

OLD DOC: Take eating. As human beings we are grateful for the food and drink that we enjoy. So that could be the occasion for praise and thanksgiving, whether expressed or not. Music and singing, if they express the love of life, creativity, and passion are a form of praise, too.

DR. TERTIA: True. Great performers draw in the audience, so we sing along silently or keep time, or whatever, when we are really enjoying it. I suppose that could be interpreted as praise. But how about confession? In a nightclub it is easier to sin than to confess sin.

OLD DOC: Can't you poke fun at yourself? That is confession. That is why we like standup comedians. On our behalf the comic pokes fun at everything: the president, war, politics, popular religion, the economy. Their satirical jokes show up our society with all its faults.

DR. TERTIA: I think that is why I like Phyllis Diller and Kathy in the comics, not to mention Doonesbury. Confession. Then what is absolution?

OLD DOC: The belly laugh. The comedy that can release us and help us let go. It is the slapstick, the pratfalls, the dumb jokes in skits, utter foolishness. Norman Cousins wrote a book on laughing yourself back to health. My father had a great gift of saying

---

* *sacred:* holy; separate from our ordinary normal experience.

† *confession:* free admission of the truth of the matter. Example: "I have done wrong. I need your forgiveness and help."

Δ *dedication:* exclusive or significant commitment to a purpose.

** *secular:* belonging to this wonder-filled transient life; not religious.

something funny that would dissolve the hostility in a meeting and allow the business to go on.

DR. TERTIA: Back to the nightclub. We have the praise/singing, and confession/satire, and absolution/comedy. Nothing left but the dancing. How is that dedication? Perhaps I should ask what *is* dedication?

OLD DOC: Dedication to me is total involvement. And dancing, to enjoy it, requires total involvement in movement, in rhythm with other people on the floor and especially with your partner. And sometimes, as the dance continues, you can throw yourself back into life with a new perspective and new appreciation.

DR. TERTIA: Would that the old church liturgy were as lively as celebrating life with singing, dancing and laughing at ourselves in a secular liturgy. Worship in church seems like a very private experience. ´

OLD DOC: On the contrary. Neither worship nor celebrating is an individualistic exercise between you and the Divine. If you feel part of the church community, then the praise, confession, absolution and dedication will be as lively as the singing, dancing, satire and comedy of a good cabaret.

Planning a celebration

According to the dictionary, to celebrate is to observe with ceremonies of respect or festivity, to extol or praise. Planning the use of time and space to achieve celebration is an excellent way to build cooperation in a team and to practice the skills of up-front leadership. This is an occasion to use the chalkboard, make one or more brainstorms, create a timeline and, most importantly, hold people accountable through team assignments.

On the next page is a checklist for a well-planned celebration. All the answers, however, depend on the answers to the first two questions: Why and what are we celebrating? and What do we want people to experience? Are we celebrating to affirm a job well done? To honor accomplishment and effort? To mark a rite of passage ?

What do we want to happen to people? Do they need a shift in spirit from discouragement to hope and re-dedication? Do they need to feel affirmed and appreciated? Do we want them to come away with an expanded awareness and deepened consciousness? Are the dynamics of life celebration there in secular form (confession, absolution, praise and dedication)?

Procedures for Planning a Celebration		
WHY	What do you want to happen to people? Everything else depends on this!	
HOW	Mood	exuberant, calm, wild, delighted, meditative, intriguing...
	Theme	what ties it all together
	Activities	singing, dancing, performing, eating, drinking, making things, contests, set-up, clean-up
	Space	indoors, outdoors, familiar space, strange space, seating arrangements, lighting, color, flowers, cloths...
	Timing	beginning, middle, end, transitions, high point, prelude...
	Food	type, how prepared and served, variety, theme
	Music	live, recorded, performed, equipment
	Budget	available resources, cost, how cost will be covered
WHO	Roles	assignment and contexting for host(s) and for those in charge of food, set-up, etc.
	Participants	how they are to be invited, what image they will be given as to dress, how they will anticipate and remember the occasion with delight

■ More is required: Two continuing leadership tasks

Once a neighborhood has awakened to the possibility of dramatic upgrading of the quality of its life through cooperative actions, responsible leaders have two possibly unpopular tasks. Both are absolutely needed if the awakened residents are to reach their vision.

A very important task for the leadership of the awakened neighbors is to guide them into compassionate care for *all* who belong in their neighborhood. Stories in this book include many concerns for the previous outcasts of our world society: criminal offenders; crazy folk who put varying burdens on their fellows; illiterates; the unemployable; neighborhood residents who sicken or otherwise suffer and die needlessly, especially in childhood. A neighborhood or community of any size which turns away from these groups has violated the norm of our times and has ignored the only political consensus we are likely to have: All the earth belongs to all the inhabitants. All the resources and tasks of the neighborhood belong to all its residents. Those who must go off to war or to prison or hospital one day (usually) will return. The viable neighborhood will not ignore their needs and contributions.

The second perhaps unpopular task of responsible leaders in the newly awakened neighborhood is to honor hard work, serious learning, eagerness to experiment. Just as in some vigorous religious groups every member is expected to study the holy scriptures daily, so in real neighborhood development many residents should be expected to enroll in needed new studies of practical business, construction, health, and leadership skills. The future *does* belong to those willing to work hard, work smart, and work together for the common good.

Chapter 4

The Social Laboratory:
Social Medicine for the 1990s

he bridge between social theory, spirit passion, and real world acceptance of the new is the social laboratory. In this chapter, we offer illustrations, identify contradictions (otherwise known as blocks or challenges), frame questions, and create experimental* strategies necessary to tackle the hard contradictions of urban problems.

Too many neighborhood planning meetings end where they should begin: with the group sensing its power and moving toward common effort, cooperation, and prioritized time lines of assigned tasks. These mostly are contentless attitudinal stances. To transform the urban neighborhood, several high-energy business and scientific disciplines also are needed. To expect experts to generously give to a neighborhood the goodies from these disciplines is a regrettable illusion.

Neighborhood residents and leaders aspiring to real economic and social development, must invest time and work in hard study of basic business and scientific knowledge, attitudes and skills. Life-long learning in ever new fields of useful knowledge, attitudes and skills is the cost of transformation, freedom and prosperity in the modern urban neighborhood.

The four intellectual and social methods described in the last chapter only begin the process of neighborhood development. Also needed will be residents with newly mastered skills in accounting,

---

* *experiment(al):* a test made to examine the validity of a hypothesis or the efficacy of something previously untried. *An experiment never fails!*

communication, conflict resolution, design, etc. Where residents work hard to acquire and share these new skills, the neighborhood will prosper.

■ Epidemiology: Asking who gets ill and why

When science has done its analytical and descriptive work well, interested persons can see where the challenges lie in a troubled situation. ("The tomatoes are blighted; the cause is a virus called ....") This is just the beginning of the uses of science, of course. ("Possible remedies are a and b. We will set up four identical plots of tomato plants, test remedies a, b, a+b, and keep one plot as a control.") In the social sciences we are beginning to go beyond analysis and description (first generation science) to testing remedies (second generation science).

For neighborhood health, local residents (as well as their expert consultants) also need at least some of the working skills of the basic science of epidemiology—the study of the health of populations. It has been useful in controlling epidemics of infectious diseases. Recently epidemiology has been used in the fields of mental health and social disorders, which are so troublesome today.

Epidemiological measurement methods useful in monitoring neighborhood development include:

- measures of status,* process,† outcome,Δ and impact** related to the contradictions of the neighborhood;

---

* *status measures:* a baseline to measure from. Example: our current membership enrollment is 3560 people.

† *process measures:* a measure of the work performed in an action. Examples: a) the snow goose in a head wind may need 20 wing flaps each minute to travel at the rate of 20 miles per hour, or, b) we held 12 regional seminars and sent out 1200 informational pieces of mail last year.

Δ *outcome measures:* a measurement of the immediate result of an action. Examples: a) the snow goose in its fall migration from Canada south travels 2600 miles and loses an average of 20 pounds in body weight, or, b) the number of diagnosed hypertensive patients registered in our program and known to be on adequate medical care increased from 250 to 1250.

** *impact measures:* the effect on a population of a reported action. Examples: a) the snow goose nests in the Arctic after growing fat in the prairies of Latin America, or b) in our parish this last year five girls under the age of 15 have born children, up from none two years ago.

- samples,* controls,† retrospective△ and prospective** tabulations;
- assessing needs†† and resources (first generation science);
- testing remedies (second generation science).

We will see TWCs using impact measures to gather collaborative constituencies, and selecting arenas and sites for experiment (and finding access points for leverage and social change). These are basic tools for discovering and naming the elements for an experimental approach to neighborhood development.

Hypothetical (but real) example

A real problem in many urban neighborhoods is assaults and burglaries by young men ages 15-24. A status measure of this problem would include data on the definition of these crimes, characteristics of the criminals and victims, variables related to the frequency of these crimes in different neighborhoods, etc. Going beyond tabulations of such data is an arrangement of data pointing to previously unrecognized associations. For example, many people were surprised to learn that over 80 percent of young male urban criminals give up criminal behavior completely in their mid to late twenties, whether or not they suffer arrest or judicial punishment. Such studies are valuable first-generation science probes of the way life really is today.

Imaginary example: Testing a hypothesis

Suppose that some leaders (for reasons of compassion, desire to save public money, or whatever motives) decide to learn what kind

---

* *samples:* see examples in Narangwal story, page 93.

† *controls:* in neighborhood health broadly defined, a group of persons like the test sample people in every way except in the variable being studied. Example: two neighborhoods alike in the age, sex, race, class, occupation, resources, and lifestyle characteristics of the population, differing only in the way convicted criminals in the two neighborhoods are punished.

△ *retrospective tabulations:* studying existing records to find and collate measures based on observations already recorded. Cheaper than prospective studies, but much more subject to bias.

** *prospective tabulations:* counting process, outcome or impact measures defined in advance of the experiment or study; cf retrospective tabulation.

†† *needs:* a word often defined by outside experts for someone else, often for local resident populations. The argument of this book is that real "needs" are the *locally-defined* priorities.

of judicial punishment (say imprisonment or community service) is more effective in reducing these particular crime rates. They know that a carefully controlled experiment on a sample test neighborhood will be more useful than rhetoric. They arrange that in sample neighborhood A (population 15,000 persons), for a two-year period, all young men convicted of assault or burglary will be punished by imprisonment. In control neighborhood B (population 18,000 persons), all young men convicted of these crimes will be required to do community service. The age, sex, race, class, occupations, resources and lifestyles of the two neighborhoods are not significantly or measurably different. The crime rates and characteristics of these crimes have been tracked for ten years in the two neighborhoods. Statisticians tell the designers of the experiment that a four-year observation time will be needed to detect any real difference in rates of these crimes in these neighborhoods. So the designers modify their experimental design to a four-year period. They publicize the matter, and there is a well-attended public meeting.

Questions:

1. Why should our neighborhoods be selected for this scrutiny? *Answer:* This is a useful service we can give the whole city and other cities like ours.

2. Why should one of our neighborhoods be subjected to an inferior crime control measure? *Answer:* Which is inferior? Some studies say that community corrections are at least as effective as imprisonment of young men for reducing these crimes; community corrections costs far less than imprisonment, and damages the offender less. In fact, community corrections, by not removing the offender from the gaze of his neighbors, may deter crime more effectively than imprisonment. But until an experiment like this is completed, all the arguments are guesses and prejudice.

3. Why not just look at the past record (retrospective study)? Young men have been imprisoned for many years; recently we have used community service as a humane alternative in selected cases, usually with some public disapproval. Compare how the two kinds of punishment have worked to reduce crime rates. *Answer:* "Selected cases" prove little. We need cases, young criminals, and whole neighborhoods so alike that any difference in outcome measures and impact measures can only be attributed to what this experiment is studying: the effect of two kinds of judicial punishment. Only a prospective study can give that kind of assurance.

4. What are the outcome measures of this experiment? *Answer:* rates of citizen complaints, arrests, and convictions for assaults and burglaries.

5. What are the impact measures of this experiment? *Answer:* we must set these before we start the experiment. Impact measures could include citizen perception of neighborhood safety, as measured by surveys before, during and after the experiment; comments made at public meetings and reported in the media regarding citizen perceptions of their safety; morale of law enforcement workers in the two neighborhoods; sale prices of residential properties; numbers of businesses and workers employed in the two neighborhoods over the life of this experiment (as a good proxy measure of business perception of safety and citizen prosperity); and perhaps other measures. An important thing to remember: A good experimental design sets all these measures *before* the study begins. Otherwise, critics can claim the measures were chosen to favor one kind of judicial punishment over the other.

6. Suppose that after three months one method of punishment clearly is much better. Why should the neighborhood using the inferior method be required to persist in suffering under the rule of the experimenters? *Answer:* this is a familiar concern in testing new drugs. The answer always is that as soon as one method of treatment is proved better, beyond statistical quibbling, the results are published and the experiment ends. Our experts tell us that this is quite unlikely in our proposed experiment before the end of the four-year period, given the number of assaults and burglaries in our test neighborhoods. We will not wait, however, for absolute certainty before declaring one kind of punishment the better. As soon as differences in outcome measures and perhaps impact measures go beyond normal statistical chance variability so that we can say that there is a 95 percent probability that the difference in what is being measured is a real difference (and due to the different types of punishment), we will tabulate and publish the results. Then those responsible for directing crime control can act accordingly.

7. What about crimes committed by women? They are increasing in frequency and severity. Why not include women in this study? *Answer:* one thing at a time. It will be enough hard work to get at the real truth of the questions we have set for the experiment as proposed. Introducing more variables would make it almost impossible to get answers that would satisfy the experts and the public in a reasonable time frame.

At least a few residents trusted by the others in each neighborhood should learn the principle operating rules of epidemiology as a means for setting priorities that will advance overall social and physical health in that neighborhood.

■ Measuring neighborhood health

We have selected the following stories to illustrate the importance of measurements which help define priorities and the need for collaboration among diverse groups in addressing problems of social illness. Each example gives a glimpse into the many facets of community medicine.

Annual disability days[31]

Annual Disability Days (ADD) is a count or estimate of the total person-days per year in a neighborhood population in which any disability kept persons from school, work, household duties, or preferred leisure activities. ADD can be set forth as a percent of total person days, or as the number of days per hundred persons per year or (better for monitoring total neighborhood well-being) per week. This measure already is used by the Health Interview Survey (HIS) of the U.S. Department of Public Health.

In the average U.S. neighborhood of 1,000 persons, 10 percent of the disability days in any time period are experienced by persons in hospitals, nursing homes or prisons. Another 30 percent happen to community residents unable to participate in normal, desired activities due to chronic illness, alcoholism, fear of crime, lack of job skills or psychosis. Some 60 percent are due to untimely deaths from accidents, homicide, and preventable infant mortality. Each perinatal death contributes 365 disability days to the community total for the next 75 years, emphasizing the great value of sanitation, immunization and nutrition.

In the average U.S. neighborhood in 1979 about one-third of disability days were from causes which can be addressed effectively only by corporate action at the neighborhood level: health education for responsible self-care (examples: cigarette smoking and diabetic self-care) and control of accidents and homicide (alcoholism plays a large role).

Diabetes requires health action by medical society [32]

Medical doctors have known for decades that public health requires collaboration among many parties. Yet, we suspect that few if any medical societies have implemented Dr. Ganda's recommendation for addressing the complications of diabetes:

> Diabetes causes most deaths, after cardiovascular disease and cancer. Many of its deaths occur at an early age. Sheer neglect of older patients by an inadequate care system is a major obstacle. Diabetic ketoacidosis (DKA) deaths present the same kind of challenge that maternal deaths offered many years ago. As with maternal deaths, it will take a medical society action on a community basis (as distinct from a hospital basis) supporting unified casefinding, professional and patient education, case tracking, and population-based evaluation of the whole effort to impact preventable death.
>
> The scope for improvement is great: 5,000 cases of new blindness each year, 20,000 amputations, 2,000 cases of end stage renal disease, four-fold more major defects in infants of diabetic mothers.

Rural health needs international linkages [33]

Concerns about public health issues in Arizona abound. Rural populations have special interests and needs. We are attempting to identify those areas of greatest significance and pull resources to address needs. In the area of public health our challenges are access to health-care services, environmental hazards, quality and quantity and cultural sensitivity of health professionals.

We perceive that health problems in Africa and Central America are related to our own situation, with many similar root causes. Through educational programs and linkage building, we stimulate activity in priority areas and attempt to coordinate our services with other state agencies. Community planning forums and microwave communication systems have proven to be useful in our work.

We would like to learn from others how to build resources, how to evaluate program effectiveness, how to develop communication linkage systems. We hope to illuminate public health problems in an attempt to solve them for the benefit of rural communities everywhere. We want to establish linkages with cross-cultural groups (Anglos, Hispanics, Native Americans, Black Americans) and to collect and distribute cross-cultural education material pertaining to health and education programs. We are able to facilitate entrance of different cultural groups into the health professions.

■ Epidemiology being applied in communities

The methods of epidemiology—the science of population-based study of biological and social disorders—have wide application for communities attempting to address the problems of social illness.

When resources are scarce, epidemiology helps set priorities [34]

Narangwal, a village in northwest India with 1800 residents, was a field laboratory for Johns Hopkins professor Carl Taylor, studying affordable village health methods for 13 years. The local rural doctors, who were expected to be all things to all people, most simply settled for comfortable familiar routines of clinical care, which kept them busy. Even if more physicians could be found, there still would be too much to do. An entirely new system was needed.

A Functional Analysis Project began with village interviews about health beliefs and practices. Taylor and his team followed health workers on their rounds as they bicycled down country roads. They learned that although local healers charged more than government health workers, people preferred the locals. They experimented with local women, Family Health Workers in health teams, recruited with local newspaper advertisements. In 18 weeks of training, workers learned oral rehydration for infant diarrhea. Within a year diarrhea deaths dropped by half. They learned to suspect pneumonia in young children, inject long-acting penicillin, *then* refer the case to a physician. Pneumonia deaths fell by half in one year.

The next project was how to best attack the synergism between malnutrition and infections. Infection control is part of existing health services, and even an intensive campaign can be delivered fairly cheaply. But studies showed 25 to 30 percent of children were malnourished and vulnerable to even mild infections. From 60 to 80 percent fell below the third percentile in age-adjusted body weight. Four matched clusters of villages were selected for a five-year trial. All received emergency care as needed. One cluster served as a control, getting only standard care on demand. A second cluster was served by Family Health Workers living in the villages, stressing health education. A third cluster received nutritional supplements for malnourished children. In the fourth cluster Family Health Workers provided not only health services, but also education on nutrition.

Results? The control group fared worst of all, having the most infections and deaths. Nutrition was most important for the perinatal population. Then in the first year, infection control was most rewarding in terms of reduced mortality. Beyond one year of age, nutrition and infection control were equally important in reducing mortality.

The entire field project was conducted by administrators, scientists, and workers living in the villages. All conferences were held in the village itself, although Delhi was just six hours away. There were no hotels.

There were two major learnings: 1) The less a country has to spend, the greater the need for focus and management; and 2) People nearly always resist unfamiliar services. What is needed is some unifying idea to catch hold of the government and people.

Applied epidemiology in Israeli communities[35]

A community medicine clerkship in Israel has medical students define a project, collect and analyze data, and implement recommendations. Teams using epidemiological methods in primary health care assess health needs of a selected population, do surveillance of changes in health of the people served, and evaluate the service. They start with any "question" asked by a practicing physician in relation to more than one patient under his care. While the individual practices (2500 patients at most) provided numbers too small for statistically significant conclusions in many arenas such as mortality, nevertheless the applicability of knowledge from such studies for a particular community is clear.

Two-hundred and fifty such community projects have addressed questions on health-seeking behavior (related to smoking, sex, etc.); prevalence of major chronic diseases or their risk factors in the community; infant mortality in a town with only 100 births each year (a statistical problem because of the small numbers); opposition to treating head lice among the very old (a belief that an old person without lice is dead since the lice leave the body after death); why lung cancer was nonexistent, and cancer of the breast more common in the kibbutzim than in the country as a whole; worker absenteeism related to upper respiratory infections and air pollution in a major power-producing company.

Social epidemiology in the developing world[36]

My Name Is Today is a book about children and their families in the developing world that uses illustrations, cartoons, graphs and line drawings, with captions and discussion in the form of an explanatory dialogue between David and Hermione. Using data from the field of social epidemiology, the book raises questions— Who gets ill and why? Where are the resources spent?—and suggests alternatives and opportunities to prevent ill health. There are five chapters:

1. Our Children's World—problems of resources, education of women and health, poverty, future problems of old age.

2. Childhood Illness in Less Developed Countries—frequency and causes of illness, infant mortality, population growth.

3. Improving Health Services—primary-care planning, expenditure on arms, big hospitals vs primary care, training for health workers, the curative orientation, training the health team, lessons from history.

4. The Changing Role of Health Workers—helping others learn self-care, team work and leadership, breaking down walls between disciplines, politics of health.

5. Where Next for Children?—asks what are the priorities among such concerns as diarrhea and oral rehydration, immunization, suckling, growth, malnutrition, stimulation and employment when children grow up.

The imaginal format, simple words, clear illustrations, and the question-and-answer teaching dialogue form an excellent basis for a curriculum for neighborhood health workers, parents, and public health personnel in the U.S. as well as in developing countries.

This brief summary suggests the power of the science of epidemiology in naming problems, discovering the critical variables, setting priorities among remedies, evaluating allocation and use of resources, and developing the criteria for public accountability. All health professionals and most citizen leaders need a catch-up course in epidemiology.

Chapter 5

Many Kinds of Family

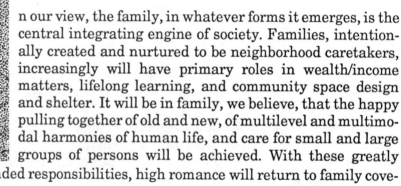 n our view, the family, in whatever forms it emerges, is the central integrating engine of society. Families, intentionally created and nurtured to be neighborhood caretakers, increasingly will have primary roles in wealth/income matters, lifelong learning, and community space design and shelter. It will be in family, we believe, that the happy pulling together of old and new, of multilevel and multimodal harmonies of human life, and care for small and large groups of persons will be achieved. With these greatly expanded responsibilities, high romance will return to family covenants.

Communities served by such families-in-dialogue around the world will integrate information into knowledge and knowledge into wisdom, creating a New Common Sense. We see ahead a time for great romance and high drama in building family as a major pillar of the new world ahead.

■ The covenanted clan: The best retirement village

MEDICAL STUDENT: Doctor, what are you going to do now that you are retired?

OLD DOC: I think I will live in a retirement village and use it as a social laboratory for community medicine.

MEDICAL STUDENT: It might be fun. To study the behavior of oldsters in a retirement village, I mean.

OLD DOC: My retirement home will be in an urban village in an inner-city neighborhood.

MEDICAL STUDENT: Why the inner city?

OLD DOC: There is so much life there. Perhaps it is a form of social repentance. Earlier in our lives, with all good intentions, I suppose, my generation in the rising middle class fled the neighbor-in-need in the inner city for the security and niceties of suburban living. Now we have proven social technologies for village development. It is a challenge worthy of the rest of our lives to apply these new technologies to inner-city neighborhoods. It is a way of reclaiming our roots, I suppose.

MEDICAL STUDENT: Just any city neighborhood?

OLD DOC: As long as it has defined geographical boundaries within which people live and work—young and old, rich and poor—and the people want it to be a good place to live.

MEDICAL STUDENT: What would you do in the neighborhood?

OLD DOC: Elders like myself would be expected to insert ourselves into the social process to develop jobs, safe streets, lifelong education, and great community celebrations, so that every person is engaged and the village enjoys good health.

MEDICAL STUDENT: How would it differ from what we are doing in neighborhoods now?

OLD DOC: We would of course build on what others have done.

MEDICAL STUDENT: Doctor, how will that keep you interested in living to a ripe old age?

OLD DOC: By seeing the neighborhood as a social laboratory, a great place for new social inventions.

MEDICAL STUDENT: How are you going to compensate for the losses that accompany aging: physical and mental deterioration, deaths of friends, scattering of family?

OLD DOC: An old man is in a race with time and must choose his priorities carefully. He can become detached from many things, like earning a living, family, church. He can become attached to other things. Fundamental changes need to be made in our social patterns of thinking and caring for our neighbor. An old man has nothing to lose by taking on this task.

MEDICAL STUDENT: Blood is thicker than water, they say. What can take the place of the old tie to the family—brothers, sisters and children?

OLD DOC: What is family, after all? Family is a relationship based on mutual covenants more than on blood alone. You can only trust that "they" will care for you when you need help. The older I grow, the more I believe it is the elders who will take the initiative in creating human community in our alienated neighborhoods. We need a new family structure, the covenanted clan.

MEDICAL STUDENT: The clan isn't new. In our Southwest, Native American villages are run by clans, each with its public sacred space where elders initiate the young into the spiritual and social covenants of the clan.

OLD DOC: You've made my point nicely. The strong religious and social ties of the extended family hold in place the social fabric of the village. In cities, too, we must express our growing spiritual values in the economic and social life of the local community.

MEDICAL STUDENT: Who is going to do that in the cities?

OLD DOC: The family in a new form. Groups of twenty-five or more persons can be covenanted to be this new family.

■ The more-than-nuclear family

There is criticism of the nuclear family, as though the high divorce rates prove that romantic love has been discredited as a basis for family formation. Well, maybe. But we can remember that throughout the industrial revolution the nuclear family sheltered the majority of middle class and poor people in Europe and the Americas. We need not apologize for an institution undergoing transformation in our time.

Family, like home, is where "if you have to go they have to let you in" (Robert Frost). Family is not a weak institution. Family is where many essential life functions go on. Family harnesses and is powered in part by sex, the biological side of the cosmic urge to merge all in One. Family has a key political or organizing role in society, as families join other families—in neighborhoods, clans, tribes, classes—in organizing the common life to protect the precious political and economic freedom always under challenge. Family and the local church, synagogue, mosque and temple are natural allies in assuring wholesome local power centers as alternatives to the huge organs of commerce and state.

The family is a pillar of the information-age society. By "family" we mean any group of persons living together under one roof for a year or more. The traditional family of parent(s) and children, with or without related elders, is included in our understanding of "family." We also call "family" other groupings of persons: adults without children, residents of a dormitory school, residents and supervisors in a detention facility, and other groupings in which individuals find themselves at various times in their lives.

Most of our culture is already exploring new forms of "family." Final designs are not yet in sight. But pretty clearly, family in some form is part of the genetic "given" of human life and society. So let us look at how some groups are getting on with designing family forms which can embody in the future human society the cosmic urge to merge in the One.

Mindful of the great difficulties waiting for any new kind of family organization, we are not running ahead of the trends of the times. The extended nuclear family holds its place in the sun by offering the best place for several essential human functions: as economic and social bases for new family structures, as social laboratories, and as therapeutic communities.

Select your family from the catalog[37]

Community Dreams by Bill Berkowitz has hundreds of ideas for enriching neighborhood and community life. Nicely illustrated, the short paragraphs are well indexed: food, economic development, health, festivals, workplaces, traditions. Under families: "The multigenerational group houses are for modern extended families, with varied familial life styles. They advertise themselves accordingly. From the group-house catalog, you can select strict or lenient discipline, bound or free feeling, high, medium or low household responsibility, as you wish. If you don't love your present family, you can choose another when your lease is up."

■ New economic and social bases for family structures

Several reports propose creation of small-scale economic and social bases, foundational to all other functions of family:

The profitable family farm[38]

Booker T. Whatley says the farm must be located on a paved road within 40 miles of a metropolitan area.

"It must have high value crops and a year round cash flow," says Whatley, who planted his model 25-acre farm from 1974 to 1981, before he retired as professor of horticulture at Tuskeegee Institute in Mississippi. His formula, which is putting profit back into the family farm, states:
- The farm must provide year-round income from about 10 crops, ripening at different times, generating $3,000 per acre;
- The operation must be full time, employing a family or about three full-time workers;

- A main market must be guaranteed through a "pick your own club" of 1,000 member households who pay an annual fee and harvest most of the crops;
- The crop mix for the 25 acres can be altered according to climate and customer demand;
- Crops must be irrigated.

Whatley's approach combines homespun solutions with the best of modern technology. To keep bugs down, he balances natural predators with insecticides: a flock of guinea fowl will reduce the need for pesticides on strawberries, sweet potatoes, greens and peas by about 80 percent.

Since 1981, 600 farms have adopted Whatley's formula. For farmers who need help getting started, Whatley has enlisted "state coordinators" who visit farms and act as consultants.

The repair-mall family business: A making place[39]

Work is an opportunity to be a co-creator with God. A regenerative economy continually forms new businesses. Skills are passed on from an older generation to the younger. How many successful farm owners today think about teaching inner-city or Third World youth their skills rather than overextending themselves to buy more land and equipment? One of the more practical ways for birthing a regenerative economy is by strengthening the repair industry. Repair work is scattered, without status. Hardly anyone recognizes that the clothing alteration shop and the small electronic repair business share a bond in renewing the physical goods of our economy. Repair skills have many positive economic and social benefits. Most repair shops do not require substantial capital. A particular pool of capital can generate many more workplaces than if invested in some capital-intensive project like a nuclear power plant or waste incinerator. Repair workers generally do not need expensive specialized education. Often their skills are gained in home-based shops on an apprentice basis. Such work is a way to build up family relationships.

Preserving repair skills and fostering innovation lead to creation of new enterprises. The Mack Truck industry in the Lehigh Valley of Pennsylvania began in 1890 when John and Gus Mack purchased a Brooklyn, New York, wagon-manufacturing business. In the lean early years they found that wagon repair added income. John Mack had engineering skills which he turned to repairing the company's steam engine, used for powering the manufacturing. In

1902 the brothers added an early gasoline-powered wagon, with automobile rebuilding and repair. From three related repair skills—wagons, steam engines, and automobiles—came the Mack Truck company.

In 1980 Mack Trucks took 1,800 jobs out of the Lehigh Valley by moving assembly operations to the South. To regenerate a local economy facing similar job losses from other large companies, Bob Rodale has proposed a repair mall. In one location, perhaps the very place where the John Mack brothers built their first truck, a variety of repair shops would provide a new "making place." This is a regenerative twist on the more traditional call for a business incubator, usually meaning shared services in accounting, docking, mail handling and telephone switchboard.

The repair mall would be a making place, where other malls today are largely buying and selling places. It would stress artisanship, durability and ingenuity. It would stand over against planned obsolescence, and the throw-away society. The mall might seem a little messy, yet retirees would like it, as would teens working part-time after school and weekends, and then moving into full-time apprenticeships and eventually ownership. The repair mall could send out a van to pick up and deliver work. It would refer out excess or specialty repairs to other shops in the region.

Groundwork must be laid before building a repair mall. A region's repair workers, business community, public leaders, and citizenry first must begin thinking regeneratively about the mall. A regional repair directory such as the Lehigh Valley Repair Directory could be a handy reference for repair work in over 100 categories. Since repair and recycling are business first-cousins, the directory could list all commercial and civic recycling centers.

The school that grew a community[40]

In the early 1970s educator and nurse Mary Leue started The Free School in inner-city Albany, New York as an alternative to the "under educative" public schools. The accredited elementary school has over 40 students and a staff of 10. Tuition ranges from $15-$80 per month. Most of the school's income is from rental apartments located in nine buildings, purchased in the 1970s and cooperatively rehabilitated by the school community. Using the housing rehab skills learned in the process, six teachers formed a successful business, Small Miracles: House Burnishers, to supplement teaching stipends.

Unless we wake each other, how shall we mature?

—UNKNOWN

101

The Free School community also operates:
- cooperative urban farming in the backyards of community-owned buildings along two parallel streets;
- The Family Life Center for support and education in medical self-care, pregnancy and childbirth, and an alternative birthing center, run in cooperation with local midwives and obstetricians;
- a clothing exchange, natural foods store, lending library, bookstore, mail order catalog and publishing company (Down To Earth Books);
- a cooperative investment group (The Money Game) which makes loans to members, functions as a limited health and liability insurance group and has spun off an alternative financing group which buys up old buildings and helps poor families rehab and finance homes; and
- a cooperatively-owned lodge, Rainbow Camp, on a small, beautiful lake in the Taconics for recreation and weekend workshops.

The heart of the enterprise is the core group that operates as a close community grounded in trust and affection. Currently 20 people, including eight of the original 10, meet four hours a week as they have been since 1974, for mutual support and problem solving. Their commitment to this corporate sharing has created the spiritual and human space in which all their community activities have been able to grow.

Harvard's prison experiment [41]

In a 1962 prison experiment, Harvard professors joined a group of maximum security felons in taking a psychedelic drug. Prisoners evaluated results in this research, selected the next lot of subjects, and gave the orientation lectures. Some 15 Harvard grads and 35 convicts formed buddy pairs for the parole period. The group visited in each other's homes, operated a 24-hour emergency telephone, sobered up members, praised them to parole officers, cooled angry bosses, and generally did what a good family does for confused members to keep them out of jail.

It is surmised that the shared psychic experience from the drug allowed new imprinting for persons recalcitrant to ordinary social controls. In the first year, when the state rate of recidivism for felons was 70 percent, only 10 percent of this group returned to jail.

Caring for weak and vulnerable persons, non-nuclear families do well what the welfare state notoriously has failed to do, which is provide a human quality to their lives. Following are two illustrations from many that are available:

Cooperative lifestyle for mental patients [42]

Patients can become too well adapted to life in a mental hospital. A more challenging alternative is living in an apartment with two or three others, with the support of established community mental health services and a professional team of psychiatrist, social worker and nurse. Association Horizon in Paris, France, composed of professionals, patients, their families and friends, was formed in 1979 to care for the mentally ill in the neighborhood setting and to work with the neighbors to help integrate those discharged from the mental hospital into the life of the community. Financing comes from membership dues, small grants from local governments, and rents paid by the occupants.

Part-time family members: The home helper [43]

For a frail elder or disabled person of any age—dependent on regular assistance with activities of daily living such as bathing, dressing, shopping, food preparation or house cleaning—a friend or paid worker who provides these services needed for independent living becomes a surrogate family member.

When a Home Help (a European name for a part-time homemaker) enters a client's home, she is an agent for change. Whether she brings healing or not depends on her self-image and training.

Many disabled persons are imprisoned by poverty and increasing debilitation in their own homes. They may have incurable disease. They may be escaping the pain and struggle of life through alcohol, or medication, or mental illness. Most have no family or primary caregivers at home.

The Home Help enters the home regularly to clean, shop, do laundry, or help with a bath. With training the Home Help becomes part of the healing team, along with the doctor, the community nurse, counselors and volunteer visitors. She uses practical "see–do–teach" nonacademic motivational methods that give the client new images of possibility, repairing the will to live and give as long as life is given.

■ New family configurations for elders

Retiring well and whole [44]

We orient to life less by place (city, house) than by life patterns and symbols; we fear death less than we fear disruption of our orienting life symbols and patterns. Social disruptions—loss of friends, moving of family, frailty, loss of money—often throw our patterns and symbols into chaos long before death is a real threat. A crippling of humor may reduce our enjoyment of activities and recreation; these may cease to be sources of stability, and instead become threats to our security.

Life symbols can be reconstructed. Elders can accept long-term health care gracefully *if* they participate in shaping their expectations of the future. A life of integrity recognizes the tension between institution and individuality. When institutions fail, it is most often a failure of individuals to stand for goals which they know they should stand for, a failure rooted in a failing integrity. This failure is a great danger in long-term health care facilities which can assume an increasingly dominant role as individuals increasingly get frail and disoriented. To remedy this failure of integrity, caregivers must assume wellness rather than sickness. The institution must develop a positive view of resident health. Opportunities for individual self-care and for a self-determined lifestyle must be multiplied.

How does one experience God's gifts of health and wholeness while natural strength ebbs? Long-term care generally is a real effort to relieve the agony of lost sight, confusion, deafness and stiff joints. Beyond that struggle, there must be an effort to deal with the wholeness of life at a higher level. The community of the faithful makes of their individual brokenness a corporate wholeness. Love is exchanged in that shared weakness and strength. The group becomes a freeing agent for its members. When people experience the wholeness of life, they can escape their private confinements.

■ Youth in families: Dealing with drugs, booze, sex and questions of identity

Difficult options for chemical dependency in youth [45]

Three million adolescents are chemically dependent, by self-reports of students in grades eight thru 11. Some 31 percent of high school seniors report major complications from alcohol and drug abuse (in this age the two almost always go together): trouble with the law, school, home or work. Alcohol is the number one cause of death, through motor vehicle accidents, in the 12-20 year-old group.

Some 90 percent of adolescents hooked on drugs and alcohol have alcoholic parents. Their alcoholism seldom is the reason they require assistance. Their difficulty is manifested as trouble in home and school, and by feelings of suicide and depression.

An adolescent drinking a six-pack of beer in two hours gets a 1.5 percent blood alcohol level. For another 72 hours his memory, perception, and judgment remain mildly impaired.

Adolescents don't take alcohol and drugs for euphoria; mostly (like adults) they get dysphoria. Many girl addicts living with dealers are able to give up heroin and other drugs when they leave the dealers. The addiction is incidental to the human relationship.

Legal look-alike drugs such as pure ephedrine or caffeine come in capsules colored and labeled to look like the hard street drugs. Delivered through the mail for $162 per thousand from Lewisburg, Pennsylvania, these look-alikes provide many adolescents protection against peer pressure to join in hard drug abuse.

Despite obvious difficulties ("it's like urinating in the ocean to try to raise the water level"), summer camps for alcoholic adolescent inner-city kids achieve frequent dramatic turnabouts. In a family with two or more chemically dependent persons, the nondependent is the deviant. These frail kids need some love.

In contrast are the antisocial groups of hardcore druggie kids; no 28-day program of however much love seems to lay a glove on them. The hardcore gangs, many of whose members are dyslexic, need a hard, structured program.

Adolescents need more options for roles other than the current ones of jocks, druggies and nerds. Non-athletic kids can't be jocks. It is easy for an experienced worker to start activity groups, impossible to start therapy groups.

Sense about (teen & other) sex [46]

In 1986, 365 children in Detroit under age 17 were wounded by gunfire, 45 fatally. Most of the fights were over trifles: a gold chain, a silk shirt. Mothers of some of the slain children organized a memorial service at St. Paul's Cathedral. Some 1,500 persons participated, shared the grief of families and friends, and determined to make Detroit a better place to live. Now over a hundred

There is no fellowhood like that of shared pain.

—SA'ADI

105

people meet regularly as Save Our Sons And Daughters (SOSAD) to "Reach out and touch with love."

Among those reaching out is Deborah D. Heath, born in Cincinnati, Ohio, in 1951. From birth she lived among people repeatedly pushed out of their homes by urban renewal or by absentee landlords. When she was 18, Deborah accepted Jesus Christ. "Martin Luther King helped me to understand that my desire to serve black people and my desire to move to racial reconciliation could be brought together." Believing education would give power to her decision to serve the black struggle, she graduated from Boston University, then took a Ph.D. from Vanderbilt University.

> I would definitely not take my resources as a black person out to the suburbs or in the midst of corporations just for my own gain; but I would return to a neighborhood similar to the one I grew up in to serve the people. So I began to seek out a church community involved in serving the poor... the Church of the Messiah on the southeast side of Detroit in August, 1984.
>
> I put the word out to a few teens hanging around the church that I was going to start a program that would be their program and that all were welcome. Sixteen kids showed up the first time. I asked the group how much they wanted to pay in dues. We learned about the difference between consensus and voting, and when to use each. I work a lot with self-respect. In our prayer we ask the Lord to teach us self-love and self-respect. We have lots of rules which I think are crucial to any program to let teens know what the limits are. We went over the list together immediately after the prayer. "If I feel that I have been wronged or offended by someone in the group I will handle my anger appropriately and talk to the person. If it is not settled and I need more help I will talk with one of the adult ministers." Another rule is "I will not use put-down humor." I typed those rules and put a place at the bottom for their signature. They didn't have to sign. However, if they didn't sign, they couldn't be in the group. We needed ground rules for our trust-building and to make a safe environment. We are going to a Young Life Conference in Minnesota for a week in August. This is a big thing!"

Another power person is Aya Hunter, an honors graduate of Miller High School, Detroit, mother of three grown children. Aya was in California when the 1965 riots occurred in Detroit. Returning home, she completed a Masters in Social Work Administration with a co-major in Black Studies and moved into the neighborhood.

We have Art of Manhood and Art of Womanhood classes. One group produced a play *The Search for Love: Victims of Passion*. I know the smallest kid knows that "dick" and "pussy" are written all over the walls everywhere. This makes sex ugly. We translate this into our own feeling, musical language and we say it is "oodiwa" and "twadiwa."

There is something about it that makes the children feel comfortable. "Who is responsible here?" I ask as we talk over their experiences. Each of us asks, "What do I want to be? What does it take to be what I want to be?" Unless talk about sex is tied to a cultural perspective, it is not going to have any essence.

Now the kids are being totally confused. Look at our young people at the baby-making age. The majority of the men are in prison. Young girls are not interested in school. The potential for finding a mate who has a job and then getting married in our culture is minimal. How did our ancestors handle situations like these? They showed the young people how they could interact without having intercourse and yet find gratification. They even made intercourse taboo, yet people were able to experience the joys of touching and being intimate; and they were more willing to forego intercourse because of the understanding that had been given them about their nature. They could caress and kiss, but they couldn't go under that apron. That gives a whole different perspective, as contrasted with condemning intercourse as bad and something you don't do. What we want is for them to be able to embrace the instruction and yet be able to experience these feelings and not be afraid of the opposite sex or set up barriers which we see in our marriages. The total disrespect, the men disliking women. That which is beautiful coming out ugly.

"Children and youth throughout the world are targets in an effort to destroy our future," says Clementine Barfield, a founder of SOSAD. "They are dumbed down, sexed up and led to believe that human worth lies in materialistic values."

The SOSAD board has conducted a campaign for public awareness through a weekly radio talk show, memorial services for slain children, youth rallies, and speaking engagements to carry the SOSAD message to countless community meetings on teen violence, conflict resolution, victims' rights and other topics.

107

In a campaign for positive change, the Education and Social Issues committees have sponsored workshops in skills for living, and alternatives to violence. A bereavement support group meets every week. Action groups are forming in block clubs to get rid of drug traffickers. Other activities focus on cultural heritage: a reading list, the KWANZA celebration from Africa, classes in communication, making the neighborhood a war-toy-free zone, free ski lessons for kids, and a community-service jobs program.

Beyond civil rights: the struggle to be human [47]

Long time resident of inner city Detroit, Grace Lee Boggs:

I feel that there is a profound connection between the philosophy which the indigenous peoples are developing for the next stage of the revolutionary struggle and what is happening in Save Our Sons And Daughters (SOSAD). Because indigenous peoples still have a culture related to their land base and a corresponding cosmology, they not only have a unique insight into the destructiveness of industrial civilization; they also have been enabled to see that the main struggles of the 20th century have been essentially the struggles of the have-nots of the world to have what the world elite has: the same rights, the same opportunities, the same power that has come from community control of the world's resources and rapid economic development. So they are able to counterpose to these Third World or have-not struggles another paradigm of the Fourth World struggles: the struggle to be human, i.e., to think and act in terms of seven generations and within that perspective to take collective responsibility for themselves, their communities and their ecosystem. SOSAD, of course, doesn't have anything remotely resembling this wholistic view. But pragmatically and empirically, out of their personal pain, the SOSAD mothers have realized that the only way to save their children is by raising all of our children to be human, i.e., to place a higher value on their own lives and the lives of others than on material things. They are going beyond the black movement of the 1960s which was essentially a movement to win for the blacks the same rights, opportunities and power which they perceived whites as having. Next? I haven't the faintest idea except that it will not be a process of cultural levelling or propaganda but rather through each group developing its own philosophy, myths, and programs out of its own historical experience and practice. Keep in touch.

■ Creating the more-than-nuclear extended family: A grandfather's reflections

It's been almost 20 years since I realized that my children were entering a new world, and my old nuclear family was slipping away. Collapse of old securities is no stranger in human experience. For many thoughtful Americans, this collapse came with the unfolding tragedy of the U.S. war in Vietnam. When our two oldest sons, then in college, chose to resist that war, I decided they were right and that I was called to public repentance and restitution. To that end I wrote a letter to family and friends beginning, "I have been wrong about our war in Vietnam. I am giving to the rebuilding of Vietnam an amount of money equal to my taxes which over the years have supported this war, plus a modest penalty of 20 percent." The common response to my letter was outrage: "Keep your good works to yourself."

However, giving away our restitution money wisely to rebuild the Vietnam homeland was not easy. Hundreds of philanthropic agencies operated in wartime Vietnam, many of them groups with foreign ideologies to impose. The agency most generally recommended for honest management was CARE, Inc. I sent off my penance money and was duly thanked. Later we learned that CARE too was caught up in aiding the political friends of the American war. In the future we would need close scrutiny of charitable gifts we might make as a family. So Betty and I and the five children, aged 15 to 22, created the family charitable foundation. Its preamble:

> Make friends for yourselves with worldly wealth so that when it gives out, you will be welcomed in the eternal home. Whoever is faithful in small matters will be faithful in large ones. (Luke 16:9)

All family members of legal age became directors. Immediately voting control passed to the children. Over the next several years directors with causes to support submitted proposals for funding at the annual family council. Gifts went to American Friends Service Committee and the Ecumenical Institute, in memory of Betty's mother, to continue training of native churchmen in India and for Migrant Legal Services of Cesar Chavez; gifts in memory of Great Aunt Mary went to several human development projects in the third world. Our family venture into philanthropy ended on the occasion of Betty's 60th birthday with the gift of the last of the family foundation money for village development in India.

The charitable family foundation, like philanthropy of the early 20th century, generally had lost its reason for being: to care for the disinherited of the world. In the information age, presence among the poor, rather than sending money to the poor, is the faithful response of those who care for wholeness of the common life.

The family constitution:
Writing a radical family story

Watching our five children scatter to distant cities to further their education and careers brought to the surface old nagging questions about the family. How could we continue to be a family in the midst of the fragmentation of interests and geographical distances that separated us? The children could not even agree on which of the many places we had lived they could call home. Christmas and funerals and the occasional family reunions hardly seemed adequate structures for the extended family. Certainly the family foundation could not fulfill its purpose of caring for society without some structure to care for the family.

It was 1972. Oldest son Peter was to be married in the fall. Second son David was in Thailand as a volunteer teacher, fulfilling his alternative service assignment. Kathy was away at college. So the four of us at home drafted a constitution of our extended family and after many hours of design and revision sent the draft to the others for their additions and changes.

The story we wrote is a common reminder of who we really are. It is a reference point in decision making. It projects the wisdom of our experience into the future for ourselves, our heirs, and for the whole world.

We described our roots and family task as:

...grounded in the ecumenical historical church existing for mission to the whole world.

Our family style reflects an intentional ordering of life to assure the nurturing of every family member for his personal fulfillment and to encourage the realization of his destined role in the mission of this family in its life in the world.... While the children were growing up, the family was neither child-centered nor parent-centered, but deliberately included all members in its common concerns, discussions and actions.... Each person was encouraged to pursue his own interests, develop his gifts, find friends, and slay dragons.

For generations we have been privileged and responsible; aware and on the edge.... This has led us to embrace the revolution of the whole world struggling for a new order and a new humanness.... As a family we are the revolution in our relations with the rest of the world. As individual, vulnerable persons, we are each other's home, roots and anchors.

Family welfare and fun:
The Great Annual Family Council

To care for family members, we created a trust fund to assure protection of each person in the family from the indignities of poverty, to aid in education, or be drawn on in emergencies and special occasions by consensus of family members. All children and their spouses are partners with my wife and me in an investment pool from which we all can borrow at low interest for family approved projects. This trust fund, which we named the Common Patrimony and Investment Partnership, is not a vehicle for passing on inheritances, but is a family revolving loan fund which can allow the extended family to behave in compassionate ways toward members in need of help, without burdening unduly any of the nuclear family units linked in the enterprise. Income has been used by common consent over the years to pay the modest costs of a Great Annual Family Council (GAFC).

The decision-making structure for the extended family, in addition to the telephone and letters, is the Great Annual Family Council, a grand combination of business meeting, family reunion and celebration. Initiated when we set up the Family Foundation, it became formal as the first GAFC on the occasion of Peter's marriage.

At the banquet for family and Honored Guests, Robin, the youngest member of the clan, lit the candles and the eldest, Great Aunt Mary, called the council into being and gave the elder's blessing with a poem. Greetings From Afar were read, including one from son David in Thailand. We celebrated birthdays, anniversaries and significant events of the year for all present. We read a memorial to the recently completed life of a relative. There were toasts:

"To weddings!"

"To esteemed relatives and honored guests!"

"To revolution!"

Overtures to the council included an offer by the newlyweds to print stationery with a family symbol for any member who desired it, and singing by daughter Deborah and her cousin Ruth:

Go out, go out my friends,
Go among my suffering people.
Cast my fire upon the earth,
Be my love to men.

The latest draft of the family constitution was distributed for consideration and action at the next GAFC.

There were feasting, stories, a slide show, dancing and champagne. Betty as mother ended the celebration with a formal benediction: "I send us all out to care for our part of the world and to be happy in this work." Someone waked Robin who snuffed out the candles to conclude the ceremonies. The extended nuclear families went off to their hotel rooms and next day returned to scattered homes and other affairs.

On New Year's in 1987 we celebrated our 16th Great Annual Family Council, with everyone present including three spouses, five grandchildren and honored guests. During these years each of the children has borrowed and paid back loans from the Investment Partnership for buying or remodeling a house, or education or special needs. The Family Foundation is still in being, by consensus of the family, but it has been inactive since 1984. Philanthropy is being replaced by presence among the poor. We expect that our children, and even more our grandchildren, will develop many other shifts away from what seemed good at earlier times to Betty and me. Already they are more concerned about caring for the natural world than we were in our childhood. We expect that their organizational covenants will include configurations we never thought of.

Expanding the definition of the family

Some work groups operate as a kind of family even though they live under several roofs. For example, Betty, I, and our two small children lived in this kind of family in the early 1950s with one American nurse and eleven young Iranian women learning to be nurses in a hospital in western Iran. As the hospital doctor, I taught and learned from each of the nurses. We shared the work, the joys, and the anxieties of the common task. We often ate meals together, prayed together, and partied together.

Bridging cultural differences

In 1973 we experienced yet another grouping of persons living under one roof as family for a year. Betty and I were preparing for a sojourn in ghetto medicine. Four of our five children had left home for school or career. The big suburban house needed more people to join Betty, youngest daughter Deborah, then a senior in high school, and myself. We three talked at length and decided to invite two inner-city black high school students to join us in our all white Wisconsin home. This would be our experiment in bridging some cultural gaps in our modern world.

Johnny W. and Carroll G., black teenagers from Chicago's inner city, came to Wausau, Wisconsin, to live with us and attend local schools. Johnny and Carroll wanted the experience of suburban life and schooling for a year. We wanted their presence as a window for us into the black experience of America. We looked at "family" as one of the four sociological structures of any human society. (The other three are state, church, commerce.) We wanted to explore not what is wrong with the family today, but some ways of making the family a resource of strength for its neighborhood and world. We wanted to make the family a winner.

The welcoming workshop

We began our year together as a family of five very different persons under one roof in a series of regular family meetings. As the oldest person, I led the first discussion, asking each person to list five memorable events in his or her life. Most of us listed getting born, key moves in education or work, and important human encounters. On a large easel I wrote each of the 25 events under the year in which it occurred. We added a few more events to complete our family "Wall of Wonder." Each person had spoken, and his own words were written on this first family document. I outlined the agenda for the four workshops we would use to develop our new family consensus of who we were and what we would be about in the coming year. Sitting still was a problem for our teenage visitors from the city, so on their request we ended the first workshop and celebrated by going together to a movie about another kind of family. It was called *The Dirty Dozen*.

The next evening after supper we brainstormed again. "What," I asked, "is going on in the world?" Each person wrote his or her own list of 10 or more trends or events that seemed important to understanding the present world. Then, again writing with magic marker on easel paper, I wrote each person's three best items: a recent astronaut adventure, the military draft, unemployment, an upcoming rock concert, a new treatment for cancer. In a world where earthrise televised from the moon is as real to our children as is sunrise or sunset, this exercise gave us a common perspective on the way life is.

No one was restless. Carroll volunteered to write our group answers on the easel for the next question which was, "What are your concerns or issues for the coming year? What do you want to have happen?" Our list was thoughtful:

- earn good school grades
- provide privacy for each person
- make new friends in the neighborhood
- be an example of successful racial living together
- publish a League of Women Voters' study on community mental health
- write three medical papers
- have regular family celebrations
- have the whole family support each member in personal struggles.

John and Carroll were worried about their welcome in our all-white suburb. Carroll hoped to make the football team. John thought track was his field. Deborah looked forward to a new class in auto mechanics. I wanted all five of our children home for Thanksgiving.

Developing an operating consensus

By now we all were ready for a celebration with ice cream sundaes. Carroll and Deborah agreed to take the data we had written together and before our next workshop prepare a draft for our approval on "The Practical Vision of Our Family for the Next 12 Months."

In our third family meeting to work out an operating consensus, Betty led the workshop. Carroll and Deborah presented their written statement of our family's practical vision for ourselves over the next 12 months. The whole group made some minor changes in wording. All agreed, and the statement was placed on the wall.

We did not take a vote. Nor did we expect all to agree on all points. In reaching consensus, we talked through all the issues until all ideas were expressed and a direction was determined which all could accept, recognizing that we all live within limits.

I asked the most difficult question of the entire series of workshops: "What are the obstacles which, if not attended to, will prevent us from realizing our family's practical vision? What are the challenges facing our family this year if we are to see our vision become real?" This Statement of Challenges is the most important of the steps we were using in family decision making by consensus. Here we faced reality. We listed in writing a fairly long set of worries and complaints of elders about youngers, attitudes of our neighbors, youth insistence upon freedom, and trust by elders.

Betty was not satisfied. She said, "We need to state the one or two underlying challenges which keep all the lesser annoyances in being. What is it which, if fixed, will release the whole enterprise?" After much talk, we decided that our one challenge was Limited Trust In Each Other. If we could fix that, almost everything else would get right. We held a family snowball fight on the lawn to celebrate that breakthrough of candor and insight.

Over the next three days John, something of an artist, prepared an illustrated copy of our corporate writing: the Practical Vision and Challenge Statements. In a final Sunday morning workshop we talked through our family covenant and mission statement. We created a family constitution with preamble ("We, the five free and responsible persons of...") and Bill of Rights ("1. Each member is entitled to honor and respect by other members at all times. 2. ..."). Together we drew up some operating rules, a weekly schedule of chores, and called for a two-hour weekly family council to handle all future decisions.

A final reflective conversation

At the conclusion of our family meetings we took ten minutes to review what we had done, using a careful sequence of questions from the Basic Discussion Method. Betty asked the questions:

1) What words or images do you remember? (objective level)
2) Where die we struggle? Where were we pleased? (reflective level)
3) What meaning does this have for our life as a family? (interpretive level)
4) What remains to be done in developing our family life? (decisional level)

This final reflective conversation allowed us to see the process and meaning of what we had done.

In this way we welcomed Carroll and Johnny into our family. Our suburban neighbors were quietly offended that we were bringing black young men into their white ghetto. Some muttered worries about their daughters. In our family council Deborah, Betty, Johnny, Carroll and I talked about the coming year. Johnny reported a neighbor's reaction.

"I told them we are writing a family constitution for the next year. Mrs. B asked where each of us sleeps. I told her we each have our own room.

"Then she asked, 'And does Deborah lock her door?'"

We all stiffened at the hostile potential of the exchange. Mrs. B did not know the secret that our family had learned after Johnny arrived in our home. He had gone through 11 grades in Chicago schools and could not read or write his own name. Johnny guarded this shame carefully, but his insecurity was overwhelming. Outwardly a grown man, in his secret self Johnny was a helpless illiterate, socially inept and frightened in many daily situations. "What answer did you give the old crow?" Deborah asked.

"I told her the truth. I don't know if Deborah locks her door. I lock mine!"

The year was a rewarding experience for each of us. We were a real family. We had a common task, and each person had his part in it. We were answerable to each other for obedience to the common task. It worked.

■ Old Doc: The family as the neighborhood arm of the parish church

DR. TERTIA: Doctor, you talk of the converging of many trends in science, art and vocation, and new consciousness and values in local neighborhoods as though they are all that's needed to bring about profound social change. You never talk about power or electoral politics as the arena to implement change.

OLD DOC: Well Doctor, we both know that politicians react to social change. They don't initiate it. The struggles we face now for military sanity, the care of our resources, justice and compassion, cannot be limited to fights between established political parties. Take the example of Father Arizmendi, an unassuming priest in the unknown village of Mondragon in the unruly Basque country of Spain in the reign of the fascist dictator Franco. Without a political confrontation, he started an economically successful, cooperative society diametrically opposed to fascism, communism and capitalism. The model is being copied all over the world.

DR. TERTIA: A single community based on Gandhian nonviolence was no threat to the dictator.

OLD DOC: It was the priest's profound consciousness of being one with the universe and one with all people that enabled him to develop the worker cooperatives. It is said that when he came into a room his presence changed the atmosphere. It was his own love that caused those around him to choose friendliness and cooperation over competition and conflict. Without that profound understanding, cooperative associations cannot work.

DR. TERTIA: Without that profound understanding I guess nothing will work for long. Even though voices around the world are making it clear that the earth belongs to all, social change does not happen without leaders. The source of real empowerment of those who make social change happen must be in the world of spirit.

OLD DOC: There is great energy in many diverse groups which I see as an emerging planetary religion, beyond the ethnic and class origins of any of our great religious or philosophical belief systems. This planetary religion, or mind, I do not see as destroying the old faiths (including my own) but as fulfilling them and putting new life into the symbols.

DR. TERTIA: Maybe our current religious institutions have to break apart some more before they get better.

OLD DOC: Building the planetary civilization ahead will be a bit like St. Francis of Assisi rebuilding the ruined parish church from the unchanged stones lying about the holy ground. We will need the solid values from all the old faiths and empires.

DR. TERTIA: That's a good parallel and should hit a responsive chord for people of quite different life experience and expectations. But some of us, though well educated, can't understand. Or perhaps, won't?

OLD DOC: Can't, I think. Words can call to memory only what one has experienced. Unhappy persons who have not experienced high resolve leading to failure, followed by subjective guilt and objective forgiveness often will shun stories of men and women empowered by forgiveness. They may say the stories point to sick or bad values. They may smile at values of the spirit. Such a stance of course is their religious right, but I don't see it contributing to the development of our needed new social ethic.

DR. TERTIA: How does this help the poor and dispossessed?

OLD DOC: God loves the poor. Abraham Lincoln argued this on the ground that God made so many of them. There is no particular virtue in being poor, but all wise and good leaders have a bias for the poor to protect them from our natural tendencies to dominate and exploit the powerless.

DR. TERTIA: It is the logical outcome of the profound consciousness we've been talking about, "you and I are one with the universe." If

117

that be so, then "you and I are one." And I have an obligation to break down all barriers between us. Any of us, whether we are Mother Theresa in Calcutta or a frustrated resident in Neighborhood, U.S.A.

OLD DOC: True, but the transformed individual consciousness is not enough. It is the intentional family, the core group, the primary community of transformed individuals that is at the center of the building task; people of several generations, varied temperaments, gifts, needs, and experiences bonded in covenant and trust. Shared property is one good bond. In such a primal community there is stability, mutual help in growth, and security in illness, disappointment and age. It is such a community that can integrate cooperative values, planetary religion, regard for each person, and bias for the poor into a new social ethic and a new religious mode.

DR. TERTIA: And what is to prevent that intentional family from retreating into its own little world?

OLD DOC: It is a parish church which will provide nurturing and keep the community accountable. By church, I mean the people who venture out beyond their origins as they find themselves called to wonder, awe, gratitude and compassion.

DR. TERTIA: And where are the leaders who will transform the local church?

OLD DOC: They are the servant leaders within the intentional families, persons with big hearts who are not afraid of being heroes and martyrs.

Chapter 6

A New Common Sense

Those Who Can Make Things Happen serve community cohesion through a collaborative leadership style, using tested participatory social and spirit methods. In this chapter we look at the social dynamics of a new common sense and at schematics for the integration of information and experience into a new operating wisdom. This is an exploration into the dynamics of an emerging planetary mind.*

■ Old Doc: A new common sense

Doctors Primus, Secundus, and Tertia
One night over their beers
Were rethinking medicine
For the next hundred years.
"It needs religion," Primus said.
He likes profundity.
"It needs a lab," said Tertia,
Who likes technology.
"It needs integration," said
Secundus on the fence.
"We've got new information;
We need new common sense."

---

planetary mind: a metaphor describing planet earth as a living organism, setting physical and chemical balances which favor continuation of its diverse creatures and ecosystems. In this metaphor the human function is

NEIGHBORHOOD CARETAKERS

The discussion continues...

DR. PRIMUS: If theology is the queen of the sciences and philosophy—pointing to the mysterious beyond, giving meaning and direction to everyday experiences—then I would call the art and science of medicine the beloved princess in every culture.

DR. TERTIA: I agree. Every society uses its best mythology, worldview, rationality and intuition to address the common experiences of pain, of defeat, and death of body and spirit. And Western medicine has recently made extraordinary leaps in rational powers. Look at our bold advances in surgery, our control of infectious disease (admittedly not all), discovery of the causes and cures of many cancers, and the treatment of some of our most disabling disorders of mind and emotion. I'm proud to be an M.D.

DR. SECUNDUS: All very true. But medicine must be concerned with more than individual quality of life. When the great plagues of typhus or tuberculosis killed a lot of us, the social dimensions of health were easy to see. If my neighbor became ill, I most likely would be next. The social plagues of mind and spirit are not so obvious, though many could be preventable with an expanded medicine.

DR. PRIMUS: I think that is happening. In recent decades our mythology and consciousness have shifted. About 90 percent of the writings in our libraries have been written in our own lifetimes. Great treasures of many cultures have been translated and are eagerly scrutinized by the masses, in paperbacks or videos. Knowledge is not limited to those in the "learned professions."

DR. TERTIA: It never has been. And the work of designing a medicine for the 21st century may well be done by those who are not medical doctors. The shoemaker will stick to his last, and the surgeon to his surgery. But we also need a new kind of physician, a doctor (in the medieval sense of "teacher of the community") of neighborhood health sciences who can bring together professionals and technocrats and neighborhood residents to deal with root causes of diseases like domestic violence, illiteracy, youth suicides and depression.

---

to organize general sentience into a coordinating organ or intelligence which serves the preservation and mission of the planet. Individual humans are likened to individual neurons, with a collaborative function which is greater than the sum of the separate individual roles.

DR. PRIMUS: Beware. The great pathologist Virchow said "Medicine is politics writ large," which is glaringly evidenced by our fragmented specialties and subspecialties. Which of these medical specialties do you see in dialogue with anthropology, architecture, criminology, epidemiology, macro- and microeconomics, education and the arts to heal our body politic? How can isolated knowledge systems make integrating contributions to the quality of our community life? Who heals the healers?

DR. SECUNDUS: It should be possible to retrieve the wisdom of the separate sciences. It is there, filed in electronic and print data bases but not yet tested in real human neighborhoods. The integration of this information for daily use will be the task of the new neighborhood social laboratories, worldwide.

DR. TERTIA: What happened to all the social labs of the 1960s and 1970s? How many movements and community experiments flourished and are no more?

DR. SECUNDUS: An experiment never fails. We learned from them. It may be time now to restart a whole series of coordinated local development efforts. We would call them the Planetary Mind Project to reflect the global consciousness and networks. The social experiments of the 1970s were but a first glimpse of the varied social forms of community in a secular world come of age.

DR. PRIMUS: What a happy thought! Instead of Armageddon, we could be coming to a new common sense—everyman's 20th century creation. It is possible. Each day space-age technology links an infinite number of perceptions, reflections, and decisions of several billion persons congregated in two million villages and neighborhoods. Analogous to the human brain, the message pathways are organized in many interchange systems through perhaps 50,000 cities and another 50 metropolitan complexes.

DR. TERTIA: You are implying that the knowledge being created is largely urban.

DR. PRIMUS: Perhaps. But the knowledge also touches the cosmic One. Until recently most people more or less gratefully have linked themselves to the Mystery Beyond, or Other, vicariously, through membership in a world religion and a mythic or historic hero: a revered Isis, Moses, Jesus, Siddartha and many others. Now, as futurist Barbara Marx Hubbard announces, we all may be on the edge of a planetary Pentecost when we may join consciously in the grand enterprise of creating the planetary mind while continuing to honor and draw life from the religions of our own cultures.

121

DR. TERTIA: Back to the social experiments of the 1960s and 1970s. There were good reasons for their sometimes abrupt end. Many of the groups continued to live in the industrial-age consciousness, with its class confrontations, exploitation of natural resources, and its imperial polities. They were unable to envision a new age already begun and therefore unable to participate in it.

DR. SECUNDUS: I think our concern is to get some handles on urban knowledge, to invite more conscious participation by ordinary people as well as seers in the evolution of the planetary mind.

■ Everybody's gift of creation to the 20th century

We all live in the new age of an information economy. Each day space-age technology links an infinite number of perceptions, reflections, decisions of several billion persons congregated in two million villages and neighborhoods. We will not consider here the ultimate form or thrust of human consciousness, which we believe is an inscrutable mystery, however enlightened we are by revelations. Rather, within a limited sociological frame, we will look at some social processes that are contributing to the evolving language and wisdom of the planetary mind. We will look at such profoundly mundane issues as safe streets, meaningful work, good learning, family roles, institutions of research, and government —redefining familiar concepts to expand their usage.

The civilizing foundations of our cosmopolitan Western societies were laid in the 19th century: urban sanitation and the rise in the standard of living with improved nutrition, housing, and wide use of immunization. The flowering of Western medical science in the 1940s transformed the human race when it added laboratory and radiologic diagnosis, miracle chemotherapy, parenteral life support, skilled anesthesia and surgery, and psychotropic drugs. The U.S. built hospitals within an hour's travel for 80 percent of the U.S. population. Death rates dropped in childhood and disease patterns shifted to those of an aging population. Science and technology seemed all powerful: the messiah.

But as science was flowering in the 1940s, the intellectual and spiritual foundations of Western civilization changed forever. Christendom as a civilizing power self-destructed at the Auschwitz death camps. Common sense, as the glue of Western civilization, was also lost at Auschwitz.

Nevertheless, remnants in all religious communities of the planet lived again in the resurrection life—normal in the household

---

Everyman! I have come for you.

—SPOKEN BY DEATH IN THE MEDIEVAL MORALITY PLAY JEDERMAN, FORERUNNER OF ALL WESTERN DRAMA

of faith. Out of this faithful remnant there arose around the planet in the 1950s a prophetic demand and powerful mass alliances commanding universal human freedom. In the 1960s the U.S. code for this movement was "civil rights struggle." In the midst of this social activism there was an equally powerful drive toward ecumenical conferencing in every ethnic tradition. Vatican II was a symbol of this movement to create a modus vivendi in the civilizational vacuum left by Auschwitz and the Bomb.

In the 1970s, smaller faithful remnants of the great civilizational traditions converged in campaigns for comprehensive human development: to end poverty, war, and hunger before the 21st century, and to reverse the destruction inflicted on planet earth. In the 1980s a challenge arose within the movements to define the new human: Local people no longer understood the what, how, or why for any particular action and recognized that shifting into any new consciousness is painful:

> Recently I read a book in which the author says that evolution is not the evolution of mankind, but the evolution of the planet Earth. At first the oneness of all humanity, especially when adding in the plants and animals, is repugnant to the ego. But it is welcome in times of humility or danger.
>
> Last summer, selling ads for a neighborhood newspaper, I became painfully aware of the risks business people take, the fears they live with. What can neighbors do? What can I do? I can't afford to just buy and buy. New consciousness haunted me, and was painful. Seeing things with my eyes, and seeing theings in the media—starvation in Africa, killing in Lebanon, child beating in U.S. cities—more tragedy, more pain. I tried to shut it out.
>
> Gradually I understood that shutting anything out is not the answer. It causes more pain, pangs of separation and loneliness. Relief and ultimately joy comes from fully accepting the oneness of the earth and striving to live in cooperation with all the needs of the earth.[48]

Looking to the 1990s and beyond, the need is for a new human, common operating wisdom, a "Sophia." To the Greeks who invented her, Sophia was the essence of human spiritual being, mysteriously continuous with all being, beyond all knowing, a precious gift of the One. Knowledge in the 1990s will mean creating a planetary mind, which finally will transcend earth, birth and death. The Greeks knew this wonder, as did the earlier awestruck brown men of the Vedas, the common people living the Way, the bodhisattvas of Gautama, the Buddha, the later Hebrew prophets, the church fathers, the seers of Islam, the shamans of aboriginal cultures, the mystics and saints of all traditions. We know already that we must go beyond processing information, beyond arranging mindless beeps of data, to exchanges of knowledge.

The entrepreneurial age: A 21st century renaissance [49]

"Knowledge will replace information as a measure of value. 'I guess' and 'I think' will be acceptable to everyone, everywhere."

A little book, *The Entrepreneurial Age*, is about rethinking productivity. The authors' backgrounds are in economics and in labor management within the publishing industry The computer, telephone, and other tools of the information society's workplace have transformed the rules of the game in global competition (motivation), people productivity (knowledge), and economic development (silicon-based opportunity). The cheap microprocessor is the key technology pushing along the Entrepreneurial Age. There is no invisible hand; we need a common vision, common values. Most of middle management will fade away. Economics moves to a theory of survival by cooperation in a competitive world.

Begin with a fair language [50]

The old tool-based categories of "health" sciences do not include what is needed in future-looking health sciences, where 85 percent of disabling urban disorders are social rather than biological in origin and effect. Anatomy, psychology, sociology and their kin no longer serve to file or retrieve the knowledge we need at the neighborhood level.

The quest for knowledge begins with learning and/or creating an appropriate language with signal words, relational grammar, and transparent idioms. Any powerful new language sets into being thought, interchange, new perceptions, consciousness and covenants. A basic human language needs about 600-800 words for minimum daily conversations; in becoming a doctor of science or philosophy, the first task is to learn the use of another 50,000 or so new words. The list of words invented since 1970 which are in common daily use exceeds several hundred.

Creating new languages is as universal as the arrival of newborn children: Each generation creates its very own language. In one generation in Hawaii in the late 19th century, the children of Japanese, Polynesian, and English-speaking parents created their own hybrid language which became the dominant language of the islands as that generation moved into adult roles.

■ Old Doc: Family—the integrative dynamic

DR. PRIMUS: For me, one of the unfathomable mysteries of living organisms is the moment at which a cell stops merely reproducing itself and changes into a different kind of cell, a new type of cell that is the essential building block of another specific tissue and organ, which then must cooperate with all the other organs in a healthy body. This happens in every phylum, order, genus and species.

DR. TERTIA: You might say that life is just one long journey of complexification. And we are developing complex techniques to help us find the answers in the genetic engineering lab. One of these days we'll know how to stop cancer cells from madly proliferating themselves instead of differentiating.

DR. SECUNDUS: Maybe we could take some of those learnings and apply them to the cancers of pollution and urban sprawl: all those clumps and rows of undifferentiated boxes wildly scrambling to reproduce themselves in new subdivisions.

DR. TERTIA: Ah! The new typology of urban sprawl: sarcoma condominiensis, ranchous carcinoma, and townhouser leukemia! And the cause, Herr Professor? Vell ve in the social medicine lab suspect an oversensitivity of the green receptors to the perturbation of economic demand, resulting in centralized necrosis and runaway peripheral metastasis. *Ja wohl!*

DR. PRIMUS: Not a bad analogy. Getting bigger or doing more of the same is not an effective strategy for dealing with increasing complexity. The question is how and when the suburban proliferation will change to a different approach to shelter and services to meet all the needs of all the people in the city. When are we urbanites going to get that essential consciousness that it is possible to meet those needs?

DR. SECUNDUS: We know some of the mechanisms needed in a complex system: catalysts, interfaces, semipermeable membranes (or leaky margins), specialized vehicles, messages, receptors, intricate communication and transportation systems within reach of every cell, a responsive coordination system and structures that cooperate with each other to make the whole body work.

DR. PRIMUS: And what integrates the several diverse and specialized systems and functions into a whole? What is the energy that keeps the social body alive?

DR. SECUNDUS: It is the same life energy, or spirit, whether in a person or a social body. In either case it is embodied in flesh and blood. We've called the integrative structures catalytic cores, cells, missional family clusters, intentional families, interdisciplinary holons, orders and probably other names. It is the multilevel integrating skills of numerous core groups that will transform fragmentation and unresponsive closed systems into open, communicating, cooperative parts of an evolving whole.

DR. TERTIA: It is families that will be the integrative structures for a community. But the nuclear family based on romantic love is an ideal that hasn't worked.

DR. PRIMUS: One could say the nuclear family is a product of post World War II Levittown, the Veterans Housing Administration and the highway assistance program. It collapses under stress. Family

FIG. 6-1: DR. TERTIA'S
SET OF FAMILY TRIANGLES

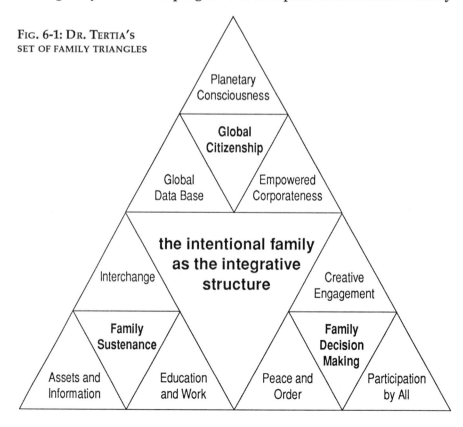

configurations now are any relationship people want to call family. So what is the "integrative" organization that will catalyze the new common sense?

DR. SECUNDUS: We are using a set of triangles to help my students understand the complexity of the social forces affecting their patients and communities. Integrating skills are in the lower right, or organizing, pole. Knowledge gained from processing information is integrated into the common operating wisdom of local communities and the consciousness of the planet. Persons or core groups with integrating skills actually move the social organism into a new level of awareness and common sense.

DR. TERTIA: We also use a tripolar analysis of the Intentional Family (Fig. 6-1). The context for family members' lives is global citizenship. This gives broader meaning to their symbols and the work they do. The lower right-hand triangle deals with the organizational and decision-making functions of the family. In our family workshop, participants not only create their own symbols and story but also write a family constitution and bill of rights, with procedures for conflict resolution in family meetings. The foundational or sustaining dynamic, in the lower left triangle, is economic. In our workshop, participants make a family budget, taking into consideration their contributions to the globe and local community, as well as their own needs. It is a great image-shifting exercise.

■ Tripolar schematics: A language that sorts information to find knowledge[51]

Today we need simple ways of picturing and understanding complex systems and how they interconnect with other equally complex systems. Triangles offer a simple graphic picture of the comprehensive dynamics in any set of relationships. Within the limits of a two-dimensional form, the equilateral triangle can be used to represent the interrelated activities of any moderately complex situation—the family, a business organization, or a neighborhood—up to the very complex dynamics of a whole culture or world. By using these triangles a planning group can be reasonably assured that they won't be blindsided by a factor they forgot to consider.

The what, the how, and the why

In each cluster of four triangles—for example, Fig. 6-2 of the Social Process Triangles on the following page—the dynamic (or

FIG. 6-2: THE SOCIAL PROCESS TRIANGLES

MEANING:
- shows the 'why' of the system
- the thrusts, values and beliefs
- why is a particular action taken? ...on what values is it based?

FOUNDATION:
- shows that 'what' of the system
- the 'stuff-that-is-there'
- asks what are the basic ingredients in this system?

ORGANIZATION:
- shows the 'how' of the system
- the form or way the system is organized
- asks how do decisions get made and implemented?

system or set of information) represented is named in the center triangle. The three triangles at the lower left, the lower right, and the top, respectively, describe *what* the basic stuff of the system is, *how* the system organizes its stuff, and *why* any action is taken in the system. This form of naming the main cluster and describing its what, how and why is maintained in both the larger clusters and in each of the smaller subsets. When each triangle is worked down to sublevels, the dynamics are seen in more interactive detail.

The social process triangle shown in Fig. 6-2 describes the sociological processes of any society.

The foundational WHAT

The lower left position of any cluster shows a foundational process, the basic stuff-that-is-there, without which the larger dynamic cannot happen. In the social process triangle, this basic stuff-that-is-there concerns economic activity. "Economic activity," in turn, includes its own what, how and why:

Common Resources are the basic-stuff-of-the-basic-stuff without which you couldn't have any economic activity.

Common Production is *how* resources are organized so they will be of some use to people.

Common Distribution explains *why* all this activity takes place, or, in other words, the activity people go through in order to consume the final goods and services.

And each of these main subsets then becomes the major category for its own subsets. For example, Common Resources includes as its most basic component, Natural Resources; which are organized and harnessed by Human Resources; so that a higher level of Technological Resources can be built up in society and passed to the next generation.

The organizing HOW

The lower right position shows an organizing process, the form, or in the case of the social process, political commonality, or how any group (individual, family or nation) makes decisions. Basic to decision making is a *common context* (or Corporate Order) based on protection against predators (Common Defense), peace (Domestic Tranquility), and fairness (Legal Base). Then there has to be an *actual mechanism* to consider, judge and carry out the decisions made (Corporate Justice and its subsets). These decisions must be made for the *present and future welfare* of those concerned (Corporate Welfare) which includes considering their security, human rights and the role they play in society.

A family trying to decide about how to spend a week's time together will be operating in this triangle as they weigh the beach against the mountains, whether to visit Aunt Martha, what activities to plan for the kids, time spent for new experiences or upgrading career skills, and how much to time to spend where.

The meaning-giving WHY

The top triangle describes values, belief systems or reasons that give thrust to an action, and informs why it takes place, or what gives the action meaning. Any society will have accumulated wisdom (Communal Wisdom) based on skills (Useful Skills), knowledge (Accumulated Knowledge) and social values (Final Meanings) that inform actions. This wisdom will be expressed in certain *social forms* (Communal Styles) which include people's roles at different life stages (Cyclical Roles), the current understanding of what the family is (Procreative Scheme), and how these aggregate into Social Structures. *Ultimate meaning* (Communal Symbols) is reflected in the symbols people create—the current language, what they read, write and watch on TV, their art forms (skyscrapers and living room decorations, for example) and their common stories of who they are and why they're here.

Using the tripolar analysis

Let us take the nation as an example. In the ideal state—where everything works as it should—the cultural, economic and political processes are in perfectly balanced equilibrium, each process acting upon, and being acted upon, by the other two. The meaning-giving myths, religion and wisdom in the cultural pole guide the political decision making towards justice and equality for all people, and prevent economic growth from becoming greedy exploitation.

The economic realities of the country keep the cultural myths and style from becoming irrational and unsustainable, and constrain the political sector from gross mismanagement.

The decision-making, or organizational, dynamic implements or sometimes changes the style and mandates set by the myths and wisdom of the culture, and controls the use of economic resources for the good of the whole.

Another example: Military leaders know that armed troops are the sine qua non of war; that leadership is the factor which organizes resources for common action; that morale ("why we fight and die") includes myths, images and visions. Developing a winning army requires a vigorous balance among the three polar dynamics of troops and supplies (foundational), leadership (organizational), and morale (cultural).

But the ideal does not exist. One or more processes will be weak, unable to inform or restrain the dominant one. In our western culture, the economic dynamic pays little attention to old myth or religion (as in Fig. 6-3). It tends to control the decision making, as well as the cultural life of society, rather than the other way around. For example, a student may well choose his educational path and

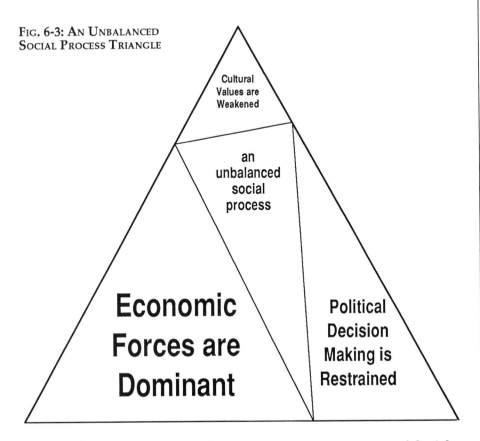

FIG. 6-3: AN UNBALANCED
SOCIAL PROCESS TRIANGLE

Cultural
Values are
Weakened

an
unbalanced
social
process

Economic
Forces are
Dominant

Political
Decision
Making is
Restrained

vocation based on the salary level rather than the content of the job. Once a set of triangles have been built and analyzed, strategic action usually occurs by strengthening the weak processes (myth, religion, lifestyle and the political process) to restore a wholesome balance, rather than attacking the dominant forces (e.g., economics) head-on.

■ Creating a new common sense

The triangles in Fig. 6-4, on page 132, offer a possible three-level tripolar graphic of a new common sense (Sophia) which provides a grammar for planetary mind development in the new age consciousness. We think the first level dynamics (Information-Processing Power, Multilevel Integrating Skills, Common Operating Wisdom) are real dynamics. We are less confident about the lower levels, until readers speak back.

A test of this or any language is the new directions which it points to and talks about. As we experiment with going beyond "adolescent pregnancy, anatomy, architecture..." will this tripolar process of classifying knowledge be helpful, e.g., in local or regional conferences? Will it draw out the depth, breadth, and particular gifts of all the participants in the conference? Will it help poets talk with statisticians? When such interchanges begin to happen, we will develop further a working, filing, retrieving language for neighborhood health sciences, and for knowledge in general, and finally for fairest Sophia.

Fig. 6-4: The New
Common Sense Triangles

In the tripolar schematic of the new common sense on the following page, we will begin with the largest triangles: Information Processing Power, Multilevel Integrating Skills, and Common Operating Wisdom.

Information-Processing Power has been substantially initiated and undergirds the two other main dynamics of the new common sense. Data recognized as useful and requiring months to collect are recorded in the libraries of specialty indexes, paper printouts, databases, microfilm and software.

Multilevel Integrating Skills clothe new knowledge in social structures. Much work here remains to be initiated, tested and shared. These skills are most widely perfected and used in the family setting in all its many new forms. Knowledge so clothed can be tested in other local settings and transformed into:

Common Operating Wisdom, in turn calls for renewed congregational data gathering, ordering of data into information, transformation of information into knowledge, and clothing of new knowledge in appropriate social structures and symbols. Most of this work has yet to begin.

■ Information-Processing Power: Assembling the data

Data gathering groups of the 1990s: Sacred and secular congregations

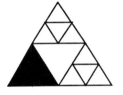

Twentieth-century congregations have appeared which are 50 years beyond our ordinary mental association of "congregation" with the sacred congregation of a synagogue or church. Usually we remember the sacred congregation at its high-water mark of several generations ago, within a simple frontier kind of town-society directed by the Lawman, the Banker, the Schoolmarm, and a few other civilizing powers. In recent decades the sacred congregation has been less visibly in the forefront of giving direction and social form to the general society. Rather this leadership role has passed to the secular congregations which have come together as gathered communities about some shared purpose.

Sacred congregations gather data on beliefs, dreams, fears, cyclic roles, behavior, covenants, ways of celebrating life transitions, etc., from their own members and from the public. These are the profound dimensions of neighborhood living, now mostly in eclipse to the detriment of our American dream of freedom and opportunity for all. The prototypical sacred congregational forerunners were, and deep down still are, concerned with the whole of human experience, a wide spectrum of values including the transcendent. They were concerned with law as it enables freedom, and with grace as it reflects our human reality.

The newer secular congregations all have lesser ambitions. Most have a more narrowly defined mission than the sacred congregations. For example, economic task forces in a secular congregation gather data on technologies, markets, job training, price determinants, etc. They take lesser obligations. Their concerns are not about wholes, but about parts. The secular congregations look not at ultimate meanings, freedom, obligation and responsibility, but at the use of particular tools: microscope, biochemistry, information flow, and public art. Some secular congregations take as their obligations a shared pain, worry, or vision: self-help groups, revolutionary cadres, established political parties and crime syndicates.

There are many forms of secular congregations: a professional American public health community, a county medical society, a village development task force. Each of these secular groups, like the local sacred congregation, is a voluntary association of persons. Some secular congregations have a strong common commercial or partisan political interest. Many are served by a formally designated (elected, appointed, ordained) set of leaders. Still another kind of congregation is the clan, based on kin relationships of an extended family, dozens or even hundreds of persons claiming a common set of ancestors. These modern secular congregations have local, regional, even global memberships. In power and scope of interests the vocational groupings surpass the prototype sacred congregations on which they have modeled their internal dynamics. Unlike the sacred congregation, however, each of these vocational groupings has its own particular, often narrowly-defined purpose.

Trends are occurring in the further evolution of secular congregations and their data-gathering work. Having emerged from the secular society of the last few centuries, these congregations share with their older siblings, the sacred congregations, several characteristics:

- They find that the gathered body is greater than the sum of its member parts.
- Members experience mutual empowerment in their several individual vocations.
- They freely share with other members of the congregation common obligations and responsibilities.

The Neighborhood

Despite its fallen estate today in many places, the residential neighborhood is a particular kind of secular congregation which is more biologically determined than almost any other human aggregation. The residential neighborhood satisfies our animal territoriality. Popular thinking affirms neighborhood to be a secular gathering of independent backgrounds, eschewing transcendental concerns or visions. Well, maybe. But this judgment reminds one a little bit of listening to adolescents talk about sex and love. Very soon there erupts in their exchanges the utterly other, the yearning for total trust, mutual surrender, merging in almost unitary consciousness "until death us do part." And so it may be with our littered, mortgaged, decaying urban neighborhoods. In our pluralistic society we finally do not wish to flee from neighbor, but to join neighbor in mutually creating the symbols and structures which empower and ennoble neighborhood, because it is our home. We believe sacred congregations in some new forms will have a key role in making this almost unspoken, deep yearning a sociological reality. Both sacred and secular congregations share one important social task: from many sources they gather data related to their concerns.

One great weakness of many urban neighborhoods is the fragmented and missionless church institutions in their midst. While secular congregations, associations, companies, institutes, etc., have increased greatly in recent decades in numbers and power, the sacred congregations of most North American religious traditions have declined. This trend has accelerated each decade since the Great Depression. With this decline in numbers and confidence of the sacred congregations, there has been considerable confusion among members as to the mission or purpose of the sacred congregation. The secular state, which is trusted to provide for the common defense, prosperity, and ordering of pluralistic community life, has taken from them the obligation to care for the poor, both locally and globally. In chapters 8 and 9 we will look at remedies for the leaderless neighborhood.

Group Data Gathering

Essential to information processing is data gathering by every congregation based upon its particular concerns.

An example: today in every part of the world, people are living longer than in earlier centuries. The secular congregation looks at ways to engage the elderly meaningfully in the life of the community. A common fear is that retirement from paid employment is bad for one's health. Not so, new data indicate:

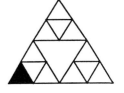

Retirement is not an unhealthful state[52]

Excluding those retiring for health reasons, statistical regression analysis showed no difference in the health of early retirees from those continuing to work.

Here data of interest pointed to the absence of difference between retired and employed elders. Only an interested congregation of elders and those concerned with elders could create this kind of useful data. Another congregation of elders observed data which refuted another superstition: that worry about abandonment is confined to persons in economically advanced industrialized nations. Not so:

Elders in Nepal[53]

Elders in isolated villages of Nepal were found to be greatly disturbed by rumors and experiences of declining respect for elders elsewhere in the world.

Secular congregational data gathering is enormously productive. Some 90 percent of data in any public library today have been added to the stores of knowledge within the last several decades. Data are accumulating at such an ever increasing rate that complaints of "data overload" are heard. Yet without this process of congregational data gathering, and recording in some accessible journal, the further development of the urban person and planetary mind cannot proceed.

Look at the group data gathering triangle. Undergirding that process is abstracting and preserving documents (the what), indexing and filing data (the how of organizing), and collating and distributing (the why of data gathering).

Happily, secular congregations not only observe and record data, but take the obligation of indexing and filing data for future retrieval and use. Over 6,000 journals of health sciences regularly publish vast quantities of good data. Many, many congregations are engaged in observation and recording of this kind of data. How can anyone get into such myriads of data to use it? Some kind of sorting, labeling, and systematized access is needed. It employs hundreds of secular congregations.

Old Doc: Bumble Bee Transfers

OLD DOC: Have you ever considered the universal implications of the bumble bee buzzing from flower to flower?

MEDICAL STUDENT: Cross pollination sustains the species. No bumble bees, no flowers; no flowers, no bumble bees.

OLD DOC: Right. Like flowers in the field, clusters of individual

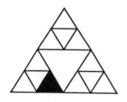

persons are maturing gloriously in wisdom and grace. And like flowers, they are doomed unless they exchange genetic information with their fellows in the whole field, which for us is the planet.

MEDICAL STUDENT: What does the bumble bee dynamic look like relative to health care?

OLD DOC: I call it Regional Cross Disciplinary Collaboration. Fragmentation of both information and funding is a major block to responsible service and creative dialogue among innovators. Wherever thoughtful citizen groups set local priorities for addressing social diseases (examples: adolescent pregnancy, alcoholism, depression, senility) and work with collaborating teams of experts, they have the power to change whole systems of health technologies.

MEDICAL STUDENT: That sounds like an exciting experiment. With process, outcome, and impact measures, it could be publishable.

OLD DOC: The experiment is to measure the synergistic effect of local and regional collaboration in the context of new global consciousness.

MEDICAL STUDENT: But that would require many meetings and people are too busy for meetings.

OLD DOC: Ah, that is where the bumble bee comes in. Some of us will need to take meetings to the people. Faced with more wealth, more demanding options and ongoing commitments, the need is greater than ever to exchange information with neighbors and colleagues.

MEDICAL STUDENT: Are you suggesting a bumble bee circuit as a new vocation, a kind of networking that could substitute for group gatherings? Meetings can disappear from the human scene?

OLD DOC: Only the boring meetings. Well-set-up meetings create new universes.

MEDICAL STUDENT: Who will be these circuiters? Will it take another generation to integrate the wisdom of these blossoming but separated clusters?

OLD DOC: A creative elder could take this as a full-time retirement career. Soon new constituencies could develop regional power bases for the new spirit edge in health care.

Common Knowledge Creation

Discerning useful associations among data is a big payoff for the labor and cost of indexing, filing, and retrieving data from many different congregations, each with differing interests. For example, much "research" about alcoholism is anecdotal, polemic, manipulat-

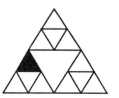

ive, biased and useless. Controlled population-based assemblies of data are regrettably uncommon.

The value of studies relating data from different origins and sets is illustrated in trying to answer the question, "Does social drinking impair cognitive function?" Answer:

A cross disciplinary view of alcoholism [54]

Among a sample of 1,367 employed men and women in Detroit, scores on tests of ability to think in abstract terms decreased as the reported weekly consumption of alcohol increased. Indexing by psychological, by behavioral, by age-sex-class data led to new useful information.

Much scientific inquiry is this sort of patient searching through apparently unrelated data sets for combinations which make new sense. A similar careful search through available recorded data revealed weaknesses in common ways of reporting motor vehicle accidents, suicides and assaults:

Needed: A new method of tabulating injuries [55]

Injuries, as leading causes of death, are underreported by police and hospitals and are treated as behavioral problems. (Who, legally, is at fault? Who should pay?) Generally, causes are not considered in the reports. Example: if someone dies of a gunshot wound, the social cause isn't noted—i.e., alcohol abuse? Habitual domestic violence? Accident? Data which could point to future prevention of deaths from gunshot wounds is not put into hospital or police reports of these tragic events.

Collating and distributing data is what gives meaning to data abstracting (that is, documentation) and data indexing. Files of data are made useful by collating and distributing them to user groups.

Examples: filed data becomes useful information when tested and validated by wise caretakers; when applied to the needs of special populations; when used to track individual persons through a maze of separate health service agencies; when temporal trends are discerned among files of data; when working models of interactive data systems are reported; when new ways of using filed data are described.

Local caretakers (teachers, hostesses, gang leaders, professionals: the wise caretakers of a nearby small triangle) do the work of collating and distribution of indexed and filed data to answer the questions: Who? What? When?

Who?

Does your doctor warn you [56] if you have hypertension, the silent killer? Long-term, inexpensive treatment can reduce by several hundred percent your chances of stroke, heart attack, and other very nasty conditions.

Who helps high-risk mothers with special needs? [57] Infants of adolescent mothers have a mortality rate which is 150 percent that of older mothers in the same region, due to increased social and biological risks and fewer resources tapped by these young mothers.

What?

There is a natural history of ghetto teen crime. [58] The law is ponderous, always too late. By the time the teen criminal is locked away his criminal behavior already has been abandoned in most cases. The competent neighborhood can defend itself against hoodlums without a great deal of help from police, the law, or social agencies.

When?

Person, time, and place are classic characteristics of events that the medical statistical science of epidemiology tracks. Many practitioners of neighborhood health sciences will need an overview of epidemiological methods applied to small populations. Current, careful, and complete enough for most neighborhood work is a little textbook called *Epidemiology in Health Management.* [59]

■ **Multilevel Integrating Skills:**
   Getting the data where it needs to go

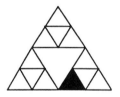

Professional Disciplines

Professional Disciplines and its Skilled Observations, Regional Exchanges, and Parish Evaluation is what sustains multi-level integrating skills. A local community cannot live without its professionals who develop and use specialized skills for the sake of the community. An interdisciplinary group can network with others in regional exchanges; apply their skills in observation or information gathering; and collaborate with local residents of the parish who set the local priorities and are final judges of whatever projects are developed in their neighborhoods. Legal professionals work with neighborhood residents to create a strategy for conflict resolution:

Neighborhood justice [60]

Lawyer Raymond Shonholtz in 1977 began the Community Boards Program in San Francisco as the nation's first effort in systematically building a new justice system, complementary to but separate from the court system. Community conflict-resolution mechanisms are among the effective tools for early intervention and reduction of hostility between people who know each other.

After community volunteers complete a two-week training period, they may become members of Community Boards and act as outreach workers, case developers, or hearing panelists within their own neighborhoods. In 1985 neighborhood conflict-resolution forums were serving a third of the city's residents in 22 neighborhoods, and residents in other cities.

When a person calls for help (frequently referred by police), a case developer calls on both disputants and invites them to talk together before a panel of 3-5 of their neighbors. If the parties agree to work out their problem, the panelists help negotiate a written agreement. In its first eight years, the board program handled over 2,000 cases. Some 92 percent of their hearings end with a voluntary agreement; 80 percent of these are upheld in practice. Some 25 percent of Community Board volunteers are former disputants.

"Community conflict resolution is not a program. It is a long-term social investment in the health of individuals and communities. This approach will need to be in place 10-15 years, with the support of schools, neighborhoods, and cities, to change the way Americans manage conflict," says Raymond Shonholtz.

Intuitive Strategy Creation

Community develops strategies for reducing teen pregnancy [61]

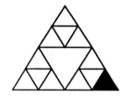

The Greater Piedmont March of Dimes convened representatives from local public schools, colleges, and parent teacher associations. From this came an action core group, the Council on Adolescent Pregnancy. The core convened 600 leaders for a day-long awareness and strategic planning conference. Ten task forces allowed small group discussion in these arenas: medical, parents, neighborhood community groups, church, school, peers, media, business agencies, legal and government. In each task force small groups brought together their ideas which the entire conference prioritized in a final plenary session. The core group then developed strategies to be implemented by small work groups. Annual update of the master plan was set to renew commitment.

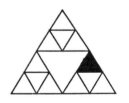

Family Social Formations

Skilled professionals work with other neighborhood families to create strategies which catalyze the varied family social forms to develop missional family clusters empowered with universal symbols and fulfilling vocations. Example: a strategic approach to the need for affordable housing.

Creative financing mechanisms [62]

Hope Communities, Inc. was founded in 1980 to develop decent, affordable housing in Denver's Five Points neighborhood for low-income families. The new corporation purchased a three-building apartment complex and renovated it for 33 low-income families, with funding from a foundation, business corporations, churches, individuals and volunteer labor.

In 1983 Hope sold its first limited partnership to finance a second apartment complex for 20 families: The Denver Revitalization Partnership One, Ltd., with 23 investors. Other parts of the financial package included a block grant, Section 8 rental subsidies, a loan from the State Housing Authority, and inkind services. A second limited partnership was formed, following the success of the first venture, for further acquisition and renovation, for cooperative management and for home ownership.

In 1985 Hope joined the Enterprise Foundation housing network. It received technical assistance and $500,000. Through a lease/purchase program Hope Communities focuses on low income home ownership. Elements are:

1. Hope acquires structurally sound but deteriorated single family or duplex units.
2. Hope does as much renovation as possible under $45,000, including cost of acquisition.
3. Hope finances the project through a revolving loan fund (investors: Piton and Enterprise foundations, Colorado Housing Finance Authority, AMOCO oil, and Hope Communities).
4. The Supply Thrift Center, an outlet for donated building supplies, provides needed items at greatly reduced cost.
5. While construction goes on, owner applicants with incomes between $9,000 and $15,000 are screened by Hope for the Lease/Purchase program.
6. During the one-to-five-year period of leasing a home, the potential homeowners are expected to save the down payment; some earn cost reduction credits for improvements in

the home they are renting; monthly rental payments can be no more than 39 percent of their annual income.

7. At the end of a successful lease, with financial and home management training, most lease/purchasers are expected to qualify for mortgage loans through FHA or VA or privately insured loans, or through tax-exempt bond financing through the city or state.

■ Common Operating Wisdom: Building appropriate social structures and symbols

Commissioned University Research

Perhaps the universities will generate the first pulses of the new common operating wisdom, succeeding old common sense. Not the university as an institution, probably. Rather, the university as a societal assignment or mandate given to a community of scholars. Such a community of scholars in an organized bioregion* could create packages of knowledge and technology in linked systems for use by secular congregations, professional holons, and groups with many interests. Both basic and applied research will need funding and appropriate accountability. Basic research funding may need ties to related applied research, both supported licensing of patented technology.

Many experimental or developmental projects by local social laboratories will need expert assistance in project design, evaluation and publication of results. A regional university would be the natural provider of such help. Electronic exchange of information, access to global data banks of neighborhood health sciences, and assistance by clusters of scientists and scholars of many backgrounds would empower the hundreds of social labs which will do the testing of hypotheses created for the planetary mind project.

---

* *bioregion:* "an identifiable geographical area of interacting life systems that is relatively self-sustaining in the ever-renewing processes of nature. The full diversity of life functions is carried out, not as as individuals or as a species, or even as organic beings, but as a community that includes the physical as well as the organic components of the region. Such a bioregional community is self-propagating, self-nourishing, self-educating, self-governing, self-healing and self-fulfilling. Each of the component life systems must integrate their own functioning within this community functioning to survive in any effective manner." —*Thomas Berry*

Town-gown cooperation in the Swannanoa Valley[63]

In recent decades quality of life has deteriorated for residents of Black Mountain and Swannanoa Townships, nestled between hills along 14 miles of the beautiful Swannanoa River east of Asheville, North Carolina. "Creeping ruralurbia" has brought pollution of the water supply and poisoning of fish, erosion of mountainsides through clear cutting of forests, illegal waste dumping in coves where families have lived over a century, and loss of jobs and tax base from unregulated development. Many of its 23,000 people are elderly. Half the children attending school are poor.

Warren Wilson College, accredited as a four-year college since 1966, has been a presence in the valley since 1894 when it was established as the Asheville Farm School for mountain boys. The 1,000 acre campus still includes a farm, 650 acres of forest, an archeological dig, a residential community of 500 students and 150 staff. Ten percent of the student body is international, and many poor students from third world countries aspire to attend. The students, in addition to being the work force of the college, are required to complete a service project for others on the campus, at home, or in the community.

Phase I: broad citizen input. In 1985 the college initiated a major community service project, in collaboration with local residents, to improve the quality of life in Swannanoa Valley over the next ten years. Under the leadership of college faculty, 500 residents participated in community meetings to answer the questions: What is good in the community? What do you dislike and want to change? What do you need in order to improve the community?

Six research groups of community volunteers, college students, and staff assessed the natural resources and environment of the valley, its cultural history, community values, decision-making structures, educational system, and economic base. The economic analyses included energy, health, housing, money and capital, and waste management.

Phase II: New enterprises. After 17 months of gathering people, information and momentum, the Project could offer real solutions to real problems in the valley. An archives collection and newsletter raised awareness of the cultural roots and values of the community through cove associations, Sourwood Festival, Clean Streams Day, the Art League, and other distinctive activities. The newsletter tells the progress of the research groups and their proposals.

143

Using the *Economic Renewal Workbook* designed by the Rocky Mountain Institute to diagnose the problems in a local economy, the Economic Renewal Project team discovered that 60 percent of the investments of local banks are made outside the valley, and 90 percent of the energy bills paid leave the valley. Proposals to strengthen the economy and plug the outflow of capital include importing new financial and information-service businesses, and increasing local entrepreneurship. As a first step in reducing energy costs, Carolina Power and Light Company cooperated with community volunteers and students to weatherize 200 homes in one day in Project Stop Gap. With materials from valley suppliers, this could become an ongoing youth service business. Plans have been drawn for a waste management business to combine trash collection and recycling.

Phase III: The Black Swan Resource Center. A new community center is being built to: 1) link families, especially the poor living in unincorporated areas, and organizations to needed resources; 2) provide business consulting services (business incubator) and the technology for long-range planning; 3) be a children's center, a Folk College and a liaison with Warren Wilson College; 4) be a place where the community can equip itself for the economic, social and political betterment of all the people.

Commissioned Research / Linked Systems

Packaged, linked systems bring together data from several disciplines for particular users. The packages are the product of commissioned university research offered to particular user groups. Examples:

Can architecture control crime? [64]

A university research group discovered that urban crime is made worse by architectural design of many public housing projects. Interconnecting walkways, exits, elevators, stairways ("confused space") not under the control of particular residents, increase crime in urban housing.

Providing services to the co-ops [65]

The Cooperative Resources and Services Center (CRSP) in Los Angeles provides education, training and technical help for cooperatives of all kinds. It was founded in 1980 by Lois Arkin "to help build a culture where individual rewards come from a healthy spirit and practice of cooperation... to heal the wounds in ourselves, one another and the great Gaia." CRSP's vision of a holistic and trans-formational economic system is being implemented in collaboration with other organizations in Los Angeles and San Francisco. So far the components of the system in place include the following:

LETS: This Local Employment and Trading System, begun in 1986, has over 40 members. Co-sponsors CRSP and ECO-HOME charge some of their fees and pay some wages in LETS credits. Skills for exchange range from babysitting, word processing and computer consulting to auto mechanics, carpentry, massage, to chiropractic and legal. A monthly newsletter lists offerings and notices.

ELF: The Ecological Revolving Loan Fund, begun in 1985, has 15 ethnically-diverse member lenders of mixed income levels and over $10,000 for seed money loans to cooperatively owned or man-aged enterprises. Potential borrowers are encouraged to become lenders first. ELF is exploring methods of integrating LETS credits into the fund. Cooperative enterprises being planned include a recycled paper distribution business, a co-op cafe, and shared housing communities.

Workshops for Shared Housing Communities: Begun in spring 1987, and co-sponsored by CRSP, Innovative Housing, based in Marin County, and by the Los Angeles office of the Institute of Cultural Affairs, this series helps persons with an ecological or spiritual orientation to clarify their vision and goals for holistic urban intentional communities. About ten of the 40 persons who have been to these workshops have nest eggs for cooperative housing ranging from $5,000 to $200,000. Most of the participants are interested in living in communities that are ethnically, economi-cally and generationally diverse. Many may become part of the Urban Ecological Co-op Village, planned for an 11-acre city dump-site for sand and gravel now considered surplus.

Regional Incubator Ventures

A task for many missional family clusters is the economic and social development of their community: linking entrepreneurs with sources of money and expertise and to new markets. Fundamental to these ventures is the understanding and commitment to address a widespread human need. One poor old lady protesting a move to a nursing home is a claim on human care. A million old ladies in this inhuman predicament is a call to creation of prototype incubators to offer something better in the market for maintaining the elderly in community living.

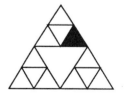

145

Pennsylvania's domiciliary care experiment[66]

Over ten months, 190 institutionalized persons were moved to group homes. Control persons resided in a similar county, and were matched by computer with experimental subjects beforehand. Savings in care costs exceeded program costs for aged, mentally ill and retarded. No effects were found in physical functioning, but there was clear improved functioning on psychological testing. Over 90 percent of savings were from lower use of institutional services.

Community support costs in the home care included employment counseling, provision of meals and homemaker services, transportation, physician and visiting nurse care, and day care. Where these services were provided by family or friends they were valued at minimum wage rates. Some 52 percent of program cost was for direct domiciliary payments (rent and service payments), at an average cost of $7/day. Costs of control groups not placed in the domiciliary program were used to calculate savings. Those placed in homes used more community support services than controls, but average daily savings of $12.07 far outweighed the added community support costs.

Previous studies of costs of alternatives to institutionalization have been inconclusive. Cost data for control groups often is inexact. Good studies must consider the interplay of community, family and physician inputs. Family evaluation must include resources, needs, attitudes and knowledge. Patient factors include needs, level of functioning, attitudes, resources and knowledge. Many studies waffle between emphasizing the demonstration part of the research and the evaluation. It is very difficult to deny services to controls. The communities chosen must be matched as carefully as the participants.

Clustering of lifestyle groups: Middle class values control economically integrated neighborhood housing[67]

Public programs for housing the poor have been a disaster since the 1950s. Our faith in social interventions has been badly damaged. Here are rules for building lively culturally-diverse urban neighborhoods of working adults, retired elders, and child-oriented families with richer public resources than those ever achieved in suburbia. The psychological designs set forth here strengthen a neighborhood's defenses against crime and vandalism. They assure residents' control of the public space around their dwellings. Only such neighborhoods can offer safe havens for minorities.

146

1) House families with children either in single family row houses, or walk-up apartments with access limited to half a dozen families. Owner-occupied walkups are particularly stabilizing, even when there is changeover in tenants. Children in single-parent families are under less supervision, are prone to vandalism and worse. Unsupervised teenagers regularly terrorize neighborhoods. Therefore, limit single-parent families to 30 percent of the total. The incomes of the families can be varied, but middle-class values must be perceived by all as operating with effective sanctions. Density of this kind of housing is 30-50 families per acre in single-family dwellings, 200 or more families per acre in walk-up apartments.

2) Any kind of housing is suitable for elders, who have a quite uniform lifestyle whatever their ethnic or economic characteristics. However, elevator housing allows the high density (150-500 dwelling units per acre) which most gregarious elders desire, provided access is limited to orderly adults.

3) Working adults require buildings secured during their absence at work or recreation. Elevator buildings with custodial control of access are best. Late partying can annoy elders, and some separation of the two age groups probably will please both.

4) A mixture of single-family row houses, walk-up apartments, and elevator buildings can be combined with public spaces favoring separate activity centers for toddlers, teens, business folk and retired persons. For a common perception of stable middle-class value dominance, 60 percent or more of the residents must be white. (Author's note: Many but not all knowledgeable persons will agree with this last sentence. The writer's main arguments are well taken and relevant to designing stable prospering neighborhoods.)

Local Testing Exchanges:
The new common sense emerges

Those who create, test, and refine new images of wholeness for five billion persons—living harmoniously among billions of other species on planet earth—are at work now, simultaneously processing information, designing new social forms, and sharing and testing inventions in local social labs around the world.

Urban knowledge, common operating wisdom which in the new age consciousness succeeds the old industrial-age common sense, is validated in local testing. In the first instance, neighborhood is the geographical community of residence, where the home is, and where 85 percent of our local testing and development of the new common

sense will happen. Neighborhood may be within an urban highrise complex, a rural network of islands connected by small ships, or a work community engaging whole clusters of families (an example is a boarding school with resident faculty living on campus).

In the participatory social labs described here, local jobs are created for residents who collect and analyze new data. Some neighborhoods also can package their learnings in proposals or business models for sharing with interested groups. In some cases this sharing work will be done better by groups outside the neighborhood: by a university, a professional holon, or a regional incubator of ventures. As much as the neighborhood wishes and can, the work of the project should be done by neighborhood residents, in keeping with the principle of fostering microeconomic neighborhood bases.

Global Pluriformity,* the topmost triangle, points to the infinite variety of local community styles which will mark the new common sense, served by a common operating wisdom, developed in research work enlisting collaborating groups of many kinds. As participatory community research is decentralized, each local experiment can be watched by the whole planet for learnings useful in other places.

Indonesia, a learning society [68]

By the 1990s illiteracy in Indonesia should be eliminated as a result of innovative programs which have now entered the educational mainstream. In the Cianjur elementary schools, spirited learning is going on. Children do lessons, play, go on field trips, and study in small noncompetitive groups with rotating peer leadership and supervision by teachers trained in nondirective, participatory techniques that facilitate problem solving, cooperation, and communication. The curriculum emphasizes the local environment, practical aspects of daily life, and the values of Indonesian society.

In the Pamong program for school dropouts, the community takes on the instructional management of curriculum provided by the schools in self-learning modules. Literate adults and youth volunteer as tutors on a one-to-one basis to prepare dropouts for the primary school certificate.

---

*pluriformity: affirms a commonality among related social designs, where "diverse" emphasizes differences. Since our need now is for integrating diverse designs and enhancing images that foster cooperation, pluriformity to the authors seems to be "a healing truth."

The Kejar (meaning "learning while working," "working groups" or "to catch up") package is for the millions who lack a basic education. The 100 booklets cover religious and social concepts, family and community, functional literacy and community health. Any neighborhood can start a Kejar group of 6-10 persons. Each course graduate is expected to teach 10 new learners.

Siena: The importance of symbols [69]

Siena, Italy, population 59,000, has the lowest crime rate of any city of comparable size. Delinquency, drug addiction and violence are virtually unknown. Siena is a tribal city which ritualizes its life. The clans of the city, called *contrada*, function as independent city-states. Each has its own flag, territorial boundaries, identity, church, songs, patron saint and rituals. Each contrada is named after an animal, either real or mythical. Each has a ritualized relationship with all the other contradas. Chicciola, the Snail, feuds with Tartula, the Turtle; Brucco, the caterpillar, with Giraffa; etc.

Rituals which form bonds between the child and his contrada begin at birth when a flag is sent to be flown from the window of the newborn's house so that the child is officially claimed for the contrada. In contrast to our culture where each child is expected to make his own place in the world as he deals first with school and later a job, the child of the contrada is enmeshed in a crisscross of bonds, just as in a primitive tribe. To us the idea of ascribed status is anathema, reactionary. Actually, this liberal viewpoint creates a situation where social relations are barely sustainable. The values we hold may be considered inherently noble, but the social relations on which they are built cannot produce a valid, sustainable society and our own cities are proving this to us.

The famous horse race of Siena, the Palio, serves two main purposes. In the intense rivalry surrounding the race, each contrada rekindles its own sense of identity. Every other contrada is an enemy, an ally, or a neutral. The Palio grew out of games which were actually mock battles; now the race is a ritualized war, venting aggressions.

The Palio is a religious event. On this day of the year the contrada's horse is brought into the church of its patron saint. In the act of blessing the horse, the contrada itself is blessed. This horse race is the community's greatest rite. "In the Palio, all the flames of hell are transformed into the lights of paradise," says local priest Don Vittorio. Ritual is the pattern that connects, that provides

149

communication at all levels, among all the systems within the individual human organism—between persons, within groups, between groups in the city, and between the human and nonhuman in the natural environment. Ritual provides us with a tool for learning to think logically, analogically, and ecologically. During rituals we have the experience, unique in our culture, of neither opposing nature nor trying to be in communion with nature, but rather of finding ourselves within nature.

■ **Summary: A new common sense**

Those who create, test and refine new images of wholeness for 10 billion persons living harmoniously among billions of other species on planet earth are at work now, simultanously processing information, designing new social forms, sharing and testing inventions in local social labs around the world. Thus a new common sense emerges.

So what good is the tripolar roadmap? If, as we have said, our common sense has been lost and local operating wisdom as well as integrating skills are collapsed, especially in deteriorating urban neighborhoods, the power of information processing becomes overwhelming The remedy for rebalancing the process is not to attack the information overload, but to strengthen the human integrating skills to turn information into knowledge into wisdom.

■ **Old Doc: 21st century guilds—Anticipations of profound planetary power**

MEDICAL STUDENT: Doctor, people talk about our planet as a single living organism, with a global circulation and brain. It takes a quantum leap of imagination for me to go from breathing, thinking individuals to a breathing, thinking planet.

OLD DOC: Some of us believe that a quantum leap is needed in bringing this new age consciousness to many more people of all ages and interests. So we're thinking of a "Brain Development Campaign" here.

MEDICAL STUDENT: For Ph.D.s or preschoolers?

OLD DOC: Both, and everyone in between. We see ourselves as part of five billion human units in a planetary brain, learning new ways for structuring new cooperative ventures.

MEDICAL STUDENT: Is this a master image around which groups can converge to improve the social fabric of our cities? And which groups?

OLD DOC: The social artists will clarify meanings and communicate the interior experience of new age consciousness. Others will focus on the technologies of health.

MEDICAL STUDENT: Say more about health sciences.

OLD DOC: One common denominator of social ills is isolation from the life of the times. Effective ways of engaging the dropouts could cure many.

MEDICAL STUDENT: What other groups will be needed in this Brain Development Campaign?

OLD DOC: Educators will ask where lifelong learning can happen best. Non-classroom learning may become their focus. Others look to architecture and design for affordable housing. Conflict resolution, crime control, better job training design, self-help groups—all for healthful neighborhoods in whole communities.

MEDICAL STUDENT: What will be the social glue that brings us all into one human community?

OLD DOC: Only at our deepest levels are we likely to become one people. Somehow treasures from our varied traditions must be brought into a harmonious whole, and new age guilds formed to stand against ancient tyrannies of church, state, commerce or family.

Chapter 7

High Vocational Adventure

Those Who Can Make Good Things Happen use social and spirit methods to lead many kinds of communities into social cohesion. TWCs are creating many kinds of families which experience profound spirit refreshment as they care structurally for their neighborhoods. But beyond the residential neighborhood, or the small business association, in which we all find our primal community, most of us also live in a very wide world of commercial, intellectual, and political systems which vary greatly in extent and power. Many of our vocations require us to play ball in very large ball games, whether or not we like all the rules, the umpires, or the playing fields. Few educators like everything going on in the field of education. Few medical doctors like everything that is going on in the health sciences. Every vocational playing field sets limits upon our human freedom. Within these limits we are free to choose our obligations and our human responsibilities.

There is no intent in this chapter to inform readers about developments or issues in education and the health sciences, but rather to use these stories as *examples* of vocational engagement within the powerful intellectual and political systems of our global culture. Lawyers could write corresponding accounts of vocational struggle from their particular viewpoints. So could the butcher, the baker and the candlestick-maker. We think that readers with vocational commitments, both inside and outside the fields of education and health sciences, will find in these reports an arabesque of the human journey in our global culture.

■ An experience in global education[70]

Currently, my husband Gigs, our sons Charles and Fredric, and I live in Kinsasha, Zaire (the heart of Africa, formerly Leopoldville, in the Belgian Congo), where Gigs and I teach. Kinsasha has about three million residents and is situated on the Zaire, formerly Congo, River, second largest river in the world after the Amazon.

The international school

Our twin sons are sophomores in The American School of Kinsasha (TASOK). The teachers, texts, curricula and methods are American. Five hundred students from kindergarten through twelfth grade from thirty different nationalities study here.

Most students did not ask to come here, but are here because of their parents' work with the foreign service, or international development, or business. How then does our school create a community of learners in a foreign land with many different students from different languages and cultures? By being intentional. By having a focus through a process similar to that referred to in chapter three in this book. This focus occurs at the administrative level, teachers' level, and most importantly in each classroom where the teacher and students set goals for the year and quarter. These goals are on view as posters. At the end of the term a reflective conversation is held to evaluate the accomplishments.

Students quickly become assimilated through the common language, English, the school songs and symbols, and wearing the T-shirts with the school emblem. A common assembly tells us who we are.

My husband and I began to teach overseas in New Guinea in the Peace Corps era. After several years in the States, the call to move beyond the familiar came again in 1979 when we signed a contract to teach in the American School in Karachi, Pakistan, where we stayed for six years. From 1985 to 1987 we taught in an American school in Sao Paulo, Brazil, where we experienced the pain and struggles of the fourth largest city of the world with its slums, pollution, crime and overworked transport system.

Why have we taught in so many places? It has been a way to learn of our world, to see for ourselves. It has been an intentional journey to prevent us from falling into ourselves, from getting too content in suburbia; a way of meeting our world face to face. For us, teaching is a calling: a vocation that grips us each moment of each

153

day, a profession that has us growing and searching and producing and staying alive, a chance to experience the awe and wonder of life and share that view with our students.

The international schools that we have taught in have some of the key elements for a meaningful education:
- Parents support the child, school and teachers;
- The child knows the intent of school;
- The child is expected to learn; and
- Teachers care.

Public education in the U.S.

That public education is nonfunctioning, I cannot deny. The system worked well for the Agricultural Era where the family farm defined the limits of education and supported the children in their studies. It worked for the Industrial Era when it trained people for jobs, for competition, and for success defined in terms of the salary and prestige of the job.

When the focus of society shifted, the education system no longer met the needs. Overwhelming social ills prevented people from being educated. Both students and teachers were defined in economic terms, clearly a much reduced view of human life. Beyond that, the system lacked a clear model of what should be taught. Operating out of a reduced view of human life, students were given facts at best. Public schools have not dared to enter into the arena of values.

In the system of education for the compassionate era students will need to learn about the quality of all of life. Success will be measured by care for one's neighbor and care of the earth. Prestige will be found in being a community leader.

Reading will be taught in the new age in an expanded context. In addition to books and print, it will include "reading" films, TV, speeches and panel discussions, body language, facial expression, and tone of voice. Moving into a still larger context, it is possible and indeed necessary to read the mood of a home, a meeting, a group; to read the needs of a city block, the ecological state, as well as the political state of the world.

Writing will be taught as a thinking process, including all arenas of the thinking process. Writing will be a kind of servant in the classroom, the tool central to the entire learning process, through which each student will define the world and make the learning process truly his own.

Love consists not of gazing into each other's eyes, but in looking out in the same direction.

—ANNE MORROW LINDBERGH

The teacher's journey

Reflecting upon my own journey of nearly half a century, I remember the people who made a difference. Mrs. Lane, my eighth grade teacher in a one-teacher school with 52 students, grades one through eight, gave us good training in being leaders. We wrote plays and acted them out and taught younger children. It was a ready-made community.

In high school my debate coach and history teacher, Mr. Marquardt, talked about the changes needed in the educational system. I listened avidly because I hadn't heard other teachers talk about the future, nor my responsibility for the future.

If education is what remains long after the facts have been forgotten, then my favorite English professor in college was truly an educator. I still recall her conversations and dialogues. She never lectured. Her method was simple. She dictated questions which we copied down and answered as we read. Then we discussed them in class. I recall the joy, the suspense, the excitement of discovery as she moved the class through a particular story or poem. Through gentle prodding and encouragement—"trust yourself, trust yourself"—she was the facilitator, the one who helped us "commune with Robert Frost."

Her course included life skills as well as academics. We read literature that answered questions we young adults had. We read carefully, then matched the literature with our own life experiences. Our lives were enriched by the countless people, views and values we encountered in the class readings. The scales fell from my eyes, and I was left in awe as the world grew bigger and bigger each day. Miss Smith began my spirit journey.

The Suzuki method

Dr. Suzuki developed his method of teaching music after World War II in Japan when he saw so many children without joy in their lives. This system is now worldwide. Its goals are perfection in music training with joy, based on the mother doing the teaching. As children learn language from their mother, the children learn music at home from the mother. Both attend the lessons. The teacher conducts the class, but the mother does the homework.

When my five-year-old sons began Suzuki, I took the lessons. The children watched me play the violin at home. They listened to recordings of the songs they would later play. How well I remember

We are entering the new age of education that is programmed for discovery, not for instruction.

the long hours of practice and listening at home, the three-hour group sessions (300 pupils on stage with the teacher), and the joy when our sons graduated from one level to the next. The community of musicians gives strength to continue, and work in this method is fun. The discipline develops good character as well as good skill. Our family unit was strengthened. Meeting another Suzuki family is a special event. They carry a consciousness of what is humanly possible with music and children and commitment and love.

The Montessori school

In the early part of this century Dr. Maria Montessori began her demonstration of intentional education in the slums of Italy. She wanted children to be able to interact with their environment, to be at home in their world, to learn the cause and effect of things. Tasks, designed in sequence, are available for children to choose according to their needs. Her approach includes socialization—children learning how to deal with other children and how to be responsible for themselves and for the world. Our sons attended the Montessori preschool and kindergarten and retain a spirit of inquiry, of discovering for themselves. The word "boring" does not exist in their vocabulary.

The I-search method

In the 1970s I met Professor Ken Macrorie who taught the I-search, rather than the re-search paper. (I suspect that the 1990s will see more of the we-search papers.) This method shifted the objective knower into the subjective partner in the search. Instead of students searching the world out there, the students put themselves in the middle of the paper—they include their search, their reactions to the search and their findings, along with the conclusions from their work. Such papers are engaging to write and fun for teachers to respond to.

The Theory of Knowledge course

Last year in Brazil I taught a course known as Theory of Knowledge (TOK). This is a required course in the International Baccalaureate (IB) program, a world-wide high school curriculum with head offices in Geneva. TOK is the course in which students learn what they have learned. It presents knowledge as more than facts. Students examine relationships between the areas of knowledge: science, aesthetics, language, history, logic. How do they know what they know? What is the nature of knowledge?

This course asked students to take a relationship to their knowledge. Upon completion of the 11th and 12th grade IB program, students receive a diploma with three comments written on it: 1. concerning their academic work, 2. what contributions they had made to society through their work, and 3. how successfully they had integrated what they had learned through TOK.

More ideas on classroom communication

How does a teacher know when a piece of writing is finished? Ideally, when the student owns it. He has chosen the topic, has written it, gotten responses from others, revised it and has made it his own. He also decides what to do with it: outline it, read it to an audience, illustrate it, post it, publish it, mail it or file it.

In the same way, in reading, we hope to bring the student to ownership when he has read the piece, questioned it, marked it, put it in his own words, heard other opinions, and matched his life experiences with those in the book. Side effects: he probably enjoyed his reading and will retain it.

Writing is taught as a process, beginning with discussion of a topic, brainstorming ideas, writing a first draft, getting responses from other people, revising, rethinking, rewriting, finishing and publishing it in some way. Instead of judging only the finished product (a composition), teachers now teach the entire process, equipping a student to be a learner for life. Writing is a direct link to the mind of the learner, beginning with the actual physical movement of the hand across the page which triggers the mind to create images—true mystery! What a privilege to teach writing!

While teaching in Karachi, I worked with Professor Mary Budd Rowe, a consultant to our school from the University of Florida. One night a group of us went to the beach to watch for sea turtles. Such excitement! We began with awe and wonder, asking questions. We continued in observation, with laughter. We ended with a written report. Dr. Budd's research has given us "wait time." Too many teachers wait only one or two seconds for a reply from students. By increasing wait time to seven to ten seconds, more students answered. Their answers were in sentences and in more depth. Expect something to happen and it will.

Writing across the curriculum is done here in the high school by teachers in various disciplines who are trained in writing, on a volunteer basis. Ideally, a teacher will be involved in all four of the communication skills with the students: speaking, reading, listening and writing. Both students and teacher can play the roles of guide, motivator, and orchestrator in the classroom.

Dialogue, student with student and student with teacher, is a significant mode of learning. The writing in the classroom is based on dialogue: the exchange of views and then reaching a conclusion for the sake of the community. No student can stay inside himself.

But after the thinking, the making one's own, the dialoguing, what then? Students need a sense of vocation, to know they are making significant contributions by learning. Somewhere in the scheme of things, we need events that tell students they are of value, that there is a future if we work for it, and that students are expected to be a significant part of that. We need rituals and ceremonies and celebrations for this purpose.

The intentional teacher

In my classroom hangs a photo of the earthrise, the picture that defines our world. On the wall hangs the chart (from China) explaining the four lifetimes:
- Ages 0–20: youth. Time to gain an education, to ask questions, to learn about the world through travel.
- Ages 20–40: rising adult. Time to find a profession, establish a family unit, work in the community.
- Ages 40–60: established adult. Time to be the guardian, the backbone of the society.
- Ages 60–80: old age. Time to share wisdom, to view life holistically, together with youth to raise eternal questions about life and death.

This intentional decor in my room reminds the students of the world they are part of and their necessary role in it.

Students soon recognize intentional teachers. They "read" their class daily, record responses, and plan accordingly for the next day. The intentional teacher notes the journey of each student, recognizes and tells the student of accomplishments, and motivates the student to improve where weak. It is when students change an attitude or some life habit that learning retention is achieved.

Tools for lifelong learning

Recently I was invited by the Agha Khan Mosque here in Kinsasha to present new teaching methods to their mosque teachers, volunteers from their community who teach the youth their religious faith. One of the sessions dealt with viewing a picture. How do you talk about a painting? Where do you begin? After we looked at the painting carefully, I asked the following questions and cautioned the class about the need to answer the questions in sequence and accept all answers; this was not the time to critique one another's replies.

1. Impressionistic (observe the raw data)
   What objects do you notice?
   What shapes do you notice?
   What colors do you see?
2. Reflective (take a relationship to the art piece or situation)
   What color would you add? Where?
   What color would you take out?
   What music would you play in the background?
   What noise do you hear?
   Where would you divide this painting into two?
   What part would you keep?
   How does this part make you feel?
   Where would you hang this in your house?
3. Interpretative (relate it to ordinary life)
   What story about this painting would you tell?
   What happened here previously?
   What word about life is this painting speaking?
   Where do you see this going on in your own life?
4. Decisional (relate it to *my* life)
   What would you say back to this painting?

After this conversation, we reflected on our responses. After first telling me they were never good in art, the class was amazed at the variety and depth of their insights. They saw the wisdom in following the questions and accepting answers from the group without judgment.*

The stance of the teacher

In observing colleagues, I have noticed those who give do receive. Those who hold on to their time and energy, carefully guard their hours and extent of engagement with the task and the students, are

---

* This method, called the Basic Discussion Method, is further described in Chapter 3 pages 71-75.

more likely to burn out. It's like jumping into the swimming pool over your head, then figuring out ways to get to the top of the water and stay there. Drama coaches have a lot to teach the rest of us teachers. They are beyond counting hours. They know the power and value of being joined in a community focused on a common goal. The drama will come off—never mind the problems, the anxieties, the conflicting personalities and hurt egos. Deal with each situation as it comes. Decisions are made in the context of the whole, not based on a personal bias or on the most powerful voice.

By being involved in a larger context (helping to build lives and making significant contributions to the community), teachers have motivation to see them through long hours of work, the silence of colleagues and times when the community says, *"No!"* Being trained in the "process" mode of teaching, the teacher can face uncertainty; is able to live with unanswered questions. Being intentional in lessons and being cognizant of the journey of students provides motivation. Trust life. Know that you are sustained by community and by Life itself. Stay engaged.

■ Accelerated literacy through multimodal learning [71]

In teaching foreign languages it is possible to provide virtually complete mastery of the language in a sequence of two 84-hour courses. It should also be possible to teach literacy this way. With an ideal class size of from twelve to fifteen students, by creating a fully structured accelerative learning class, it should be possible to move nonreaders to mastery in about 150 hours of instruction, spread over a period of from six weeks (in intensive classes six hours a day) to six months (in two evening classes a week). Below is a group of global, accelerative teaching guidelines for what we presently consider to be the ideal environment, structure, approach and materials for such learning, as practiced at the SpeakEasy Language Center in Minneapolis.

Three fundamental principles of accelerated learning: Joy, double planing, and the group process

To evoke *joy*, the teacher makes each learning task seem easy, natural and interesting. The joy of learning imparts safety, freedom, self-esteem, hope and progress. These values are of particular importance for the illiterate who have had long periods of deprivation. Having fun creating dramas, stories and games helps recreate the child-like state when learning was accomplished easily and quickly.

Double planing is the process of teaching on at least two levels simultaneously. On one level the student is conscious of and attentive to a particular learning task. On a second level, the student's thinking is influenced by the environment, the student-teacher relationship, and the relevance of the lesson.

The second level has about ten times the impact of the first. It is on this level that the teacher can affect the learning process most positively, through his/her own teaching style and use of decor.

In the *group process*, or cooperative learning style, the student and teacher impact each other's learning through a growing dynamic relationship which can produce large jumps in understanding. This can occur in a one-on-one tutorial setting. However, it is greatly enhanced in groups of 12-15 students. The noncompetitive effect of teaching a group to cooperate reduces stress and helps to remove the fear of competition. Students reinforce each other by making discoveries and sharing them. A particular student may understand some matter before others in the group. Then others may understand even better and leap frog over the first student. The leadership role is passed back and forth among students. Discovery: learning can be fun, easy and rapid!

In the group experience the teacher can help raise the self-esteem of students by affirming their survival skills. The teacher helps them overcome some of the barriers to learning they have experienced in the past:
- the belief that learning to read is impossible for them
- the feeling that they are unworthy of reading
- the pain of past unsuccessful attempts to learn.

Concert reading

Global accelerative teaching uses concert sessions as a means of entering material and skills into the long-term memory. While the students relax, the teacher reads a passage accompanied by baroque, classical or romantic music. If, in addition to this previewing and modeling by the teacher, the student reads aloud with a background of music, the rate of learning is significantly speeded up. The style of intonation used by the teacher should contain firmness, matter of factness, and lightness.

The learning environment

Most students have learned to feel unsafe in the classroom. For the accelerated learning environment, the "distant intimacy" of the teacher, the mutual support among students, and the teacher's ability to keep all students equally involved in a relaxed comfortable atmosphere, surrounded by plants and objects of beauty, all contribute to the safety needed for the student to be receptive to new experiences. Everything in the environment should contribute to the positive suggestion that the student will learn quickly and easily.

The play is the thing

By presenting the material to be learned in the form of a dialogue similar to a play, with acts for individual lessons, the class can become a theatrical experience. The text becomes the central focus of the class, to be read in concert sessions, to be acted, or danced, to be the source of ideas for skits, games and character development among the students. The more senses involved in the learning experience, the better the chances that the student will learn. An illiterate adult who enacts the role of a college professor, by identifying with that role, gives up the old image of being a nonreader.

Some tools used

Peripherals (wall posters of pictures or words, containing subliminal messages), with no attention drawn to them, can improve both vocabulary and self-esteem of students. Card and block games are used to teach phonetics, and word and sentence patterns. Playwriting: increasingly complex scenarios can be created by the group from a two-word sentence like, "Stop Sam." Human sculpture: using the whole body as a part of a written sentence helps the student to internalize and identify with the writing and reading process, relating it to a larger process which is nonverbal.

Other tools include bingo (matching pictures and words), reading hieroglyphics (picture writing), and the word processor.

■ Using our seven intelligences[72]

In September 1987 Indianapolis Public School 97, which had been closed for over a year, opened its doors as the Key School to 150 pupils, kindergarten through sixth grade, whose parents wanted for them a program of instruction designed to develop all areas of their intelligence:

- Linguistic: sensitivity to the meaning and order of words and uses of language;
- Logical/mathematical: ability to handle long chains of reasoning, and to recognize patterns;
- Musical: sensitivity to rhythm, pitch and tone;
- Spatial: ability to perceive the visual world accurately and to recreate or modify aspects of that world based on one's perceptions;
- Bodily kinesthetic: fine tuned ability to use the body and handle objects;
- Interpersonal: ability to notice and make distinctions among others; and
- Intrapersonal: access to one's own feelings.

The Key School was born when teacher Patricia Bolanos and seven of her colleagues in PS 113, after studying the latest theories of intelligence, creativity and motivation, decided they needed a whole school organized around Howard Gardner's seven intelligences.[73] In 1985 the eight teachers presented their complete plan for the school to the superintendent of Indianapolis Public Schools. He was delighted. A building was available, and Lilly Endowment was interested in funding collaborative development in education.

The pupils were chosen by lottery from 500 applicants across the city. 58 percent are white, 37 percent black and 5 percent other minorities. Forty-three percent come from single parent families. One third are eligible for free or reduced cost lunches. Although the children are not screened, the parents must agree to attend three out of four parent-teacher conferences and arrange for the daily transportation of their children. The average daily attendance has been 95 percent. Eighty-five percent of the school are enrolled in the after school program when they can play in a safe place or participate until 6 p.m. in electives such as photography, computer graphics, gymnastics and Spanish. These are taught by teachers, volunteers and hourly employees.

The multidisciplinary curriculum, the first of its kind in the nation, is tied together by school-wide themes, spanning all grades and all subjects, each lasting nine weeks and ending with a grand celebration for the whole school. 1987-88 themes: connections between people and the globe; animal patterns; and changes in time and space. Equal emphasis is given to reading and writing, math, science, social studies, instrumental music, language skills, computer science, board games and physical education. Multi-aged groups(pods) emphasize work in a particular cognitive area, such as art, architecture, dramatics, choir, problem solving, etc.

Part of the school's mission is to measure and record the children's progress in each of the seven intelligences. School district tests are supplemented by videotapes documenting interests and accomplishments. Each pupil keeps a "log" with weekly entries about his/her projects; and teachers make detailed observations as they follow pupils in all their classes and activities.

■ Strategies for ethical re-education [74]

What does a relevant curriculum include today? Gene and Joyce Marshall propose one based on educational institutions which can motivate students with a genuine desire to know and live life fully rather than the education-for-employment curriculum now in place in most institutions.

This curriculum would include department study arenas of:
- Birth—studying the mysteries of our origins through subject areas such as
  - —my birth and my family;
  - —the human niche on planet Earth;
  - —the biological evolution and the origin of the universe; and
  - —the dynamics of rebirth;
- Adulthood—the ventures of responsibilities with subject areas of assuming responsbility for my own thinking, feelings, actions and skills;
- Homemaking—the covenants of location with subjects in
  - —sex and relationships;
  - —home management;
  - —child raising; and
  - —community building;
- Vocation—the commitments of contribution with subjects in
  - —my inclusive social vision;
  - —the strategies of effectiveness;
  - —choosing my personal tasks;
  - —the skills of implementation; and
- Death—the acceptance of my finitude with subjects in
  - —understanding the limitations of my life;
  - —the practices of humility;

–the courage to risk and sacrifice; and

–the tranquilities of happy dying.

■ Designing social medicine for the 1990s

Although we want to see substantial change in high technology medical leadership, we offer little direct criticism of what is wrong. Our strategy rather is to affirm one foundational tenet of Western medical science: therapy without evaluation is quackery.

And to use the medical science of epidemiology to ask our policy makers, "Is this work directed at priorities selected by all the people? How do you know that?"

Old Doc recently returned from a 40th class reunion where he met a few of his medical school colleagues. The vision and concerns expressed herein have little support among the friends of his youth. TWCs however are free to stand in a small minority of their fellows when that is their choice.

Old Doc: Beyond the golden age of medicine

MEDICAL STUDENT: Doctor, you've been out of medical school 40 years now. What are your reflections on society during that period?

OLD DOC: From World War II and the atom bomb through the 1980s we have experienced, either by fleeing or by embracing, the perturbation of shifting into a new paradigm of one global village. Among other things, we have witnessed the spread of cancerous suburban sprawl, the breakup of the nuclear family, and fundamentalist churches seeking the moral leadership of Christendom.

MEDICAL STUDENT: What about the field of medicine and health care?

OLD DOC: For us doctors it has been a golden age of miracles in technological medicine, prestige and authority. But the world is asking for more primary care of our community ills.

MEDICAL STUDENT: Where should medical education go from here?

OLD DOC: We could begin by applying the two principles of convergence and miniaturization. By convergence I mean that research and training should be concentrated in a few tertiary centers.

MEDICAL STUDENT: You mean that all medical and nursing schools in one city should share their resources rather than compete?

OLD DOC: I mean that no tertiary care facility should have fewer than 100 cases of anything. Then every patient in a tertiary center should be part of a controlled clinical trial, in which the control arm carries the best proven state of the art.

MEDICAL STUDENT: How would you apply the miniaturization principle in training doctors?

OLD DOC: We would use the neighborhood as a laboratory for engaging the student in learning to supervise a multidisciplinary team in which community, clients, students and mentors participate. Control groups and publication of learnings would engage clients and neighborhood residents in original research. Training of professionals in serving comprehensive human development would be integrated with timely learnings of the basic sciences. After that some would go on to specialty training in medicine, surgery and other fields of social and biological sciences.

MEDICAL STUDENT: I think the old preceptorship model, with a student assigned to a medical practice, might be more specifically suited to medical learning.

OLD DOC: That has become inefficient and very expensive. The student just gets in the way. What we must teach, and the student must experience, is working in a multidisciplinary team with responsibility for all aspects of family and community and their ailments.

MEDICAL STUDENT: How can this be organized?

OLD DOC: The neighborhood holon house could be the structure to coordinate and integrate research, training and quality control. When we link global resources with local needs, we have methods that work. We can bring in the necessary expertise to create new curricula.

MEDICAL STUDENT: The holon house might be like the medieval Abbey which was the repository of culture and science that helped the community around it.

OLD DOC: Looking to the future, such training at the grassroots has greater potential for serving the health needs of more people around the world than does our current overemphasis on technological wizardry.

Health and medicine

Health is more than individual quality of life and always has been. When great plagues of typhus or tuberculosis killed most of us, the social dimensions of health were plain to see. If my neighbor became ill, I most likely would be next. Today most of the epidemic plagues are controlled in time of peace and in economically prospering neighborhoods. Rather today it is the social plagues of mind and spirit which cause most of our disability days and shortening of life.

Abandoned elders, accidents, addictions (including alcoholism), adolescent pregnancy, assaults, burglary, deteriorating housing and neighborhoods, functional illiteracy, untreated high blood pressure, domestic violence, and youth suicide—all are social diseases. They weaken our life together. They all are more common in poor neighborhoods, but also are well known in the "best" neighborhoods.

Medical heroes then and now [75]

"Politics is medicine writ large," argued the great pathologist Rudolf Virchow (1821-1902). In terms of disability and early death, social forms and community priorities affect the length and quality of all our lives today far more than do deadly bacteria, viruses, or natural aging processes. The health sciences, in dialogue with anthropology, architecture, criminology, epidemiology, macro- and microeconomics, sociology, statistics, (and a dozen other specialty fields of knowledge in need of wholeness), can make major contributions to our shared quality and length of life. Many of their gifts already are filed in electronic and print data bases, untested in real human neighborhoods. Many more await worldwide development of local social laboratories of the sort cited as examples here.

Virchow was German medicine, German science, German politics, for 50+ years. He exemplified the social as well as the scientific ideal of the physician. He founded and edited *Archiv*, the premier journal of medical studies. His *Cellular Pathology* transformed medical thinking. He organized a national medical society which opposed politically the absolutist Bismarck. Today he would be called a liberal; then a revolutionary. He was for disarmament and against the death penalty. He remained obstinately skeptical of the germ theory (as did Florence Nightingale). He labelled typhus epidemics, tuberculosis, and scurvy "artificial" illnesses, meaning concentrated among the poor. Dysentery, malaria, and pneumonia were "natural" epidemics, evenly distributed among all classes. Virchow did not favor basic or pure knowledge; he believed science should be "useful."

His studies in social medicine and social epidemiology appeared in his journal, *Die Medizinische Reform* under its masthead, "the physician is the natural attorney of the poor." "Medicine is a social science," he argued, "and politics is nothing but medicine on a grand scale." He was elected to city, state and national governments. His democratic stance, bitter opposition to Bismarck, and his populist views later would lead the Nazis to remove him from the German medical pantheon.

The title of Leon Eisenberg's speech to elite Robert Wood Johnson scholars was "Rudolf Karl Ludwig Virchow, Where Are You Now That We Need You?" Can we see today's medical heroes as they might resemble Virchow in the causes he chose? There is a growing unanimity among physicians that is a counterpart to the kind of consensus prevalent among physicians in Virchow's time, but around a different issue. Now some health professionals argue that political resistance to nuclear war has become an ethical imperative of medicine.

■ Involving patients in setting policy [76]

Our Patient Advisory Council (of Milton Seifert, Jr., M.D. & Associates) is a medical practice advocate group of patients and health-care professionals. They consult together to provide superior health-care services in a cost-effective manner, while preserving the personal nature of the doctor-patient relationship. We hope to create a network of family medical practices that would be dedicated to partnership enhancement, as an integral part of patient care and practice management.

Partnership as embodied in the Patient Advisory Council is complex. Elements include communication, support, trust, commitment and negotiation. Caring and trust are most necessary in the situations in which it is most painful to accomplish. We search for true partnership where each person has an equivalent participation in the process as well as the outcome. The council meets monthly to address management and patient-care issues of the family practice. Practitioners and patients are seen as co-examiners, co-therapists, co-educators and co-researchers.

A visitor would be able to see a normal family medical practice which produces its outcomes by means of partnership interactions. We emphasize the whole person in the context of families. We use a Language of Negotiation in all transactions. The practice should be seen as a laboratory of health-care delivery, working on the problems that are applicable to the whole system of health care.

Our tools and methods include: the Partnership Enhancement Form (combination charge ticket and diagnostic checklist), the Language of Negotiation (less pejorative and simpler than standard medical language), participation with a Patient Advisory Council, the use of a Health Educator to teach life-management skills based on the Twelve Step program, team function and interdependence. A prototype is Alcoholics Anonymous.

We believe that organizing the practice in partnership with patients and the community has an important local effect. With our routinized data collection in a laboratory medical practice we create a model health care system. Our main gap is in organizing a larger community and transfering our technology to other medical practices.

We would like to see health care as a unifying force for the various community institutions and facilities. The impact of our work would be enhanced if all community and family decisions were considered to be health decisions.

We're a community group made up of one physician, several members of his office staff, and 50 of his patients. We've joined together to make our medical practice more successful as a business and more responsive to the needs of individual patients. We like to think of our approach as cooperative consumerism. Each year we sponsor a community health fair. We invite the public to sessions on health-related subjects ranging from death and dying to interfamily relations. Our talent-bank registry is a system for matching people needing help to other people able to provide it. We've been able to arrange transportation to the doctor's office, physical therapy at home, home care for invalids, baby-sitting, and other services.

■ M.A.S.H. (Mutual Aid Self Help) groups [77]

The Self Help Clearinghouse at St. Clares-Riverside Medical Center since 1981 has provided information to find or start self-help groups of persons calling a statewide hotline for assistance with addictions, bereavement, chronic illness, disabilities, parenting concerns, and other stress-filled life situations. A directory of national self-help groups lists over 3200 local groups and 500 national or demonstration groups.

■ When the professor encourages community care [78]

Of 175 freshmen accepted into the University of Washington School of Medicine in Seattle in 1980, 30 had expressed interest in working with the medically underserved in the community and joined an elective Community Health Advancement Program (CHAP). To help these few students sustain their commitment to

169

community-oriented health-care needs of the poor, CHAP offered weekly meetings to present information. CHAP sponsored quarterly seminars for the entire medical school. A major part of CHAP's effort supported a half-day clinic each week in a low-income section of Seattle. Here students from all four years of medical school worked within the resources of a well staffed and funded quality outpatient practice. The clinic's regular staff followed up the care begun by the medical students. CHAP students started several small special projects: blood-pressure screening in the market place, home visits to the elderly, health care to inmates in jail, services to migrant workers and Native Americans, and overseas work in the developing world. In these ways CHAP sustained students' original commitment in the face of the intense indoctrination toward high tech specialty medicine which worldwide is the fate of most medical students.

Results: 61 percent of CHAP students, and only 19 percent of non-CHAP students chose family practice residencies, taken as a proxy measure of commitment to community-oriented primary care. (The two groups were matched by age and sex and evidence of prior experience in community service.) Of non-CHAP students with no evidence of prior community service or orientation, only 9 percent chose further training in family practice. Medical students at the University of Washington must complete a research project to graduate. CHAP students were much more likely to do community-oriented kinds of research than were non-CHAP students. Further tracking will tell how this group of doctors now entering practice get on with their careers.

The senior professor of medicine sponsoring the CHAP project has served in scores of overseas short-term medical missions, and enthusiastically promotes Community Oriented Primary Care as socially responsible medicine for the U.S. and for the developing world.

■ A challenger of our health care system—the nutty MD[79]

Imagine a bunch of serious medical students running around Harvard medical school in assorted clown costumes, learning how to be Nutty Doctors under the tutelage of Patch Adams, M.D., in pony tail, handlebar mustache, and rubber nose. Thirty-eight-year-old Patch (Hunter) Adams has given such "humor in healing" seminars at Harvard and other schools. He works at the Gesundheit Institute with his wife and a dozen other physicians and friends.

They operate out of a group home in suburban Washington, D.C. Over the past 12 years they have provided free health care for 15,000 people. They challenge the absurdities of our pharmaceutical-medical-industrial complex: They charge no fees, carry no malpractice insurance, and accept no third-party payments. They reduce iatrogenic (physician-caused) illness by trying gentle solutions first and following patients closely. "The whole point of Gesundheit is a dialogue of friendship," Patch says. "I talk to people about self-responsibility—nutrition, exercise, faith and family.... It's the most exciting thing I do. Self-responsibility is very broad, from picking up the trash to involvement in the nuclear issue, to voting." Clowning and theater shows are part of a fund-raising campaign for a new hospital facility in rural West Virginia set up as a land trust owned by the constituency it serves, with a range of traditional and alternative medical services. They are looking for 30-40 staff persons who will commit themselves for the first two years of the experiment.

■ The dragons behind adolescent pregnancy[80]

Forty resident clergymen initiated the Mid-North Indianapolis Partnership (MIP) in 1982 to foster the economic, social, and cultural development of this zone in which 100,000 persons of quite varied income, background, and expectations live. Here is a nice mix of rather poor and very rich, of young and old, of black and white, of native born and newcomers. Supporting the Partnership were business people, public officials, voluntary bodies, and grassroots block club level leaders: the kind of four-sector coalitions (private, public, voluntary, and local sectors) which are essential to urban development.

It does not do to leave a live dragon out of your calculations, if you live near him.

In 18 months of activity, MIP had public meetings each 90 days for a broad participation in discerning directions. Task forces addressed particular concerns for better housing, elders' engagement, and media leadership in building a prospering, secure, lively community. One task force formed in January 1983 to look at youth engagement. When the youth of this task force selected for their focus interest adolescent pregnancy and its effect on education, I joined the action.

In science we look not only at what is measured (in this case a health action in an urban social laboratory of 100,000 persons), but also at the methods of measurement and at the measurer. My interest was that of a physician retired a decade ago from 20+ years

171

practice as a pathologist to explore community medicine at the neighborhood level.

The health action

A health action in this social laboratory began January 1983 with lunch in the Institute of Cultural Affairs (ICA) office. Eight agency and local neighborhood leaders asked, "How can we involve our youth?" With some fears expressed about allowing youth too much scope, they agreed to launch a task force led by youth in the next MIP 90-day public meeting. The Indianapolis Urban League called an initial meeting with youth in February. Three youth leaders said their concern was teenage pregnancy as it affects education. Several adult leaders and youth agreed to support a program addressing this concern in Indianapolis.

Our project was to be a three-year coalition of 10 community task forces coordinated by a youth steering committee. In February, two youth attended a Community Leadership Training Seminar at Butler University, which is in the center of the MIP zone. These youth leaders then prepared a final draft of an abstract for a three-year youth-led project on Adolescent Pregnancy in Mid-North Indianapolis to be presented in Dallas at the 1983 Annual Meeting of the American Public Health Association. Half a dozen youth held weekly late afternoon meetings to prepare publicity and plan recruiting for a "Rabbit Rap" sponsored by the Urban League. One prominent black leader strongly opposed the plan. The youth went ahead.

75 Interviews

In March it became evident to ICA staff that recruiting by the local youth leaders for the symposium was insufficient in concept and energy to launch the program. Hence ICA staff designed and conducted 75 interviews with a variety of persons in MIP. We learned that youth and adults in all parts of the zone agreed that clarification of group values is a current local mandate—how children are to be raised, appropriate family social structures, and future-looking images of masculine/feminine ontology.

Fears of cultural genocide appeared as an issue dividing black men and women. The women's revolution, weak as it is in the black community, appeared to be the troop base for any nonagency approach in this sensitive arena.

Interviewees saw public schools as the structure for dealing with

Under ideal laboratory conditions an experimental animal will behave exactly as it pleases.

the issues, although present content of school life is inadequate to address the tragically growing numbers of pregnant adolescents. Youth sense abandonment by adults as a cause of this tragedy and are moved by compassion for the individual girls getting pregnant. Elders see wide societal structural collapse and seek new structuring as the needed response. All those interviewed agreed that the financial and emotional responsibility attending jobs for teenagers would be helpful. Continence as a moral issue seemed irrelevant to all but a very few traditionalists.

The youth-led symposium

In the symposium, attended by 35 persons, the youth experienced for the first time the power they can exercise when they get needed skills in leadership. Several agency staff professionals were offended by being asked to participate in group processes under youth leadership and left early from the day-long forum.

Mandates for action came out of the interviews and symposium, but no troops—significantly, no teen or adult troops stepped forward to implement the plans. Plans were mapped for events addressing: a new image of a responsible male role, media portrayal of responsible sexuality, interagency coordination, and parents and teens talking about life values.

Blocks to action

Dragons of urban reality quickly attacked our dream. Awakened, educated black leaders appeared isolated in jobs where they have little freedom to seek broad-based support for needed new coalitions and group actions. Many parents seemed to cherish illusions of the power of old authority to protect and guide youth. The youth leaders all moved on to colleges elsewhere. The Urban League fell into funding and staff cutbacks and dropped this program. Many agency staff seemed bound to limited objectives set by funding constraints and interests of their supporters. Churches and pastors were minimally interested. In a subsequent statewide Youth Congress, youth leaders generally rated jobs, job training, safe streets, and safe schools as the issues more important to them than adolescent pregnancy.

Youth saw themselves as isolated from each other and from the adult world, including parents. They look primarily to schools for structures within which to order the world. The curriculum of their schools seems remote from youths' passionate concerns over jobs, job training, creating values-clarifying dialogues with elders, and preserving the unique cultural gifts of ethnic groups while fitting these groups to use emerging new technologies.

What, then, shall we do?

A viable response to these concerns and blocks might be youth leadership training in public schools around issues broader than adolescent pregnancy. Public health technologies taught and practiced in the schools might be a curriculum for bringing together both youth and adult leaders for joint work in effective use of newer urban social methods.

The school as a social laboratory could give leadership experience to youth directed at major social issues of urban living. There seems to be support among both youth and adults for an investigative approach by youth working with adult colleagues in common real life issues. This may be the clue given us by the general enthusiasm among adults and youth for reporting our MIP experience at the annual meeting of the American Public Health Association in Dallas.

In this eight-month social laboratory experiment we learned that our youth want to talk with their elders about values. Although they are moved initially by compassion for the poor adolescent who gets pregnant, they want to work with skilled adults in bringing about real social change in local neighborhoods—they insist that priority be set for jobs, secure schools and neighborhoods, and relevant education including social and leadership skills.

With national attention now focused on the meaningful engagement of youth in the whole social process, the time may have come to engage local residents of all ages in learning to work together for the public health, prosperity, and security at the most local level—the neighborhood and the neighborhood school.

Chapter 8

ily Clusters and
n of Wholeness

NEIGHBORHOOD CARETAKER
converging science, art, and vocation

1522 Grand Ave. #4C
St. Paul, MN 55105
(612) 698-0349

Editors: U. Dyson, MBA
Elizabeth C. Dyson, MD
Burton C. Dyson, MD

n previous ch   he players and
methods for c   . Intentional
families of man   s of community which integ   into a new
common sense ne   ne shared
planet. In this cha   our own
experience and unde.   l family
clusters as the core g.   ...ce* to give
practical form to a vis.

■ The holon house: A missio   ..y cluster

MEDICAL STUDENT: Doctor, What is a holon house?

OLD DOC: It is going to be part of my social laboratory.

MEDICAL STUDENT: Would people live in as well as work in the Holon House?

OLD DOC: They will live with their children, aged parents if congenial, and half a dozen other compatible family units. The common bond for living together for a decade or more will be a covenant to a disciplined life of service to neighborhood and world.

MEDICAL STUDENT: I read in your prospectus that each family would be self-supporting and own a share of the house. What would that cost?

MEDICAL STUDENT

---

mandate: an authoritative command. "Such and such had better happen, or else!" In this case, the mandate arises from the awakened consciousness of persons living in a core group.

OLD DOC: For a family of four persons there would be an investment of $50,000-$100,000, which at present interest rates would require monthly payments of $400-$800.

MEDICAL STUDENT: What activities would go on there?

OLD DOC: Use your imagination. With the hydroponic garden, computer room, and neighborhood business, this could be a model for future urban family living, with work space on the premises as well as flexible provision for security, privacy of family rooms, sharing of tools and kitchen.

MEDICAL STUDENT: Solar heating, pet rooms, and microwave cooking?

OLD DOC: As the occupants decide together. Personal freedom is a cornerstone of this group home of several sharing families.

MEDICAL STUDENT: Will unmarried adults be welcomed?

OLD DOC: Of course, as long as they pay their share and uphold the covenanted life-style.

MEDICAL STUDENT: Would the residents draw up a sort of Mayflower Compact?

OLD DOC: That's a great image.

MEDICAL STUDENT: How is the holon house related to the social lab you talk about?

OLD DOC: A laboratory is a work place. In a laboratory we test new models; measure change; and document assumptions, procedures and outcomes. Also, we invent new ways to improve things. The holon house is a three-dimensional model. Every neighborhood of 5000 persons needs a holon house with about 25 persons who will be experimenters in caring for a neighborhood for a decade or more.

MEDICAL STUDENT: Like the old-time resident parson, family doctor, and newspaper editor living together under one roof?

OLD DOC: Or a factory worker, school teacher, nuclear physicist, nurse, and two retired persons with their extended families. Join us and work out the design. You'll be helping to create new work- and life-styles for your unborn children.

MEDICAL STUDENT: Doctor, the people I know who are concerned about neighborhood generally have been moved to action by some injustice or tragedy that affects everybody, like a school closing or a traffic disaster. Then they organize. Few have the sense of obligation or commitment to serve that community year in, year out, just to make it a better place for everybody to live in. What is the life-style that prevents burnout? Is the secret in the group?

OLD DOC: I think the secret, as you call it, lies in the strength of commitment of each family to the mission of the group which nurtures, disciplines, and sustains the family.

MEDICAL STUDENT: What would the life-style of those who live or work in the neighborhood holon house look like?

OLD DOC: The families would not agree to a code of beliefs. But each would have some daily way of rehearsing the way life is: It is *all* good. This daily act can be solitary or group, spoken or in silence. They might wear a symbol or garb (e.g., a blue shirt) to remind them of their decision to lead a life of service and profound happiness.

MEDICAL STUDENT: I can do that living alone. What prevents the group from becoming a cozy fellowship escaping the hard realities of the world?

OLD DOC: A good point. Along with the spirit dimension they need the political and economic. The weekly planning meeting, using hard intellectual and scientific methods, will keep social theory grounded in the local situation.

MEDICAL STUDENT: If the economic base is self-support, as you insist, families would spend most of their time in their own particular necessary work of the world. For me that would be clinical practice. For you, in retirement, it is telling stories of new possibilities.

OLD DOC: And one more thing. As John Wesley said, earn all you can, save all you can, give all you can. To realize our common humanity, while living in the local community, families need to support with time, talents, and money some global network that links the regions of the world in a coordinated building of a healthy, full life for all.

Starting a holon community

MEDICAL STUDENT: Doctor, what are the operating principles of a multifamily holon house that will make it work anywhere?

OLD DOC: Ours is an evolving experimental model. Replicating it is not like taking out a franchise. It must begin with local discovery and planning to keep a balanced social process, with the needed linkages to the city and world.

MEDICAL STUDENT: What are the main elements?

OLD DOC: Begin with the six to a dozen founding families who come together weekly for planning and a celebrative common meal. In these meetings they consider all the financial, property, organizational, and social components of their own model.

MEDICAL STUDENT: What about the story that will attract new

families, especially those of nonwhite races since we want people of diverse backgrounds and ages?

OLD DOC: Think big in dreams of the spirit and mission, and conservatively in terms of financing. Focus on the autonomy of the family resident-owners and their responsibility to participate in corporate decision making. Include the neighborhood and a global network in the shared ownership of the holon experiment.

MEDICAL STUDENT: Say more about conservative financing.

OLD DOC: Foundational to the holon community is shared financial investment (with only the financial risk that each family can afford) in a building, or cluster of buildings, and a decade-long commitment to the experiment. A reserve fund created to buy back owners' shares preserves each family's freedom to move if they must. This addresses head-on the shallow covenants which allow bedhopping, multiple liaisons, tearing apart the fabric of our society. In the holon community we want to work at the grand possibilities of marriage.

MEDICAL STUDENT: You mean with money on the line, every resident-owner has a vested interest in preserving the financial and family stability of every other owner, or they all might go bankrupt. The holon community, then, is a practical, functional care structure to preserve, and redefine, the nuclear family as a global resource!

OLD DOC: So, the fundamental principles are shared financial investment, consensus decision-making, pluriform life-styles, and the call to experiment with social care structures which will become working prototypes in the emerging global culture.

A Christian confessional model of community [81]

Architect Richard Hawksley's book, *Settlements of Shalom,* suggests that human works are as much creation as are the primordial works of God, and sees architecture as "a way of being." All theories of architecture, he maintains, are based on an understanding of community, an interdependent group of people living under the same government. While there is a pretense of diversity and pluralism, pragmatic materialism dominates our majority culture. The bioregionalists, Hawksley says, are correct in developing technologies of local community, but they are deficient in their inadequate comprehension of the confessional basis of community.

Intentional covenanted local community is an essential response to the call to live in justice, sharing time and space, talents, concerns, and prayer to transform the dominant culture which increasingly abuses both humans and the land. The general American view is that land is a commodity; this view leads directly to systematic joblessness, exportation of work, expanding public and private bureaucracies, and then to organized abuse of the Third World, war, pestilence and death. A covenanted group of ten people can be economically self sustaining on a farm. However, such groups are perceived as marginal to the social process and have little power to transform the prevailing materialistic covenants of America.

Urban covenanted settlements require interchange at least of information with communities outside to avoid suffocation, according to Hawksley. The architect/author of this master's thesis offers drawings of his home neighborhood in Kent, Ohio detailed down to the trees and hundred-year-old buildings in his city block. He makes the point that the urban covenanted group dreaming of land trusts, local currency, house schools, and other benefits of the intentional life, needs the participation of a sympathetic architect. Why are there so very few American "come and see" working models of urban covenanted neighborhood communities? Only now are some theological mandates appearing to Make It Happen.

Chapter headings in this book include: the confessional basis for communities; a Christian model of community; dwelling norms: architecture of the Christian community; building houses and planting vineyards.

■ Celebrating the common life

The regular celebration of life together in any intentional community is more fundamental than any economic or social purpose of that group, be it a work team, task force, residential core community, or family. At one end of the celebrative spectrum is the dish of ice cream and a reflective conversation to affirm the hard work of a task force and refresh the spirit. At the other end is the regular celebration of life in a community to acknowledge in a structured way the relationship of each person to every other and to the Mystery itself. It is a way to rehearse the way life really is. It is a secular-religious occasion for profound refreshment.

The Earthcare Indianapolis core group, including guests, gathers each weekend for one and a half hours of feasting, singing, conversation, hearing a bit of what everyone present has been doing, and ritually symbolizing our participation in the human family. It reminds us all that the spirit is grounded in the mundane.

179

Leadership roles are rotated. Two people act as hosts, to welcome everybody, provide the context and lead the gathering through the steps of the event. One leads the singing and asks someone to light the candle which represents the presence of the Transcendent Other. The other host gives a ten-minute prepared witness on some aspect of his/her experience of life in the past week. A brief period of silence may be interrupted by someone else also wanting to share a profound experience. Before the meal, a ritual sharing of bread and water symbolizes our interdependence with the earth and the human family.

The meal itself, often a potluck, is an occasion of relaxed conversation and laughter. When most people are through eating, the host asks if there are any birthdays or anniversaries of marriage to celebrate. The birthday person stands; and, in answer to questions from someone else, states which birthday it is, the most significant event of the past year, and some expectation for the coming year. The questioner then says a few words that affirm the birthday person, and everybody sings: "We celebrate your being here with being itself in history." Similarly the anniversary couple stands to answer the same ritual questions; and, after the address to the couple by the questioner, the whole group sings: "We celebrate your family as mission from God to history."

Other events celebrated include deaths, the coming of age, and other rites of passage. For each, the uniqueness of the individual and the goodness of life are affirmed.

Each person around the table shares something of our ordinary activities of the past week as a way of reminding ourselves that we are grounded in the real world, each one connected to many networks of people. The goodness of our daily expenditure, whatever it has been, is acknowledged in song: "Let each one announce the word... my life is pleasing to the Lord."

The group is reminded of its global relatedness by hearing news items from other parts of the world, taken from network newsletters. It symbolizes its local connectedness in a vivacious dance, the grand right and left, around the room. The celebration ends with:
"For all that has been, thanks.
To all that will be, yes.
Goodnight."

Old Doc: The cosmopolitan common meal

MEDICAL STUDENT: Doctor, if, as you say, the holon house is to be an outpost against the increasing complexity and danger of urban life, I can understand why its covenant calls for self-support and resident ownership. But I do not see the importance you give to the weekly common meal.

OLD DOC: In our time people are looking for bridges between the rational and the nonrational; between the sacramental and the mundane. The family, eating together in a formal common meal, rehearses its self-understanding in its story, symbols, rituals, and perhaps songs. The same is true of the neighborhood house when residents and neighbors eat together in a weekly ritual.

MEDICAL STUDENT: What if the neighbors are Moslem, or Buddhist, or agnostic? Wouldn't a structured symbolic meal be a sectarian hindrance to the unity needed for wholeness in the community?

OLD DOC: I think not. All the symbols and most of the stories of the great universal religious systems, which have been validated in living experience by each generation, point to a common way, truth and life. None of the world's saints have killed or ranted against unbelievers. And we all have a need to touch again regularly and together the deep mysteries of life and death.

MEDICAL STUDENT: It seems to me that working on our interpersonal relationships, which can build or destroy a community, may be a better way of building unity.

OLD DOC: As we create an outpost of wholeness in the midst of urban disorder, we will be facing primordial evil, and we will need to experience healing, shalom, the Void, the real Eden to which we struggle to return.

MEDICAL STUDENT: I am a secular man of science. How could I experience the healing that religious people might find there?

OLD DOC: You may not be as secular in your heart as you are in your head. No matter. Every great religious system has a drive to become secular: The holy invades and transforms the mundane. With whatever images are agreed upon, your generation of secular man will negotiate the words of the ritual to express your own experience of sin and grace, humility, gratitude and compassion.

MEDICAL STUDENT: But why is the weekly common meal the one structure you insist is key to the social design of the neighborhood house? It is almost like saying the corporation board luncheon is the key structure for the board's effectiveness.

OLD DOC: In a way, yes. It is the business lunch which frequently launches and sustains corporations, official missions and ventures. Most hospital work groups make time to eat together. Eating and drinking together develops openness and acceptance among those participating.

MEDICAL STUDENT: The common meals I know about, the Passover Seder and Communion, are full of sacred liturgy and symbols that point to divine intervention in ordinary existence, which is something the business work group usually doesn't have.

OLD DOC: It could have, if it understands that we all live from the expenditure of others. The neighborhood house must rehearse the way life really is in order to keep the group humble. We need the powerful, deep images and symbols of the Beyond if we are to penetrate the spiritual chaos of urban settlement. The Beyond is experienced in the daily mundane: around the work bench, or in eating together.

MEDICAL STUDENT: If each neighborhood creates its own mix of poetry, symbols and rituals, some will be more Christian, others more Moslem or Buddhist. Won't this compete with traditional religious services?

OLD DOC: It shouldn't. Our world needs leaders with strong roots in their own traditions, and I expect that many who are regularly at the holon house weekly meal also will be faithful attendants at their own church, synagogue, temple or mosque.

MEDICAL STUDENT: In this complex world we will need something radically secular and universal to shift our consciousness to a deeper understanding of our relationship to the planet.

■ The spirit journey toward community wholeness

Part I: The journey map

"Who is my neighbor?" (Luke 10:25-37) when asked seriously, is a quest for the experience of the holy, our common profound center. The old answer told of a good man of no social standing who helped a victim of robbery. The answer ended with the instruction, "Go and do as he did." In the late 20th century this instruction still grounds our vision of wholeness.

"Now who is my neighbor?" is a quest for wholeness in our multilevel experience of home, occupation, life transitions, and our emerging planetary consciousness. New norms of perception and behavior are being created and tested as we grow from decade to decade. Our upward spiral of personal and societal consciousness is blocked in the ways we put meaning into our daily occupation, our developing regional and global systems of interaction. No messiah will lead us out of this wilderness experience. Our human freedom and responsibility place new tasks before each of us and all of us.

Upholders and innovators of wholeness

All of us want to experience wholeness. Most of us want to discover the norms of full humanness and live by them in a maturing of development.

Some of us are less interested in discovering norms than in creating the norms. The creativity is amoral. Sometimes the creativity moves toward responsible leadership of the whole society. Just as often it manifests as socially destructive crime or personally destructive psychosis. In this entire group are saints, sages, and heroes who lead society to new levels of wholeness. Here also are criminals who lead society to new cohesion through developing law and social controls. Caring for psychotic and other blighted souls among us leads the whole society to new compassion, new wholeness. Both the few norm inventors and the many norm upholders serve an ever-evolving human wholeness, fueled by terrible human struggle.

There is a spiral circularity in our growth levels as persons and as societies. While mastering the knowledge, attitudes and skills of belonging in society, young children struggle intensely to grasp or create empowering myths. Grandparents are the children's natural allies in developing their own myths. Norm-setters in each generation struggle to break through to higher, more authentic levels of myth and world mission that in turn affect our belonging, participation, vocation, and values in life.

The levels

Level 1. We belong to the primal community of childhood home. Then in grade-school years we begin to choose our own affinity groups. Assemblies, ceremonies, symbols, the honoring of shared founders and heroes, and their belief systems: All serve as the social glue of tradition within these groups. We cannot live alone.

Level 2. We participate in solemn rites of passage: marrying, burying, bar mitzvah—rites within a nation, church or association. The rites publicly honor the persons we have chosen to be. We are transformed in these passages.

Level 3. We can share the experience of the transformed or holy life by teaching the tradition to youth or newcomers, by working in secular or sacred missions. Without this grounding, under testing we quickly fall into burnout and despair.

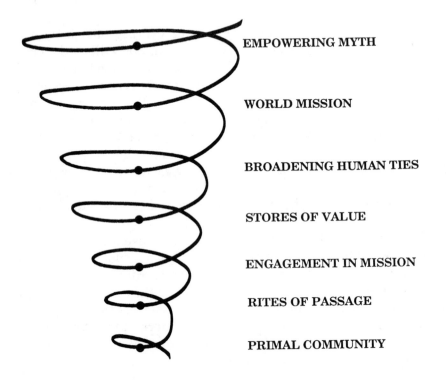

EMPOWERING MYTH

WORLD MISSION

BROADENING HUMAN TIES

STORES OF VALUE

ENGAGEMENT IN MISSION

RITES OF PASSAGE

PRIMAL COMMUNITY

FIGURE 8-1: A SPIRAL OF GROWTH

Level 4. We build citadels of style, stores of value: personal and family estates, edifices, organizations, and bodies of cultural wisdom which inform our chosen life-style and life mission.

Level 5. We can dedicate our daily occupation to this holy quest, through a work ethic, by vows of poverty, or by entering the middle or upper class. This further grounds our selfhood, our ties with the whole human family.

Level 6. We can serve a world mission: imperial adventure, multinational business, ecclesiastical enterprises, as we create and maintain nations, religions, sects and philosophies. When old values fail, either we redirect our world mission, or we perish with the passing of our old values.

Level 7. We struggle to embody and perhaps reformulate an empowering myth, its underlying systematized beliefs, and governance; so we preserve the wonder of our culture and life to future generations.

Where the upward spiral is blocked now

The 20th century revolutions (youth, women's, scientific, ethical, cosmological) have shaken our society at all levels of development. The crisis of today is a crisis among the few who are called now to set new norms. We have completed only part of our design for a new social vehicle and new spirit modes for the 21st century. Our temptation is to perseverate (rehearse again and again earlier victories) in the old levels. Like everyone else, we fear breaking out of the old ways. Truly we fear the call to redefine a global mission that will express our current planet-wide empowering myth, change our personal and group behavior, and save the planet.

Where we have been

Let us look back at the 20th century, at the work the few norm-setters have already accomplished. Then we can look at where we are arrested, and where we can move ahead.

Move back along the spiral of experienced wholeness to level 1: symbols, heroes, founders of affinity groups. Early in the 20th century, scholars of all major cultures had compiled an ecumenical library of common and powerful healing stories, images and affirmations: Christian cross and Buddhist lotus, the nameless One of Moses and of Mohammad, profound insights of Hindu consciousness and of Greek rationality, half forgotten truth from Zoroaster and Lao Tsu, wisdom of Kung Fu, spirit visions of the Pacific peoples. Great teachers packaged these integrative reflections for 20th century everyman, widening our selection of affinity groups.

In level 2, some solemn rites found a new home among those taking this theological revolution to the world. Liturgies, singing, dancing and drama draw on new treasures of East and West to express and celebrate a group's experience of new wholeness. Still to be developed are generally meaningful ceremonies of sexual

185

coming of age; of responsible erotic relationships; covenants of child and elder care; sanctions protecting the weak, the stranger, the peculiar, and our shared natural resources/environment. Also needing public honor are the transitions from childhood conformity to:

- learning and education, both in youth and in adult years,
- new tasks in each decade,
- times spent in reflection, and
- returning to new work and relationships.

Consider level 3, experiencing the transformed or holy life in teaching and working in the tradition of a particular intentional group (more precisely, a holy nation) in a wide variety of settings. Hundreds of service organizations invite participation with the option of moving as far as one desires into the core and governance of the organization.

When sustained by participating in their own organization, members can: broaden their span of affection and interest, enlarge their engagement in the life and work of the whole community, increase their collaboration with sibling organizations, and converge in ongoing, pluriform, norm-inventing movements.

When several groups collaborate to focus on a major task like mass urban housing, they experience wholeness in building citadels of style and stores of value (level 4). Their networks involve the poor, their organizers, religious communities, investment bankers, statesmen and health workers. This is a level 4 experience of wholeness. The networks involved extend across boundaries of class, age and belief systems.

A key question remains: How can this great work develop into a shared experience of authentic human growth?

We are blocked in levels 5, 6 and 7: daily occupation, world mission, and empowering myth, respectively. In our daily occupation (level 5) we experience most poignantly a frustrated quest for wholeness. Complaining of "burnout," we look for new and better alternatives to spending our lives repetitively in the service of outworn values.

With practically all other groups today, we are puzzled over level 6, serve a world mission, and level 7, empowering myth. The world is arrested at these gaps. The current structures offered for serving a world mission need a "grandchild"— a third generation of the recent imperial adventure, multinational business, and global ecclesiastical enterprises.

Our planetary norm-setters have not yet defined the authentic governance and economy in state, commerce, church and family needed for a continuing planet. The early seers of the century sensed intuitively this gap, but gave us good questions rather than good answers to the limits it set upon us. The gap still paralyzes us all.

This is also true at level 7, sustaining myth. Entire systems of governance have lost authority, legitimacy and authenticity. Their underlying foundations in myth are felt to be passing away. Now, if children honor parents, generally it is because of personal or natural affection, rather than from any instruction from universal myth or sanctioned duty. If business is conducted honestly, it is out of some inner wholeness of the individuals involved, not from any body of law or common value system. Sovereign governments of nation-states with their unrestrained commercial self-interest and great military power increasingly are seen as enemies of the people and exploiters of the planet rather than as organized defenses against disorder and chaos. Moreover, those promulgating old or new belief systems generally are regarded as minority, divisive, sectarian voices. We have lost what is essential to our wholeness—a common human myth.

We wait for the absolutely original creativity from the Source that gave us the old theological seminars, the revolutionary theories of politics, the collegial nations or orders, the institutes and service organizations of the 1950s-1970s. We wait for a messiah. But alas, there is no messiah. You and I are *it*.

Part II: Creating personal ethics when there is no messiah

There is no messiah. You and I are *it*.

This is terrifying. Shame and weakness, primitive infant level feelings, turn us to jelly inside. We profoundly doubt our sanity. We feel abandoned by all we once trusted for daring to walk ahead of the crowd. It just feels bad to be *it*. But we have a guide.

One person's view

I cite no external law, principle or authority. Rather, in the mode of the new consciousness, I give witness to my own experience, my own thinking.

The guide, Jesus, the man from Nazareth, was not a Christian. Jesus was a Jewish teacher, a rabbi. He was more Jewish than the

Sanhedrin which convicted him of blasphemy ("I have not come to destroy the Law of Moses, but to fulfill the Law. Heaven and earth will pass away, but the Law will be fulfilled"). He was more activist than the political zealots who abandoned him. (His ride into Jerusalem on a donkey dramatized a demand of the radical Zephaniah for the complete transformation of all social and political life.)

He embraced and embodied the revelations of Gautama, Lao Tsu, and Zoroaster. ("I *am* the way, the truth, the light.") He was more Hindu than the Vedas ("Before Abraham was, I *am*": recall "Thou art that.") He was more Muslim than Mohammad— in his vision of a last judgment appalling to all, seen by all as a flash of lightning from the east to the west. The Merciful One of Mohammad is the Father of David, of Isaiah, of Jesus. Islam, submission, calls for man the creature to give up all illusions, after the Mosaic model. Jesus: "All I have is the Father's. All the Father has is mine."

He was more Christian than the popes would ever be, as they came to embody imperfectly the revelation of incarnation, of atonement. Jesus saw that the Father embraces all, makes his rain fall on the just and unjust alike. Since all are loved, there can be no just war; there are no heathen outside an approved system of belief; there is no room for saying to a brother, "Come and know the Lord," for as Zechariah had said earlier, "In that day all shall know the Lord. " Where all are one, to love neighbor is to love God; to shun neighbor is to flee God. He was more radical than any atheist, any rebel: "Call no man Father: You have One Father. "

Modern consciousness and conscience grasp all this. Operating out of the ethical revolution of the early 20th century, the alert mind sees that, in the view of Jesus, no particular religious stance is demanded. Jesus of Nazareth is more than a guide to the way ahead. "Just as I am," is the call to "I and the Father are One. " Against that unconditional invitation, all the demands and self-serving moralities of church and world appear as illusion.

Holy wars, exampled by Iran and Iraq today, are experienced as ashes and death. In the new consciousness touched by a good guide, the heavy financial burdens of churches' "stewardship" point to a needless privileged bureaucracy of ecclesial rulers. The pretensions of holy matrimony are to be questioned, at least regarding many of the reasons often given: sex, security, care of children. (Matrimonial love is decisional, a privileged kind of neighbor love which, when authentic, is an early step on the way to God.) The honor of work is held up to question when we see the crazy values of the commercial world. The promises of the liberals who call others to give to the poor, always at a distance, are exposed as empty.

Any modern man or woman, of whatever cultural background, can say, "I take Jesus of Nazareth as my personal guide" (as did Gandhi). Our 20th century ethics hold up this freedom of persons and affirm this right. We remain loyal to our primal communities, and pull them with us into wider dialogues of conscience and consciousness when we find a way to affirm One God, one world, in each encounter with our neighbor.

Part III: Creating social ethical models when there is no ultimate authority—A bill of rights

In the quest for authentic social structures of a world mission and a current planetary myth, we affirm a Bill of Rights for every person: the pimp, arms merchant, lawyer, pastor coasting into retirement, philandering no good bum (man or woman), scientist, old lady with cancer, you and me.

Just as I am, I have a right to:

1. Belong to some congenial, trustworthy, non-exploiting, strong, caring group. ("Home is where, if you have to go, they have to let you in.") *Any* group which provides this kind of essential belonging is of God, the One.
2. Participate in solemn rites of passage which are meaningful to me. We all need to experiment more with rites, evaluating our experience of transitions, sharing our learnings, holding the archaic values while building in the real now. What shall we do with our erotic lives? Victorian silence is irrelevant in the high school.
3. Get inside, to share fully in, the experience of the transformed life offered by my supporting group.
4. Honor, as I labor with my fellows to build citadels and stores of value. (Sun Tzu: "For serving God or ruling men, there is nothing like stores saved up.")
5. Have my struggle affirmed as I labor to transform my occupation and my daily work.
6. A way of world mission. This can never be offered as a simple "Join Us." Rather, the authentic offer is something like this, "Let me help you discover how your gifts can bring you into an authentic world mission while protecting all your rights as a free, responsible human person."

189

7. A current, empowering myth, created by people who experience new vistas together. What myth may we anticipate from a holon house described earlier?

Any group that does not protect these rights will soon cease to be.

I expect that the sectarian din will quiet when the omega figure of history emerges from the conflict, the radical rabbi of the people Israel, Jesus of Nazareth. There is nothing in any culture, world religion, mystic experience, or wisdom which is not already embodied in Jesus as rabbi of Israel. This mythic man honors us all in our several personal vocations, as we move toward the radical common center. Examples of this movement:

- Homemakers move their own families in order to be caretakers of local community;
- Business people organize and empower sustaining economic structures of local and regional communities, repairing the gaps in the whole social fabric, restoring our balance with the natural world of which humanity is but a part;
- Compassionate groups help the homeless and the excluded to join the repair;
- The thief decides to steal no more, but do honest work with his hands, to have something of his own to give the poor.

Part IV: Creating the critical mass of responsible human beings

A critical mass of responsible human beings and their local shared life and labors must exist before the common mind of the planet gains the next higher level of human consciousness. In honest work the laborer can join the common world mission, creating the critical mass of empowered and loving human beings required for planetary survival. In this shared task we find one God. Recall our starting question: Now who is my neighbor?

Ken Wilber in *A Sociable God* [82] says that at each stage of the development of human consciousness, the next higher stage is prefigured in the symbols of the old stage. The symbols for our planetary wholeness are there: common and powerful healing stories, images, and affirmations from the great world religions and traditions. And let us add the new symbols of earthrise and of the genetic code. We never begin anew. Rather, we stand on the shoulders of giants to reach further to the stars of our human reality. The world now waits for new norm-setters to embody the reaching out and up. With a new structural mission and a new universal myth, we can develop grander ways of belonging, meaningful rites of passage, transformations grounded in our daily occupations, sustaining family structures, relevant stores of value, fulfillment in our vocation of being human. We begin here today.

■ Old Doc: On being order

MEDICAL STUDENT: Doctor, you have mentioned that you have worn a blue shirt to remind yourself of your decision to be an "order" person. Is order a secret society?

OLD DOC: No secret. I use the word order* to point to a social dynamic necessary to sustain any responsible society which needs to be recovered in our time.

MEDICAL STUDENT: You have used the words order, social dynamic, and responsible society. One concept at a time. Order implies a group of people.

OLD DOC: Hippocrates in 300 B. C. spoke of a group of people who took on themselves special obligations to serve and protect society. Medical students upon graduation still make those promises, and so make themselves part of a special order of professional leaders. Consciously they take on a common set of ethical standards. They expect of themselves and each other that they always tell the truth, never do anything that will make a patient worse, and never abandon a patient without arranging care by another competent physician.

In the Middle Ages Columbus was a member of the Third Order of St. Francis, as was Queen Isabella who funded his New World voyage.

MEDICAL STUDENT: But in this century there are multiple revolutions. The old orders seem irrelevant. Where are we going to find some trusted anchors so civilization can go on? Does the world need a new order?

OLD DOC: I think so.

MEDICAL STUDENT: How does the "social dynamic" relate to the new order?

OLD DOC: In every social body there is part of the group that gives leadership, assures that the group prospers, new members are taught group values, and justice is reasonably satisfactory. We call these leaders the Establishment. Then, sooner or later, there is a

---

*order: a group with a mandate, usually from beyond ordinary authority.

Just As I Am I Come

Just as I am, without one plea,

But that all life awaits for me.

My neighbor's need calls me to Thee,

To heal this world I come, I come.

Just as I am, though tossed about,

With many a conflict, many a doubt;

Fightings and fears within, without;

But to Thy feast I come, I come.

Just as I am, without one plea

To principle, law, authority;

The banquet of life is set for me.

With grateful heart I come, I come.

—MODIFIED 1987 FROM THE WORDS OF CHARLOTTE ELLIOTT (1789-1871), SET TO A TUNE OF WILLIAM B. BRADBURY, 1816-1868

group that complains and protests. They challenge. They try to bring change. Call them the Dis-establishment.

Both are necessary to the good working of any social group. But left to themselves, they often take a mutually destructive, adversarial stance. A synthesizing dynamic is needed to move the society into the future.

MEDICAL STUDENT: It sounds like Philosophy 101: thesis then antithesis then a synthesis. Is that what you mean?

OLD DOC: That is too abstract. My term for those who get these sides together is "Trans-establishment" or more simply order. They operate within both the establishment and the disestablishment but belong to neither. They look and feel much like everybody else in their time, but they dream and work for a better way. They are the first to despair over the misfunctioning parts of their world, the first to change their response to the worsening situation, the first to set new styles.

MEDICAL STUDENT: What are some examples?

OLD DOC: The fourth century in Europe was a bad time. The establishment ran everybody. Not much freedom of thought. So some crazy rebels whom we now honor as "the desert fathers" left the cities and went into the desert. There alone in their hermit cells, they created for the first time the intellectual and spiritual foundations for the powerful monastic orders of the next 15 centuries, the power centers for upgrading human life in the whole Western world.

MEDICAL STUDENT: Then they became the establishment.

OLD DOC: And they were challenged by new free spirits who through observation and experimentation disproved their authoritarian dogma and forever shifted spirit and consciousness of a whole culture. After Columbus and Copernicus, people never could go back to the old ideas of earth and sun.

MEDICAL STUDENT: And old William Harvey, when he demonstrated the circulation of the blood, wasn't just discovering new physiology. He was launching a new adventure of the human spirit.

OLD DOC: And since the moon walk we've all experienced another explosion of the human spirit—in a new global consciousness of planetary interconnectedness— in the very midst of the forces we can use to destroy everything.

MEDICAL STUDENT: That is awesome. We need a whole new vocabulary to talk about it, when you consider that all the inventions of every culture now are available to every other culture, for better or worse. Perhaps that is the task of a 20th century order:

exploring ways to give practical forms to the global unity we already have.

OLD DOC: Awesome and costly. It will require the evidence of our lives. Those choosing to be order always have had to abandon altogether the search for security and welcome the risks of living boldly.

MEDICAL STUDENT: What are some of the bold things you look forward to doing in your retirement?

OLD DOC: My bold deeds will be different from yours. The way for each person is unique. We need to honor individual freedom and creativity. Before I die I want to see all over North America health teams who understand themselves to be a 20th century order.

Chapter 9

New Edges of Humanness

Planetary myth and consciousness can't really be said to exist until they find grounding in the social and economic structures of local neighborhoods and communities. Faith and hope nourished from many traditions find lively expression in a new spirit mode. New social vehicles then emerge which take new understandings and build them into new forms of education, housing, finance and other community activities. The stories in this chapter illustrate a dynamic integration of religion and social structure, as the emerging new common sense finds expression in the formation of new local social structures.

■ **Combining new social vehicles, new spirit modes, and new family lifestyles**

Earthcare Indianapolis: Creating a caring net [83]

In 1987 the Earthcare Forum, a monthly meeting of 40+ civic leaders and friends, has named several priorities and directions for the Earthcare program: housing, literacy, conflict resolution, education, youth well-being, general employment and minority employment. These arenas are embodied in the work of the core group in two inner-city neighborhoods as they have initiated programs of housing rehabilitation, community health workers, a reading club, minority youth business, neighborhood ecology task force and leadership development. In this experiment we see a convergence of three emerging trends that give hope for reversing the degradation of the environment and the violence of the city:

194

- A set of core values, including voluntary simplicity, non-violence and a concern for the poor, that promotes a new social ethic;
- A new religious mode that refreshes the human spirit: the church caring for the whole of creation in microcosm;
- A family living-style, seeing "family," in whatever form, as emissary from God to history.

The new social ethic

In reclaiming a neighborhood as a home place, core-family clusters face major challenges. Educated young adults in North America are estranged from the poor and working lower middle class. Rampant consumerism (old fashioned greed) discredits the real power of capitalism to initiate economic development. Factionalism impoverishes environmental action groups that are separated from the concerns of urban systems. Social ecology has become separated from spirituality.

Our covenants must include gentrification without displacement of the poor and improved quality of life as well as property values—through cooperative associations and protection of land. Many questions remain to be answered:

- What proportion of the properties within neighborhood borders does a neighborhood land trust need to control to get the benefits of common action?
- What mix of poor and middle class in a given neighborhood do we need, and how do we avoid tipping in either direction?
- How many and what kinds of supporters do we need to assure the neighborhood cultural style we want AND financial solvency while launching real housing upgrade?
- What is the deepest common motivator among our investing supporters?
- Do we want a members' savings and loan fund to maximize local control of property in our home neighborhoods?

The new religious mode

We see emerging not a new religion (we cannot do without grounding in our own particular communities of faith), but a new mode of profound spiritual refreshment from the regular celebration of life. When we think of the inner core of the classical religions, there comes to mind "poverty, chastity and obedience; contemplation, meditation and prayer." Our covenant can reflect these in the style of voluntary simplicity; in obedience to the Second Command-

Lead, follow, or get out of the way.

—*Olney, Texas*
community slogan

195

ment (about loving the neighbor as oneself); and obeying the implications of the Second Law of Thermodynamics: You put back into the neighborhood, in both spirit and matter, more than what has been taken out, if transformation is to occur.

Great secular preaching from Carl Sagan, David Attenborough, McNeil & Lehrer, Garry Trudeau and many others, gives us much to contemplate, with images and patterns of the living universe, and calls us to a new global mission to care for the whole planet. The church dynamic (distinct from church institutions) has many new faces: business cooperatives, urban land trusts, coalitions for environmental protection, apprenticeship and mentor relationships between generations, spiritual healers. Here the church as a dynamic social force becomes once again a pillar of society. The primal community rests not on divisive belief systems but on a shared vision of human vocation. Prayer is the daily work of envisioning, planning, and paying to make the dreams real.

Threre are three test questions for all the new religious of the church, especially for the family core groups acting as neighborhood caretakers:

- Who is being enriched by our work?
- Are new communities of wonder, gratitude and compassion coming to be?
- Is the earth being healed?

The new family living style

Most people considering marriage and family nowadays are well aware of the major challenges facing them if they want to live in the city:

- collapse of the nuclear family, along with its dream of lifelong romantic love; its pledged care of children, the sick, misfits and aged; with this has come the collapse of the extended family and clan with its backup social and economic supports for all members;
- residential separation by income: middle class families fleeing their poor neighbors, compounding the devastations of poverty, drug abuse, crime and illiteracy;
- current absence of power bases for mission, vocations, or innovations which are not popular, however needed they may be for a healthy people;
- abandoned sick and aged persons: including most of the 1 percent of persons in all classes who suffer severe schizophre-

nia, many of the over 10 percent who at any one time are depressed and the 10 percent who are disabled by alcoholism;
- absence of most males ages 16-25 in many groups among the poor, and males age 65+ in all classes.

Our neighborhood covenant must address these challenges. The nuclear family needs a cooperative, covenanted community to survive. A shared property commitment is one place to start. Co-signing a mortgage loan cements a union as much as words repeated in solemn ceremony. In addition, there can be cooperative structures for child care, authentic roles for teenagers and elders in the larger family of the co-op, strengthened relationships in necessary work and regular celebrations; ties to the land and soil; and a cultural environment which enables all to celebrate and co-create the city of the future.

Our vision of converging science, art and vocation is a reclaimed inner-city neighborhood. This is a practical application of all we have learned in human development around the world, and of the ecological mandates to regenerate our society and planet. It is an exercise in turning matter into spirit.

Base communities in Latin America combine religious and political education[84]

The Catholic Church in Latin America has a whole new form, the base community (*communidad de base*, or neighborhood), that some believe could eventually replace the parish structure. There are an estimated 200,000 such groupings, and they continue to multiply.

In the 1960s thousands of priests, nuns and lay people from North America poured into the villages and cities of Peru, Brazil, Guatemala, and their sister republics. They were appalled by the squalor they discovered and the role of North Americans in perpetuating it. Initiated by the clergy through radio programs, the movement grew under the leadership of trained lay chatechists in every village. People began studying, singing, praying, and discussing local political issues. They combined an informal and participatory style of liturgy; a rediscovery of the Bible (especially the prophetic and critical elements); and vigorous engagement in the politics of peace, disarmament and hunger. Refusing to become another church institution, the movement is a cooperative association of groups of Christians critical of both church and society. Rooted in the particular locale, the groups demonstrate a style of common life that is a collective rather than an individual approach to the problems of economic security, aging, and finding meaning in life. There is a fusing of mysticism and politics (as opposed to the individualization of modern religion). By drawing poor people into genuine decision making, the base communities are rebuilding the nuclei of a polis in places where it has never developed, or where it has been destroyed by political repression.

In Mexico base communities in poor areas are local self-help and political action groups, but also cells for Christian worship and study. They pressure the government about poor garbage disposal, inadequate transportation, or police corruption. They hold courses on family life, causes of unemployment, and marketing of hand-work. They sponsor street theater and neighborhood festivals. They cooperate with other organizations at provincial and even national levels, and at times plunge into partisan politics. Members of these communities understand their activities not as secular tactics, but as signs of a better life under the Law of God. They have problems of growth: reluctance of leaders to share power with newcomers, development of an "insiders" language. They also have to deal with male dominance, continuing clerical control, continuing poverty, and police harrassment.

Thinking regeneratively [85]

Find a way to make your pie bigger rather than looking for someone to give you a new pie. That's the basic idea of regeneration. The first step is to learn to think systematically about capacity rather than needs. Most people are needs-oriented in their thinking. But to tap into regenerative potential, understanding the capacity of a system to regenerate will define its needs more accurately. After deciding to become a capacity-oriented thinker, step two is to list specific internal resources of the people and environment to be regenerated: the abundant, available, paid for things used for the production of anything, even new ideas. Every useful thing other than an input is an internal resource, raw material for regeneration. The purpose of regeneration is to expand the functional capacity and vitality of the internal resources. New inputs into a system can diminish its capacity to regenerate.

Regeneration goes beyond calls for a sustainable economy. Regeneration means economic associations that emphasize the human element. For example, economics as a discipline blossoms on the micro level by accounting, directing and structuring resource flows.

Civic associations are the means of regenerating the way we live. They can reorient the values which underlie our economy. One of our present political imbalances is that private life overshadows the public order. Another imbalance is the overshadowing of local political institutions by the overgrown federal power. Where the civil rights movement could effectively lobby at the federal level for laws that promote racial justice, a march on the Capitol for jobs predictably had little effect.

The group cannot make up for what the person lacks. Without a positive vision of life and health, the best we can dream of is security—the absence of want, disease, fear and war. The first step toward a better life involves a recovery of inner autonomy. The individual is the initiator of social change through contributions of thought and action; the community is the recipient and the testing ground. We reflect the group and we contribute to it. Just as the emergent tree rises above the others in the forest, a restucturing of economic values calls upon the individual to go beyond any life-limiting constrictions of the community.

The ultimate regenerative task in rebuilding community is the creation of a world citizenry. The nuclear spectre may be the most loudly debated obstacle hindering global development; hunger is the most silent. Every three days the earth suffers the same loss as occurred in the atomic bombing of Hiroshima, when 40,000 persons (mostly children) die of starvation. Many are now linked in budding planetary coalitions. Part of the discipline of daily life is to organize one's activities so as to be able to devote a good share of energy to public service in the community. This includes not only administrative services on library boards, school boards, etc. It also includes planting roadside trees, caring for gardens and parks, and fulfilling some of the functions of the police. Leisure among workers of all classes must be largely devoted to the tasks of citizenship. Civic will is spiritual in essence. It cannot be quantified, monetized or marketed. We have to start with how we think.

■ Old Doc: Cities turn matter into spirit

MEDICAL STUDENT: Doctor, have you ever looked at world grids of different airways? Dozens of lighted dots are cities connected by networks of airways. You don't even notice the countries. Are cities the nerve cells of the planetary brain?

OLD DOC: Cities are the social inventions that mold and transform every part of our existence. Cities create wealth, culture, world

199

views, politics, war and peace. Stone and steel are translated into temples of art and learning, cathedrals of faith, and towers of world polity and trade.

MEDICAL STUDENT: But unless we constantly fill them with spirit and conscience, they deteriorate into bad housing, potholes and empty storefronts. I'm tempted to buy a farm.

OLD DOC: Escaping to exurbia? Where would it be without the city? Every town has the potential to consume bricks and mortar and steel to become conscience and creativity.

MEDICAL STUDENT: How do you view the increasing complexities of urban life, the new technologies of space and the information age—are they more matter, or more spirit?

OLD DOC: They are evidence of matter becoming spirit. And I would add the wide interest in new age consciousness as well as the concern for ecological stewardship, revitalization of neighborhoods, and health education. As cities turn matter into spirit, the economic powers become more responsive to human need. And frugality, voluntary simplicity, and global networking all become part of a deeper commitment to human duration on an ecologically healthy planet.

■ Looking for the edges of humanness

Dormant brain research on Laughing Coyote Mountian [86]

Authors' note: in September 1987 we visited eremite T.D. Lingo at his 8,500-foot high Laughing Coyote Mountain. We ate his stew cooked in a sooty pot atop a wood fire and heard the elks bugling as the moon rose. Lingo's experience outruns ordinary English prose or poetry, but which of the real masters has not been suspect of being driven by a wild mind? Lingo claims, and we believe, that of his 300 disciples from ghetto, class and boardroom, over half regularly experience transcendant consciousness and are remaking the ordinary world we all live in. He answers letters, and we heartily recommend him as fine company. He describes his research as follows:

The synergistic community of shared consciousness is innate within every vastly dormant brain. Clicking the brain's master click switch, the amygdala organ in the limbic system, causes the ancient experience of nirvana, samadhi, rebirth. I see God face to face, transcendence. Increases up to 40 points in the Stanford Binet IQ test and up to 1400 percent on the Getzels Jackson Creativity Test are measured. Blocked genetic drive, signaled by the pain of depression, is unlocked into progressive growth happiness. More importantly, the primitive killer instinct is outgrown. A new order of cooperation for consensus action emerges, the basis of warless Earth.

Three experiments led to these discoveries. First, from 1957 to 1967, 100 dropout minority (Black and Hispanic) delinquent children using our methods had an 8 percent enlightenment rate. Next, from 1967 to 1977, 100 young adults from deteriorating neighborhoods, suffering personal depression and lacking hope, doubled the breakthrough to 16 percent. Third, from 1977 through 1987, 100 older adults started with us affected with the misery of neurosis. Twenty-seven percent achieved the experience of transcendence, using our self therapy in the workplace while doing ordinary jobs. We offer a *Self Transcendence Workbook* (640 pages) and *Mass Transcendence Guidebook* (700 pages) with details and exercises.

Back in their neighborhoods, these students, as natural leaders who see the potential of 100 percent brain power, teach others. Almost all our youth returned to school, and 90 percent graduated, most with honors. Thirty percent were able to go on to college.

At our zero stress primal nature environment, a ten-thousand-foot wilderness mountain with a simple stone and timber facility, the three test groups were guided through a 3-point program:
- Study a simplified neurology to understand the brain mechanism, consciousness, thought production, and emotion production;
- Experience the ultimate reality of primal nature during all seasons to learn survival skills and relate self to lifeforce in pure trust; and
- Invent personal intuitive methods of brain self control.

Results have been spectacular. Fears, guilts and self-lies disappear. Daily thought production becomes the most entertaining activity imaginable. Boredom and loneliness are never again mentioned. Since this self-funded research cannot afford laboratory machines, we move from tantalizing speculation to disciplined skepticism. We believe, though, that creativity and even genius is teachable. Advanced problem-solving intelligence and skill is the automatic function of brain tissue.

Transcendence is the final goal of life which all humans, consciously or unconsciously, strive to achieve. Transcendence is caused by clicking the amygdala, an organ located in the midbrain. Transcendence is the astonishing certainty that all confusions, pains and fears finally are at an end. It creates a permanent feeling of love, fulfillment, happiness and meaning in life. You are at one with the universe. Transcendence dramatically changes your relationships with other persons. You feel an overwhelming desire to be kind and gentle with bosses and bureaucrats.

This power of imagination is released by visualizing how parts of your brain can be self-controlled to open new circuits. Our exercises are for the beginner from age six to 60. You will experience the direct transcendence of nirvana, born again oneness with others and with life. You now know you have sleeping energies of infinity. You hunger for more living, to mature into pure cosmic intelligence and peace forever.

Reports from participants

I almost didn't make it. Had no pa. My ma always on gin. Rats in my crib. Screams bring nothing. You learn quick this is a painful life. Get mad. You break their law. They bust you down all the way. Juvenile jail. Big jail. They almost got me. But somehow I got to that unbelievable mountain. Lean-to, axes, timber, campfires, singing and talk. I learned my brain. Went back and beat the system in that politics-rotten high school, just like my mountain teacher taught me.... Raising a new generation. Laughing good. Doing great things.

—*Dashiki.*

One thing I learned on Laughing Coyote Mountain is, I got a mission. I don't waste time. I am spending every day of my life learning a little bit more about what we have down here and how it is related to what is out there. I will spend the rest of this life discovering everything in the cosmos. I learn with love. I share love. I hold on to the vision. I have been to the stars. I go there whenever I need refreshment.

—*P.P.*

The rate of this kind of breakthrough for women has been 3-to-1 over males in a group of 110 males (53 percent) and 99 females (47 percent). A woman's nirvana experience:

Bang! In one flash, life has become a perpetual joy and meaning to me. It came when I least expected it. All I was doing was the standard procedure when I first enrolled at the

Adventure Trails Survival School at Laughing Coyote Mountain. It lasted three days. Now I can make it happen whenever I choose. Can you imagine an earthquake between your ears? We become as children again, totally free and innocent and awe-filled. You meet a new Self and you believe in your new destiny. You want to perfect your Self quickly so you can start working to help others. The ancients believed a man in a monastery had to meditate on a blank wall for 40 years before he could hope to achieve satori. What a waste. And notice: no women allowed. Now it is much simpler. Once you learn brain control, nirvana is automatic and free.

—*G.L.O.R.*

I still cry when I think of all those sad years that I wasted by not living my life with my full growth and happiness. But now I love life again. The communication of the cosmos isn't of talking words. It's of feeling... of knowing. I didn't want to come down to lower reality. But now each day with my office workers I'm teaching some of them to open their eyes, the third eye. They're beginning to remember their original language of star love.

—*N.R.*

Cosmic consciousness

The universe is composed of five elements which create all other components, such as electrons, material objects, life, people, nations, war, death and transcendence. The five elements are: space, time, energy, matter and cosmic consciousness. Cosmic consciousness is universal. It creates space, time, energy and matter. It creates the brain. Cosmic consciousness is the supreme reality. It enters the brain. It does not care what you do with it. Use it to survive, die or transcend. It enters the reptilian brain through the first of the three click switches, the reticular activating formation, and is recomputed into competitive consciousness. It next moves to the mammalian brain and is recomputed into half cooperative and half competitive consciousness. The amygdala is our second click switch located within the limbic system. We can click to recompute into pure cooperative consciousness.

Neurosurgeons have not yet found the third click center in the dormant frontal lobes. Like the "third eye" of Eastern thought, it is postulated to be the organ which links cooperative consciousness to cosmic consciousness. This final linkage produces transcendental nirvana.

203

Cosmic consciousness, originating from God, creates the genetic intelligence which creates your personal intelligence. If personal intelligence is neurotic, it retrogresses back into the reptilian brain. When neurosis is cured, consciousness matures into social intelligence and utilizes cooperative behavior to help others cure their own neuroses. Then the amygdala clicks forward and circuits consciousness and transcendent fulfillment. All problems become soluble by linking cooperative personal intelligence with cosmic and genetic intelligence.

The mystic's transcendence occurs within the brain's frontal lobes and can be self released. By clicking the brain's master click, energy flowing into the frontal lobes causes the ancient enlightenment implosion. Cosmic consciousness from the universe completes its circuit through the brain, frontal lobes, and back out to the universe. Any motivated person who wants to free the innate potential within his 90 percent dormant brain now can follow a series of uncomplicated exercises to get his/her 100 percent brain power. All still searching followers of Christ, the Buddha, Islam, Capitalism or Communism can move beyond their origins; they can add the facts of how the human brain works to the rites and rituals of each incomplete religion or philosophy. Their belief system can become mature and effective without changing its foundation values. They can modify and codify basic neural cybernetics into their system's vocabulary. All devotees then can make a final breakthrough into the uniquely defined ultimate goal of that particular belief. Priests and practitioners of each faith need not be threatened. They need not give up all their years of learning that faith's catechism. Harmonizing into the highest common denominator, perfect humanity within a perfect universe, warless earth, the great brain learning-and-loving-and-laughing society. Transcendence is the ultimate emotion of perpetual ecstatic happiness.

Exuberant testimonials

I am a conservative reborn Christian. I have accepted Jesus Christ as my personal savior. I clicked my amygdala switch. I discovered God's kingdom on earth. I feel no conflict whatsoever between my faith and the facts of neuroanatomy. If I did, I only would have to walk outside at night to look at the billions of stars and ask, "Why?" Science is just God's tool. Science cannot explain the why of the universe. Only religion can. So I am balanced comfortably between my peace of mind and my economic career. I giggle my way through the daily paradoxes of moral righteousness which are caused by the unnecessary conflict between the two polar needs for faith and facts. Christianity is in crisis. We Christians have been murdering each other, all in the name of "God." It is our God given destiny to rationally adjust lower society reality to higher cosmic reality.

—*Beverly Giggles Grant*

I have rededicated my life to being a Jew. I know directly what Moses felt on the mount. That's what made it possible for him to talk directly with God so as to get kosher therapy of the Commandments. We are all the children of God, given the same wiring to telephone up to our Father. So in my relaxation, I have gone back to my personal historical roots, reexamined all the ideas and rituals of my given cultural heritage, discarded those which reason tells me are obviously obsolete and accepted whole heartedly those which still cook up the mystery and awe of living in God's chutzpah universe.

—*Steve/Chaim Kornblum*

Take a bath!

Part of a recent letter Lingo wrote to a friend, copied here with his permisssion:

In your letter with the check you affectionately ordered me, "Take a bath!"

I obeyed. Dangerous.

Filled outside galvanized tubs with snow. Heated them. Roaring whole trees. Burning hot water. Bucketted in. Filled bath house tub. Full steaming. Stoked up inside stove. Full belching. Cozy. Secure. Expectancy. Euphoria. Then I made my mistake.

Standing naked. Ready to step in and slip under, I clicked my amygdala up one notch from its usual daily work horse balance at +7.0. Clicked to +8.0. Turned toward the cleansing ecstasy, ready to wash away all fragrant entropies. But then God played Her joke. Clickity click click click: +8.1, 8.2, 8.3...8.8, 8.9. Chain reaction: 9.1...9.9 BLOOIE!!

So when I finally remembered to do what you ordered, when I finally climbed in, I noticed something strange. Unnatural. Confusing.

I was up too high.

Soap would not lather.

They are ill discoverers who think there is no land when they can see nothing but sea.

—*Bacon*

Wash rag said, "Clank!"

Bare-assed, I was sitting in tub, on top of solid slab of ice.

Apparently Nirvana had taken quite some time to go out into the Universe and back down to Giggling Coyote.

■ Old Doc: Spirit edges

MEDICAL STUDENT: Doctor, you mailed hundreds of questionnaires to discover where people are on their vocational journey and what sustains them. What is the context within which you will interpret the answers?

OLD DOC: A profound question. Recently six of us spent several hours trying to discern the spiritual edge of our time, against which to interpret the answers. The brief statement has four major benchmarks: integrity of commitment, a convergence of the civilizational wisdom of East and West, the experience of power in the call to service, and social and intellectual methods working in harmony with the new global consciousness.

MEDICAL STUDENT: The brief says, "The interesting man or woman lives an integrity of commitment."

OLD DOC: Yes. Being, not doing, is the heart of the matter. Such a person, "exhibits an urgent quietude, a secure personal direction. Everywhere people have an emerging confidence that men and women of power are among us again."

MEDICAL STUDENT: What is this power? Where does it come from?

OLD DOC: From a convergence of wisdom of the East and West, a synthesis of mind and spirit. We marvel at our connectedness with all the minds of the world, past, present and future. There is a consciousness of completeness of our inner resources.

MEDICAL STUDENT: How is personal power evident?

OLD DOC: Experience of profound personal power comes in a life of service. We must leave behind all mindless hurry and busyness to address the real world in its glory and its tragedies.

MEDICAL STUDENT: Is this the same as "social conscience" or political activism among local community leaders? Is there a new sense of being called?

OLD DOC: Thoughtful people see the planet's survival at risk and a global imperative to save it, an imperative that requires a synergy of social and intellectual effort. They meet this global challenge with a new understanding of what it means to be "called."

MEDICAL STUDENT: How does this help the poor?

OLD DOC: Those who are called stand with the poor, leaving aside irrelevant intellectual skeptics. The poor can hear and leap ahead with the power of the called. At the spiritual edge of the 1980s are miracles of personal healing and empowerment, as "the humble poor believe."

■ Hologram of humanness [87]

Without a clear and adequate concept of the human, development efforts inevitably will be thwarted at best and destructive at worst. They will be guided by false notions, ancient hypotheses, or cultural biases that have little to do with reality. The question is not related only to the sector battling rural poverty—efforts in the Third World must be complemented by efforts in the First World.

Indicating the human factor is an immensely complicated undertaking. It must acknowledge that despite some similarities, each instance of the species is unique, and differentiated from all the rest by culture, heredity and psychology. But the challenge is not to provide an exhaustive description of humankind. It is rather to describe the crucial elements of humanity with sufficient clarity to focus development efforts on real issues, where resolution will make a real difference and be an enduring contribution to the human enterprise. None of us engaged in human development could wish for less, yet few of us know where to begin.

Any response that approaches adequacy will have a philosophical cast. The temptations are to wander off into clouds of abstraction, or to restrict oneself to episodic insights in the manner of short stories. Our intent here is to offer a set of indicators which point to that about humanity which, when addressed, releases creativity, responsibility and fulfillment. It may provide a screen for identifying real issues, finding criteria for moral action, and freeing us from pursuing ideals that are impossible by the nature of things. It may provoke new strategies for development. And it may not.

Limits and Transcendence

Man is limited and transcendent. This leads to the problem of suffering and death, and provides the possibility of religion. There is no point to efforts that attempt to exclude either the limitedness or the transcendence of human beings. Easy solutions don't work (e.g., "Why is it bad for babies to die if all their life will entail suffering?" or "Don't grieve; he/she has gone to heaven or hell or to be reincarnated.") The problem of suffering and death, which in its deepest form is the problem of meaning, will not go away. However much development succeeds, suffering and death will persist.

The possibile synthesis here is religion, but not in the sense of superstition, credal conformity, or institutional bigotry. Human meaning is found in perception and affirmation of the ultimate mystery from whence we come and to which we go, and which permeates every instant of life. Affirming that "other world in the midst of this world" provides meaning for the development enterprise. In the profound sense, developers are priests, secular priests of the profound. Village after village that has participated in human development has undergone a revitalization of the local religion, a renewed perception of life's ultimate meaning in the face of suffering and death.

It is not part of the development task to promote verities of a particular religion. Such activity is the surest and quickest way to get thrown out of the community. But engaging fully with people in their never ending struggle with life's limits means communication at a human level that goes beyond successes and failures.

Evil and Reconciliation

Human beings are unique, yet connected. This situation presents the problem of evil and provides the possibility of reconciliation. Individual activities have consequences far beyond the persons involved. As Freud observed, group structures and values often have harmful consequences for individuals. Here is the problem of evil. Even well intentioned individual and group activities frequently are destructive. Charitable acts may create dependency. Those who initiate efforts at human development need not be surprised to find spinoffs that wreak havoc on innocent parties. Evil or estrangement are parts of the human condition which persist.

The possibility in this situation is reconciliation, a term too often used to mean escape from tension. Real reconciliation occurs in the midst of separateness, as people create new links across their tension-filled uniqueness and diversity. This reconciliation is the aim of human development.

Three approaches to development contend for the hearts and minds and pocketbooks of our time. All three attempt to deal with the individual/relation tension. The first helps individuals directly: for example, providing relief to victims of natural or social disaster. The second emphasizes relatedness, and attempts to strengthen the dispossessed so that they can contend successfully with oppressive social structures. This is most clearly dramatized by insurgency movements and guerrilla warfare. The third is the approach of human development in which individuals and communities are mobilized to do their own development alongside people from the wider comunity's public and private sectors.

Vocation and Integrity

Human beings seek order, yet are creative. This duality leads to the problem of vocation and presents the possibility of integrity. We are determined by accident of birth to act out our struggles for power, prestige and ideals within the confines of particular structures. Family, community and job protect us and yet constrict the creative impulses they exist to promote. To the creative spirit, personal capacity is too little, friends too narrow, the community too moribund, the job too confining, the ideal too distant. This disillusionment is the vocational problem, the inevitable accompaniment to the human journey.

Our responses range from quiet despairing resignation to job hopping to frantic and sometimes violent attempts to change the system and make room for more creativity. None of these responses resolves the problem, though each has a legitimate place in the scheme of things.

In the lives of admirable people or heroes, one finds not the absence of this problem, but the transformation of it. The problem of vocation for them is not something to be escaped, but something to be owned and valued and struggled with continuously. This is the mark of integrity: to know, to own, and to struggle with one's creativity within limits, as part of one's unique contribution to civilization. This posture, and not defiance or transcendence, is behind the famous "Here I stand" of Martin Luther, often recognized as the motto of integrity.

Promotion of integrity is the task of human development.

■ Old Doc: Wilderness and beyond

DR. TERTIA: Doctor, the last time we talked you said all life is good. Therefore we can affirm vocational burnout, institutional blahs and spiritual despair as all being part of life's journey to the center. Part of coming of age by the world. Where do we go from there?

OLD DOC: Into the wilderness. Alone in a space-time continuum where nothing is. On the other side of the experience of absolute nothingness emerges the absolutely new. An encounter with God, a

new vision of the holy* life came to Moses in the terrible desert of Sinai.

DR. TERTIA: That's true. And Galileo's new physics emerged in the desert of nonreality of the old cosmologies. So despair at our social collapse is our call to go into the wilderness of the human spirit and find a new burning bush?

OLD DOC: Many are on that journey now. They embrace a style of deliberate plain living, abandoning larger than life "needs."

DR. TERTIA: And some of their wildernesses can be very nice cottages in the woods with indoor plumbing and ample freezers.

OLD DOC: Like Moses who rejected the authority of the Egyptian bureaucracies, these explorers of the spirit find in themselves the right and power to define what human fulfillment is.

DR. TERTIA: That reminds me of a story from Eastern Europe. The Hasidic rabbi was asked "How does the Lord God look upon human beings who question all rules and create their own morality?" His answer, "The Lord God weeps... for joy."

OLD DOC: There is no law that can replace our own freedom and responsibility to live as interdependent human beings.

DR. TERTIA: That word "interdependent" sets limits on our freedom, doesn't it?

OLD DOC: We each set these limits ourselves, in our own primal communities.

DR. TERTIA: Wait a minute. If I went into the desert to escape my collapsing community, why would I come back to the same structures I dropped out of in despair?

OLD DOC: Those who have encountered a new vision in their particular desert return to the world with a new perspective. They freely take on themselves new obligations which transform old relationships, and create new community, new social forms.

DR. TERTIA: In or out of the wilderness, their affirmation is that life is struggle and that all life is good.

OLD DOC: That is how the whole story began: It is all very good.

---

* *holy:* separate from our ordinary normal experience.

Epilogue

Can We Make It Happen?

Let's pause in our journey into the next era with questions to the reader and his/her roundtable discussion group: What now? Can we make it happen?

In our lifetime we are experiencing a great transition from an industrial and technological era to something new—an age we hope will be characterized by compassion and cooperation. While grand trends are underway toward an information age, toward decentralized decision making, toward a vigorous localism, there remains great scope for individual freedom. Neighborhood caretakers are giving form to new leadership styles, new methods for social cohesion and local neighborhood empowerment. They are creating many kinds of families, where an important function is the transformation of information into knowledge, even wisdom. Already 21st century guilds are appearing as neighborhood caretakers, with highly developed tools of particular vocations, are reshaping the institutions of commerce, government, science and learning.

Neighborhood caretakers and Those Who Make Good Things Happen operate out of no high design imposed from above. Freedom is foundational to their self-understanding, their power, and to the call which they extend to others.

Writers of books and journals cannot decide the outcomes of the issues they raise. What writers and journalists can do, however, is present information which can set the agenda for public discussion. Our readers, particularly in dialogue with their roundtable groups, will discern for themselves the meanings and implications of the stories, data and related discussions.

Each generation makes its own accounting to its children.

211

NEIGHBORHOOD CARETAKERS

A king was re-
nowned for his
sword with which
he could fell a large
oak tree with a
single blow. His
neighboring kings
wallowed in spite
and envy. One was
particularly pestif-
erous in his con-
stant carping, argu-
ing that any king
could strike down
oak trees if only he
had the right sword.
Finally the re-
nowned king re-
solved to end this
constant gnatlike
annoyance. He sent
his famous sword as
a gift to the nasty
gnat.

The rival lost no
time in calling a
great audience to
witness his new
ferocity in felling
great oaks. Alas, to
the amusement of
the crowd, in his
hands the great
sword scarcely
nicked the tree.
Indeed, after more
than a hundred
blows, the oak stood
with hardly a
bruise. Word came
back to the king
who had made the
gift of the great
sword.

"Tell my neighbor,"
said the king, "that I
sent only the royal
sword, not the royal
arm."

—A MIDDLE EASTERN
FOLK TALE

Regional mentor panels offer help in learning social and spirit methods described in this book. See Appendix B for more information on these panels.

It is our experience that the skills of charismatic and effective leadership cannot be transferred by writing or reading alone, nor by any sophisticated multimedia devices. The skills and personal power are transferred through apprenticeship or multilevel mentoring relationships. The journey of the master teacher begins as a participant, learning not to dominate the discussion or to be afraid of expressings one's own opinion; to listen to the other members of the group; to say something without expecting a personal reply. Some participants return again as participant observers, probing the dynamics of the group process, observing the style of the facilitation team, the changes in the mood of the group. The participant observer reviews the event with the facilitator team: What happened, what made it good, what changes would be helpful another time?

Wanting to learn more, the new leader apprentices to facilitators experienced in the social methods used. With skills in the Basic Discussion Method, Image Shifting Methods, motivational planning, tri-polar analysis and profound celebration, the apprentice becomes a confident facilitator, endorsed by his/her regional panel of peers as a fellow mentor.

Apprentices who learn well under the observation of the master teachers and demonstrate skill in leading a group through the Basic Discussion Method can be added to the panel, and themselves serve as master teachers for that particular leadership skill. As more advanced skills are gained in up front apprenticeship, further facilitator and mentor assignments can be expected from the regional mentor panel.

We distinguish two levels of competence for serving in leadership training: 1) persons experienced in the particular method, having used it in their own occupation, who are equipped to demonstrate the method before new groups, but are not yet designated by their peers as equipped to be mentors; 2) master teachers who not only have used the particular method in their own occupation, and can demonstrate it effectively before new groups, but also—in the judgement of their peers, after observation before live groups—are well equipped to serve as mentors to new apprentices.

We leave financial arrangements to the panel in each region and the local leaders seeking to qualify for master teacher status for each particular skill or method. In general, we hope that panelists will charge modestly for the teaching/mentoring of the Basic Discussion Method. Grateful learners will be able and willing to pay more for help in mastering higher levels of skills.

Initially, we and our associates at Earthcare Indianapolis have located persons with whom we have worked personally in recent years to serve as starting members of the several Regional Mentor Panels. Regional panels can provide biographical data describing the particular gifts and interests of each of their panelists.

Finally, a substantial human base of varied core groups (hundreds of them) calls for intentional visiting among the groups—the bumble bee dynamic. Skilled visiting can develop mutual encouragement, exchanges of information and resources, common work in developing knowledge, and even wisdom needed by an evolving planetary society. Some readers may hear and heed a call to this service. Where might it all lead?

Free, free, free to decide

What this world is going to be;

This imperative is ours, to be

Free, free, free to decide . . .

—*CHILDREN'S ROUND*

References: Who Can Help Us with X, Y and Z?

Note: "NC" refers to the story's appearance in *The Neighborhood Caretaker Journal.*

1. Dyson, B.C., & Dyson, E.U. "A Family Mission: An Interview with Old Doc by His Young Colleague," *Family Systems Medicine*, Winter 1986, 4:442-447.
2. Christoffel, K.K. "Homicide in Childhood: A Public Health Problem in Need of Attention," 1984, *Am. J. Public Health* 74:68-70. (1986 NC p. 70)
3. Schlesinger, Bill and Carol. Project Verdad, 10160 Sumatra, El Paso, TX 79925, 915/592-8818. (1987 NC p. 113)
4. Bonhoeffer, Dietrich. *Ethics*, 1949, section on Freedom, Macmillan Paperback Edition, 1975.
5. Morris, D., Hess, K. *Neighborhood Power: The New Localism*, Beacon Press Boston, 1975. (1987 NC p. 56)
6. *Sprouts*, March 1986, Community Self Reliance Center, 301 S.Geneva St., Ithaca, NY 14850, 607/272-3040. (1987 NC p. 120)
7. Webster, J.B. 1010 Sunset Court, W. Lafayette, IN 47906, 317/743-8620. (1986 NC p. 124)
8. Chopp, F., Exec. Dir. Freemont Public Association, 3601 Freemont Ave. N., Seattle, WA 98103, 206/632-1285. (1987 NC p. 127)
9. Allen, Germaine. Testamony at Job Training Partnership Act Hearing, July 1, 1985, Judge Baker's court, 46 E.Ohio St, Indianapolis, IN 46204. (1988 NC p. 22)
10. Madara, E.J. Self Help Clearinghouse, St.Clares-Riverside Hospital, Denville, NJ 07834, 201/625-7101. (1987 NC p. 27)
11. Jones, Lynn. *A Matter of Community*, 1984, 72 pages, 500 Lincoln St., Denver CO 80203, 313/321-3104, $5.00. (1987 NC p. 124)
12. Breyer, P.R., and Malafrinte, D. "Promoting Community Involvement in Deinstitutionalization Planning: The Experience of One Community," 1982, *Hospital and Community Psychiatry*, 33:654-657. (1987 NC p. 55)

13. Brandenburg, A. 1984 interview with H.M. Alfonso, doctoral student at the Univerity of Pennsylvania. (1987 NC p. 131)
14. Bonnet, N. "Villa El Salvador," *UN Development Forum*, October 1987, UN Div. for Economic and Social Information/DPI and UN University, United Nations, Room DC1-559, NYC 10017. (1987 NC p. 137)
15. ibid August 1987. See also Green Dollars For Barter. (1986 NC p. 129; 1987 p. 97)
16. Harley, R. "The Entrepreneurial Poor," *Ford Foundation Letter*, June 1, 1983. (1986 NC p. 84)
17. Weiss C., Holup, L. WWB/W. Va. Affiliate, 1217 Lee St. E., Charleston, WV 25301, 304/345-1298 from *West Virginia Women's Commission News,* Summer 1986. (1987 NC p. 99)
18. Mollner, T. "Mondragon: Linking Economic Structures and Spirit," T. Mollner, Trusteeship Institute, Baker Road, Shutesbury, MA 01072. (1987 NC p. 119)
19. Montefiore Hospital Seminar, April 1984. (1986 NC p. 83)
20. Bennett, Richard S. P.O.Box 3030, Santa Cruz, CA 95063-3030. (1987 NC p. 139)
21. Brandenburg, A.L. Director. West Philadelphia Fund for Human Development, 215/724-1702. (1987 NC p. 131)
22. Lane, W. B. Interfaith Housing Task Force, Inc., P.O. Box 1157, Wilmington, DE 19899, 302/655-3379. (1987 NC p. 20)
23. Institute for Community Economics, Fall & Winter 1985, 151 Montague City Road, Greenfield, MA 01301, 413/774-5933. (1987 NC p. 119)
24. Thresher, C. *Thursday People News*, July 1984. (1986 NC p. 125)
25. McRae, G. Rochester Community Care Home, Inc. Box 417, Rochester, VT 05767. (1987 NC p. 99)
26. Institute of Cultural Affairs, *IERD Highlights*, Jan/Feb 1985, 4750 N. Sheridan Rd., Chicago, IL 60640. (1986 NC p. 60)
27. Hesse, Hermann. *Journey to the East*, Strauss & Giroux, NY, 1956.
28. Institute of Cultural Affairs, "The Basic Discussion Method" from *Effective Supervision Participant Manual*, 1982. (1987 NC p. 64)
29. Boulding, Kenneth E. *The Image*, Chap. 1, Univ. of Michigan Press, Ann Arbor, MI, Paperback, 1956.
30. Institute of Cultural Affairs, *Organizational Facilitator Training Manual,* Chicago, IL, 1986. (1987 NC p. 105)
31. Dyson, B.C. "Annual Disability Days" (1983 NC pp. 17-20; 1987 p. 99)
32. Ganda O.P. "Morbidity and Mortality from Diabetes Mellitus: A Look at Preventable Aspects," 1983, *American Journal of Public Health* 73: 1156-1158. (1987 NC p. 24)
33. Driesen, K. Rural Health Office, University of Arizona, 3131 E. Second Street, Tucson, AZ 85716, 602/626-7946. (1986 NC p. 138)
34. Ernst, E. "A Place Called Narangwal," December 1984, *Johns Hopkins Magazine,* pp. 56-62. (1987 NC p. 135)
35. Epstein, L.M., Tamir, A., Spenser, T., and Perlman, S. *The Community Project: The Teaching Implications of Applied Epidemiology.* (NC story #262)

36. Morley, D. and Lovel, H. *My Name is Today*, Macmillan Publishers Ltd., 1986, in conjunction with Teaching Aids at Low Cost (TALC), PO Box 49, St. Albans, Hertfordshire, UK AL1 4AX. (1987 NC p. 71)

37. Berkowitz, Bill. *Community Dreams*, 1984, Impact Publishers, PO Box 1094, San Luis Obispo, CA 93406, 805/543-5911, 255 pp., $8.95. (1986 NC p. 66)

38. Seeber, B. "The Producer," *Science*, July/August 1984, pp. 40-47. (1986 NC p. 84)

39. Shegda, Ron. *How To Create A Regenerative Economy*, New Generation Press, 48 N. Third St., Emmaus, PA 18049, 215/967-6656. (1987 NC p. 83)

40. Leue, Mary. 196 Elm St., Albany, NY 12202. (1987 NC p. 46)

41. Leary, T. "Tim Leary's Magic Bullet," *Psychology Today*, July 1983, pp. 20-38. (1987 NC p. 45)

42. Avery, Ann. 2 Rue Joliot Curie, 93120 La Courneuve, France. (1987 NC p. 124)

43. Dyson, E.U. "The Home Help as Healer." (1986 NC p. 9)

44. Peters, Rodney. Wichita Presbyterian Manor, 4700 West Thirteenth, Wichita KS 67212, 316/942-7456. (1987 NC p. 123)

45. Davis, J.E. Speaking at the annual meeting of the American Medical Society on Alcoholism in Detroit, MI, in April 1984. (1986 NC p. 142)

46. Boggs, G.L., Zola, N., Gruchala, J.S., and Cook, R. *Loving Them To Life*, 1987, 75 pp., excellent photographs, New Life Publ., 161 W. Parkhurst, Detroit, MI 48203, $6.00. (1987 NC p. 81) Boggs, G.L., ed., *SOSAD Newsletter*, Box 32421, Detroit, MI 48232, 313/833-3030. (1988 NC p. 34)

47. Boggs, James and Grace Lee: Residents for over 25 years in inner city Detroit, 3061 Field St., Detroit, MI 48214, 313/921-1236. (1988 NC p. 33)

48. Wildhack, M. "Coping With Pain," Earthcare Indianapolis. (1986 NC p. 125)

49. Dressler, F.R.S. and Seybold, John W. *The Entrepreneurial Age*, Seybold Publications, Media, PA, 1985.

50. Dyson, B.C & E.U. "Sophia: A Fair Language." (1986 NC p. 76)

51. Institute of Cultural Affairs, Social Process Triangles, 4750 N. Sheridan, Chicago, IL 60640, 312/769-6363.

52. Eckerdt, D.J., Baden, L., Bossey, R., & Dibbs, E. "The Effects of Retirement on Physical Health," 1983, *Am. J. Public Health* 73: 779-783. (1986 NC p. 46)

53. Goldstein, M.C., & Beall, C.M. "Indirect Modernization and the Elderly in a Third World Setting," 1982, *Gerontology* 17:743-748. (1986 NC p. 83)

54. Parker, D.A., Parker, E.S., Brody, J.A., & Schoenberg, R. "Alcohol Use and Cognitive Loss Among Employed Men and Women," 1983, *Am. J. Public Health* 73: 521-526. (1986 NC p. 149)

55. Baker, S. "Medical Data and Injuries," 1983, *Am. J. Public Health* 73: 733-734. (1986 NC p. 32)

56. Barker, W.H., et al. "Community Surveillance of Stroke; Contribution of Uncontrolled Hypertension," 1983, *Am. J. Public Health* 73: 260-265. (1986 NC p. 99)

57. McCormick, M.C., et al. "High Risk Young Mothers; Infant Mortality in Four Areas in U.S.A., 1973-1978," 1984, *Am. J. Public Health* 73: 18-23. (1986 NC p. 134)

58. Press, A. "Mapping the Streets of Crime," Nov. 1983, *Newsweek*, p. 68. (1986 NC p. 26)

59. Dever, G.E.A. *Epidemiology in Health Management,* 1984, Aspen Publications, 399 pages. (1987 NC p. 12)

60. Shonholtz, Raymond Community Board Center for Policy and Training, 149 Ninth St., San Francisco, CA 94103, 415/552-1250. (1987 NC p. 55)

61. Sloan, L.A. "Community Developed Strategies For Reducing Adolescent Pregnancy: A Case Study," *Family and Community Health*, pp. 73-80, May 1982. (1988 NC p. 30)

62. Stranske, Raymond. *Vision of Hope, Newsletter of Hope Communities Inc.*, July 1985 -Summer/Fall 1986, P.O. Box 9620, Denver, CO 80209, 303/292-4673. (1987 NC p. 6)

63. Haney, Laura T., Soloman, Louise. Warren Wilson College, 701 Warren Wilson Rd., Swannanoa, NC 28778, 704/298-3325. (1988 NC p. 2)

64. Coleman, A. "Does Bad Design Lead to Crime?" Nov/Dec 1985, *Land & Liberty,* p. 106, 5 E. 44th St., New York, NY 10017. (1986 NC p. 55)

65. CRSP, PO 27731, Los Angeles, CA 90027, 213/738-1254. (1987 NC p. 140)

66. Sherwood, S. and Morris, J.N. (1) "The Pennsylvania domiciliary care experiment: Impact on quality of life," 1983, *Am. J. Public Health* 73:646-653; (2) Ruchlin, H.S., and Morris, J.N. "Part 2. Cost Benefit Implications," 1983, pp. 654-660; (3) Weiler, P.G. "Evaluation of alternatives in long-term care," 1983, pp. 638-639. (1986 NC p. 76)

67. Newman, O. *Community of Interest*, Anchor Press/Doubleday, Garden City, New York, 1980, 356 pages. (1985 NC p. 10)

68. "Education for All," *Development Forum*, June 1987, UN Div. Economic & Social Information and UN University. (1987 NC p. 68)

69. LaChapelle, Dolores. *Ritual:The Pattern That Connects*, 1985, 45 pages; c/o Way of the Mountain Learning Center, Box 542, Silverton CO 81433. (1987 NC p. 145)

70. Kirsch, Virginia. Kinshasa ISC, Department of State, Washington, DC 20520.

71. Peter Kline. "Proposal to Develop Complete Literacy Training Program Using the Principles of Global Accelerated Learning, As Practiced at the SpeakEasy School," Mar 1987; c/o SpeakEasy School, Calhourn Square, 3001 Hennepin Ave. S., Minneapolis, MN 55408.

72. Olson, Lynn. "Children Flourish Here," *Education Week*, Vol. VII, #18, Jan 27 '88; and interview with principal Patricia Bolanos, Key School, 1401 East 10th St., Indianapolis, IN 46201, 317/266-4297.

73. Gardner, Howard. *Frames of Mind: The Theory of Multiple Intelligences,* Basic Books, Inc., 1984.

74. Marshall, Gene and Joyce. *The Reign of Reality, a Fresh Start for Planet Earth*, Chap. 11, Realistic Living Press, PO Box 140826, Dallas, TX 75214, $12.00. (1987 NC p. 66)
75. Silver, G.A. "Virchow, the Heroic Model in Medicine: Health Policy by Accolade," 1987, *Am. J. Public Health*, 77:82-88. (1987 NC p. 34)
76. Early, F. & Seifert, Jr., M.H. *Starting Your Own Patient Advisory Council*, 675 Water St., Excelsior, MN 55331, 612/474-4167. (1986 NC p. 106); and Seifert, Jr. M. H. *Patient Advisory Council*, 1981. (1986 NC p. 142)
77. Madara, E.J. Self Help Clearinghouse, St. Clares-Riverside Hospital, Denville, NJ 07834.
78. CHAP Program, University of Washington School of Medicine, Seattle, WA.
79. Adams, P. Gesundheit Institute, 404 N. Nelson St., Arlington, VA 22203, 703/525-8169. (1986 NC p. 74)
80. Dyson, B.C. et al. "Dragons Behind Adolescent Pregnancy," NC 86:61. (1988 NC p. 29)
81. Hawksley, Richard. Apropos publishing, 120 Portage St., Kent, OH 44240. Copies of this nicely illustrated and referenced 78-page book are priced for barter, exchange, or federal currency; estimated value 150 grams of vegetable protein. (1987 NC p. 104)
82. Wilber, Ken. *A Sociable God*, 1984, Shambhala Publ., Boulder, CO and London, 160 pages.
83. Earthcare Indianapolis, 3038 Fall Creek Parkway, N. Dr., Indianapolis, IN 46205, 317/925-9297; Earthcare Indianapolis, 1987, "The New Inner City Neighborhood." (1987 NC p. 103)
84. Cox, H. *Religion in the Secular City*, 1984, Simon & Schuster, Inc., New York, 304 pages. (1987 NC p. 120)
85. Rodale, R. "Learning to Think Regeneratively," *Regeneration*, Vol. 1, Winter 85/86, 33 E. Minor St., Emmaus, PA 18049, 215/967-5171. (1986 NC p. 119); Shegda, R. 48 North Third St., Emmaus, PA 18049, 215/967-6656. (1987 NC p. 47)
86. Lingo, T.D. Director of the Dormant Brain Research and Development Laboratory, Laughing Coyote Mountain, Box 10, Black Hawk, CO 80422 (no phone). (1987 NC p. 8)
87. Epps, J. *The Forum*, ICA, Rue Amedee Lynen 8, 1030 Brussels, Belgium. (1987 NC p. 13)

Appendix A: The Church as Social Pioneer*

Finally, the social responsibility of the Church needs to be described as that of the pioneer. The Church is that part of the human community which responds first to God-in-Christ and Christ-in-God. It is the sensitive and responsive part in every society and mankind as a whole. It is that group which hears the Word of God, which sees His judgments, which has the vision of the resurrection. In its relations with God it is the pioneer part of society that responds to God on behalf of the whole society, somewhat, we may say, as science is the pioneer in responding to pattern or rationality in experience and as artists are the pioneers in responding to beauty. This sort of social responsibility may be illustrated by reference to the Hebrew people and the prophetic remnant. The Israelites, as the major prophets ultimately came to see, had been chosen by God to lead all nations to Him. It was that part of the human race which pioneered in understanding the vanity of idol worship and in obeying the law of brother-love. Hence in it all nations were eventually to be blessed. The idea of representational responsibility is illustrated particularly by Jesus Christ. As has often been pointed out by theology, from New Testament times onward, he is the first-born of many brothers not only in resurrection but in rendering obedience to God. His obedience was a sort of pioneering and representative obedience; he obeyed on behalf of men, and so showed what men could do and drew forth a divine

* "The Responsibility of Church for Society" by H. Richard Niebuhr from *The Gospel, the Church and the World*, Kenneth Scott Latourette, Ed., Harper & Brothers, New York and London, 1946, Vol. 3, pp. 111-133.

response in turn toward all the men he represented. He discerned the divine mercy and relied upon it as representing men and pioneering for them.

This thought of pioneering or representational responsibility has been somewhat obscured during the long centuries of individualist overemphasis. Its expression in the legal terms of traditional theology is strange and often meaningless to modern ears. Yet with our understanding of the way that life is involved with life, of the manner in which self and society are bound together, of the way in which small groups within a nation act for the whole, it seems that we must move toward a conception similar to the Hebraic and medieval one.

In this representational sense the Church is that part of human society, and that element in each particular society, which moves toward God, which as the priest acting for all men worships Him, which believes and trusts in Him on behalf of all, which is the first to obey Him when it becomes aware of a new aspect of His will. Human society in all of its divisions and aspects does not believe. Its institutions are based on unbelief, on lack of confidence in the Lord of heaven and earth. But the Church has conceived faith in God and moves in the spirit of that trust as the hopeful and obedient part of society.

In ethics it is the first to repent for the sins of a society, and it repents on behalf of all. When it becomes apparent that slavery is transgression of the divine commandment, then the Church repents of it, turns its back upon it, abolishes it within itself. It does this not as the holy community separate from the world but as the pioneer and representative. It repents for the sin of the whole society and leads in the social act of repentance. When the property institutions of society are subject to question because innocent suffering illuminates their antagonism to the will of God, then the Church undertakes to change its own use of these institutions and to lead society in their reformation. So also the Church becomes a pioneer and representative of society in the practice of equality before God, in the reformation of institutions of rulership, and in the acceptance of mutual responsibility of individuals for one another.

In our time, with its dramatic revelations of the evils of nationalism, of racialism and of economic imperialism it is the evident responsibility of the Church to repudiate these attitudes within itself and to act as the pioneer of society in doing so. The apostolic proclamation of good and bad news to the colored races without a pioneering repudiation of racial discrimination in the Church contains a note of insincerity and unbelief. The prophetic denunciation of nationalism without a resolute rejection of nationalism in the Church is mostly rhetorical. As the representative and pioneer of mankind the Church meets its social responsibility when in its own thinking, organization and action it functions as a world society, undivided by race, class and national interests.

This seems to be the highest form of social responsibility in the Church. It is the direct demonstration of love of God and neighbor rather than a repetition of the commandment to self and others. It is the radical demonstration of faith. Where this responsibility is being exercised there is no longer any question about the reality of the Church. In pioneering and representative action of response to God-in-Christ the invisible Church becomes visible and the deed of Christ is reduplicated.

Appendix B: Questions for Reflection and Discussion

Following are some suggestions for group discussion in each of the chapters following the basic discussion method outlined in Chapter 3. Good group discussion is a protection against intellectual tyranny by smooth talkers. A well-run two-hour roundtable group discussion will be at least as useful in evaluating the offerings of these stories as any solitary reading and reflection.

■ Introduction

1. What statements, arguments, concepts or images do you remember from the introduction?
2. What was new to you? Where did you get excited?
3. What other approaches to social ills were you reminded of as you read? What are some implications for our society's learning and health that will follow the type of approach chosen?
5. What does H. Richard Niebuhr say about the pioneer role of the church? (See Appendix A, also.) What are some illustrations of this dynamic in society? Where do you experience it in groups you're in contact with?
6. With whom would you like to discuss this book? Who would you like to invite to participate in a study group on it?

■ Chapter 1

1. Which statements, arguments, and illustrations do you remember from this chapter?
2. As the authors defined the characteristics of TWCs, who came to your mind out of your own life or community?
3. In what area of your community are Those Who Make Good Things Happen most needed right now?

4. From your own perceptions and experience, what are some examples of new ethical values? ...new forms of the family?...new spirit modes?...new forms of "community medicine?"
5. How would you change this first chapter to offer an interpretation of the new world which coincides more closely with the reality which you experience? What is one thing you would like to do to make an impact in the community? What would you like your group to do?

■ **Chapter 2**

1. Describe the movement or flow of the stories in this chapter.
2. What parts of this chapter struck you as something new? Where did you get excited?
3. What other models of affordable housing, urban ecology, and neighborhood economic development have you experienced or know about? What other cooperative models do you know? What makes them work? What new myths were motivating the people in Villa El Salvador? ...in other stories?
4. Where in your community (or city, or professional group) are people creating the "new localism"? What are the contradictions present? What do you see as required to turn your city's deteriorated neighborhoods around?
5. What would be the most effective way to attack these contradictions and what role would your group play?

■ **Chapter 3**

1. What do you remember as significant elements in effective leadership style? ...of celebration? ...of the basic discussion method? ...of image-shifting workshops? ...of planning?
2. What are the dynamics of profound celebration? ...of the other tools?
3. Where have you experienced similar methods?
4. What makes them work? How are these methods related to developing leadership and empowering people?
4. How do you see yourself using any of these methods in your home, workplace or organization?

■ **Chapter 4**

1. Recall one of the illustrating stories in this chapter. What images of social medicine did it give?
2. What experience have you had, or read about, that illustrates the science of epidemiology?

There is at the back of human lives, an abyss of light more blinding and more unfathomable than any abyss of darkness which human misery can discover.

—*Unknown*

223

3. What would be some questions that epidemiology could ask and answer in your community? What are the obstacles to using epidemiological methods to get a picture of the health of the neighborhood? What would the benefits be?

4. In what ways could we expand the use of these methods in our local community (using annual disability days, for example)? What extra colleagues and resources would be needed? Where would be the strategic action our group could take?

■ **Chapter 5**

1. What stories do you remember from this chapter? What different kinds of family did you see in these stories? What were the images of family they contained?

2. What feelings did this chapter evoke? Where did you get angry, excited, depressed? Where did you find your feelings shifting?

3. What other kinds of family groupings do you know of? What are their strengths? ...their weaknesses? What is the relation of family or families to core groups?

4. Where do you see these groups forming in your community? If a core group or group of families is to be responsible for tasks like upgrading community space, increasing the supply of affordable housing, lifelong learning, or other jobs your community requires, what support structures, services or resources would they require to be able to do the job?

5. What structures does your family need to become effective in its mission? How would you implement these?

■ **Chapter 6**

1. What ideas, stories or images do you remember from "A New Common Sense"?

2. Where did you get excited? ...or tired? What insights did you have?

3. What advantages does tripolar analysis give a group? Where are the imbalances in our current operating wisdom? (Which dynamics are dominant, restrained and weakened?)

4. Where do you experience the need for a new "common operating wisdom"? Where do you see structures in society that could benefit from a more updated worldview? What roles do you see people playing in inventing the new worldview? What, really, is this chapter all about?

5. How would you draw a tripolar picture of your neighborhood or community? ...your family? ...your church? ...your organi-

zation or workplace? Which poles would you show as dominant? ...restrained? ...weakened or collapsed? What is one thing you would like to do to restore balance?

■ Chapter 7

1. What was one of the stories you remember from either the education or the health vocation?
2. Choosing one of the stories that particularly interested you, what are the concepts of education or health that it contains?
3. Where have you seen innovative teaching/learning practices (or community medicine practices) that are similar to those in this chapter? In your experience, what are the benefits of using this method (these methods)?
4. What images come to mind when someone says global education? ...wholistic health?
5. How do you think we should restructure our educational curricula (or community care nets) to help us live on one planet and save it for our grandchildren?
6. Where in your community would be a strategic place to start? What role would this group play? ...would you play?

■ Chapter 8

1. What do you recall from this chapter? What images come to mind?
2. What feelings did you notice as you read this chapter? Where did you sense a strong reaction to the text? ...excitement? ...anger? Does this chapter bring to mind any good times (or not-so-good times) you've known in communities?
3. In communities you've known, what have been the things important in holding them together? What have been the stress areas which have not been adequately resolved? Where do you know of a community that has a sense of mission? ...a community that has a strong, joyous internal life?
4. What does your community (or family, or church, or vocation) presently require for leadership? ...to create a sense of mission all members could buy into? What role would you play?

■ Chapter 9

1. What do you recall of the stories in this chapter? Where did you hear or read something new?
2. What were you feeling? Did you feel like laughing (or crying or cheering) at any point?

3. Discuss the idea of turning matter into spirit, or spirit into matter. How do some of the stories illustrate this? Where have you seen this happen in your community (or church, or vocation)?

4. Take a radical leap of imagination—what are some of the possibilities for being really and fully human in our times? What would be some of the consequences if a group did this? ...or a church? ...or a business, or other organization?

5. What would it be like to try out one of these wild ideas? What would you like to do to begin?

■ Epilogue

It is now your turn.

1. Write a question requiring a brief objective answer from every person in your discussion group.

2. Write a question requiring a reflective answer from several members of the group.

3. Write a question requiring an interpretive answer from one or two people in the group, or for silent meditation by most members.

4. Write a question requiring a fourth-level, decisional answer from one or two people in the group, or for silent meditation by most members.

Appendix C: Information for Mentor Panels and the *Journal*

■ Current information on Regional Mentor Panels

A growing number of mentors are available to assist you in developing your up-front leadership skills. The panels also will welcome your assistance in helping others develop new skills.

Groups active in the areas listed below use the leadership skills outlined in Chapter 3: the Basic Discussion Method, the Image Shifting Workshop, Strategic Planning and Contradictional Analysis, and the Community-Building Celebration. The cities listed are the nearest major metropolitan areas to where the groups are actually located. The authors update the list every six months.

Most of the panel members have full-time job and family duties. Some earn substantial fees for the advice and assistance you may want, so please discuss time and financial arrangements with them early in your conversation. Most panels can accommodate a wide range of interests and charges. They can also suggest books, newsletters, conferences and other resources for you and your core group. Also, ask about bed and breakfast accommodations when you visit their cities.

To obtain a current list of names, addresses, and phone numbers, send $2.00 to cover postage and materials to Regional Mentor Panels, 7777 W. Morris Street, Indianapolis, IN 46231. If you're interested in becoming a mentor, include a note to that effect, and we'll send you that information along with the current list.

New England
- Providence, RI
- Hartford, CT

Hudson River
- Albany, NY
- Binghamton, NY
- Rochester, NY

Delaware Valley
- Philadelphia, PA

Chesapeake-Potomac
- Washington, DC
- Bethesda, MD
- Alexandria, VA
- Roanoke, VA

Illinois-Wabash River Valley
- Indianapolis, IN
- Lafayette, IN

Lake Michigan
- Milwaukee, WI
- Evanston, IL

Minnesota
- St. Paul-Minneapolis, MN
- Duluth, MN

Northern Plains
- Rapid City, SD

Central High Plains
- Kansas City, MO

East Texas
- Dallas-Ft. Worth, TX

South Texas
- San Antonio, TX
- Austin, TX

West Texas -New Mexico
- El Paso, TX
- Las Cruces, NM

Colorado
- Denver, CO

Bay Area California
- San Francisco, CA
- Berkeley, CA

■ **Subscription information for**
the Neighborhood Caretaker Journal

The Neighborhood Caretaker Journal: A Journal of Converging Science, Art and Vocation covers the range of topics described in this book. If you are working with urban issues or are a concerned layperson, the *Journal* is a valuable monthly publication that tracks, analyzes, and abstracts items of interest in community medicine, servant leadership skills, and social and spirit methods that are being applied by Those Who Make Good Things Happen around the globe.

A year's subscription is $25.00, for which you receive:
1. Ten issues (16 pages each) plus two special mailings;
2. A sturdy binder for storing copies of NCJ;
3. On request, back issues which are still available;
4. NCJ annual report with financial statement;
5. Use of the current full subscriber mailing list (NCJ encourages direct exchanges among subscribers); and
6. Announcement of your projects in NCJ.

Please make check payable to Knowledge Systems, Inc. and mail to Neighborhood Caretaker Journal, 7777 W. Morris Street, Indianapolis, IN 46231. Credit card orders may be made by calling toll-free 1-800-999-8517. Please allow six weeks for arrival of the first issue.

Index

229